ORDINARY LIVES, UNCOMMON ENDINGS

Colin C. Carriere

Carriere, Colin C.
Ordinary Lives, Uncommon Endings - First Edition
pages cm.
Library of Congress PCN No. 2018911067

Ordinary Lives, Uncommon Endings, by Colin C. Carriere. Copyright © 2018. All rights reserved. Printed in the United States of America. For information regarding obtaining copies, address Amazon at www.amazon.com/books-used-books-textbooks.

Front and back cover design and illustration by Raenell Pollard
Back cover text by Niloc V. Carriere

TABLE OF CONTENTS

Introduction -General Statement............................1

Chapter 1- Bomber –His Heart was Bigger than His Stature..19

Chapter 2- My Body Tells Me – It's All About The 11's..66

Chapter 3 - Killing of the Mediator for Conflict Resolution and Non-Violence................................110

Chapter 4-They Killed the Body but the Spirit Did Not Perish 156

Chapter 5-Brittany Ray...198

Chapter 6-The Other Jackson Family....................238

Chapter 7-Bloody Red..277

Chapter 8-General Eulogy and Honor..............., 327

Endnotes 347

INTRODUCTION

GENERAL STATEMENT

*Jesus said, "I am the resurrection
and the life; he who believes in me,
though he die, yet shall he live,
and whoever lives and believes in me shall never die."*
John 11:25,26

A Time for Everything: Ecclesiastes

*There is a time for everything,
and a season for every activity under the heavens:*

*a time to be born and a time to die,
a time to plant and a time to uproot,
a time to kill and a time to heal,
a time to tear down and a time to build,
a time to weep and a time to laugh,
a time to mourn and a time to dance,
a time to scatter stones and a time to gather them,
a time to embrace and a time to refrain from embracing,
a time to search and a time to give up,
a time to keep and a time to throw away,
a time to tear and a time to mend,
a time to be silent and a time to speak,
a time to love and a time to hate,
a time for war and a time for peace.*

GENERAL STATEMENT

My journey began several years ago, when I thought about several relatives who had been killed. I did not have to go canvassing neighborhoods to discover murder victims. Either I reflected upon what I had experienced as part of family tragedies or the topic continued to come up in conversations with relatives, close friends

Introduction

or neighbors. The refrain was usually sad but strikingly familiar - my son, or brother, or cousin, or baby's daddy had been killed. I was shocked when I began to write down the names of the victims – more than 60. Wow; I either knew them, one of their immediate relatives, or knew a close associate. I had grown up or gone to school with a few of them. And as a few more years wore on, the list grew to more than 70.

I shocked myself because even though I had grown up in a rough neighborhood in New Orleans, been attuned to violence in a few other urban environments, where I had lived, and had several family members arrested and "served time", I was not a thug, nor had I lived a thug life. Nor for the most part were the friends or relatives with whom I spoke, and listened to their accounts of each murder, considered thugs. In my mind, they were survivors, or as one researcher has coined it, "co-victims of homicide".[1]

I wondered immediately about those who had lived "hard" lives, or lived most of their lives in the "projects", or been involved in criminal activities, or had been shot or incarcerated – how many victims did they know and remember? What about gang members who had many of their "hommies" killed, or ministers and priests who had presided over services for so many homicide victims? I also thought of the devastating and broad impact which each murder had on society – parents and grandparents, siblings and friends, and cousins and classmates and co-workers, and, most importantly, surviving children.

Then I read that there are (or were) some young men, half my age, who knew- directly or indirectly- more than 100 men who had been murdered.[2] Or there were parents who had lost every son to gun violence.[3] With these stories in mind, the uniqueness of my personal accounting suddenly disappeared. That was even more indicative of the devastation of murders, than my indirect accounting.

With further discussions and reading, I discovered that knowing 60

Introduction

or 70 victims, or being one level removed, was neither unique nor unusual.

Some polls have found that as many as 40 percent of Americans indicate they know at least one person who has been killed. Post-911 that number undoubtedly grew, since Pew Research Center found that 11% of citizens knew someone killed or hurt in the 911 attack. However, 911 was an act of war, like Pearl Harbor, and not representative of the daily potential for a person being a victim or survivor. Poignantly, and by comparison, there are some persons or communities where the likelihood is much higher, with the number of known victims for each person polled, an average far greater than a single person.[4] For those persons, having someone killed, whom they know or are associated, is ingrained in their everyday lives.

Similar to serial murderers, there are individuals who have lost scores of family or friends to murder. Are they considered chronic or ongoing murder survivors, or better yet, "serial survivors"? One such person, Camiella Williams in Chicago, describes losing 24 friends to murder in the last 12 years.[5] Only 27 years old, she says, "Imagine,... "They're your friends on Facebook one minute, and then they're gone the next." And the persons to whom she referred were friends, not merely persons she knew indirectly.

Then there is the youth football league coach in New Orleans who maintains a sheet of paper with the names of all of his former players who have been killed. The list contains 28 names of players who have been killed in a 14-year span.[6]

Or consider the 23-year-old young man in New Orleans who claims he can list 60 acquaintances, family and friends who have been killed.[7] Then there is the high school senior in Newark, New Jersey, who had four close friends who were killed in a four-month period in 2013.[8] The point is most dramatic when you consider that nearly every hand is raised in response to a question, in many classrooms across the country, (often elementary schools), regarding how

Introduction

many knew someone who has been killed in street violence.

But their woes may be mitigated when compared to that of Frances Davis and Clara Saunders, of Brooklyn. Clara is Frances' mother and lived in the Tompkins Housing projects in Bedford-Stuyvesant. Between 1987 and 1993 all three of Frances's sons were murdered in the projects. Then in January 1996, 2 of Clara's other grandchildren (and Frances' nephews) were ambushed and killed in one of the project's lobbies. Clara Saunders then calculated that she had lost 5 of her 15 grandchildren to murder, all in the same location (Tompkins projects). She died a year later, at age 66.

Gun violence and murder is deeply personal to all of them. For many, death by gunfire or murder is the norm and not knowing someone murdered, even if they are young, is the exception. In today's mass shootings climate, the mourner could be a person who lost many people whom they knew in one incident, such as the Principal at the Columbine High School shooting incident, or a friend and patron at the recent Orlando nightclub shooting incident.[9] In speaking to a couple of classrooms of inner-city high school students recently, when I inquired how many of them knew of someone who was shot or murdered, every student raised his/her hand.

Essentially, whether one lives by the lyrics of Snoop Dogg in his song *Murder was the Case,* or President Obama in his eulogy of the Charleston, South Carolina church racial hatred victims, one hardly can escape murders' impact on society.

Unsurprisingly, research has found that the impact is disproportionate in the African-American community, such to render it not uncommon for some communities.[10] One study has concluded that nationwide, on average, African-Americans experienced the homicide of loved ones at least 2.5 times during their lifetime.[11] Inexplicable to me, particularly given that I had live the vast majority of my life in "safe neighborhoods, the rate I had

Introduction

experienced was far beyond the rate noted above.[12]

Apparently, hidden inside my soul was a hurt, concern or curiosity about the emotional impacts on survivors, and why more was not done to stem the murderous cycle this country has experienced. Psychologically, it was necessary for me to break the wall of silence. The tipping point for a debate is here. Otherwise, we risk complacency about a critical social, health, and human justice issue.

The questions for those survivors interviewed in connection with this book were more difficult for some to answer than for others, just as the manner of grieving varies. Questions concerning what occurred were not as demanding as those pertaining to why the killing occurred or their handling of loss or grieving.

There has been a tremendous amount of research about murder and there is a nearly daily barrage of news coverage in metropolitan areas of senseless killings. Indeed, the local nightly news in cities across the country often begins with an account of a shooting and, more recently, mass shootings.

One of the difficult aspects of addressing homicide is the imbalanced media coverage of murders based upon various factors such as sensationalism, entertainment value, class and race. For countless years, newspapers merely identified most urban murders in a few sentences. Now, however, many news media often give somewhat fuller descriptions of the circumstances, motives and relationships between victim and perpetrator. Moreover, there are blogs on the Internet and social media where the lives of victims are catalogued and photos presented and in places, such as Facebook "RIP" memorials are laid out, or Go Fund Me pages are posted.

What is still missing for most victims, particularly the "ordinary" citizen, is more media providing some life to their life or deeper, insightful depiction of the affect upon the survivors. Many are

Introduction

identified after the "He/she left behind ... portion of an obituary or news story. In many ways, outside of social media or their families, they had become faceless "John Does" or "Jane Does" or murder no. "xxs", for purposes of the uniform crime reporting system. They are invisible. Yet, the byproduct of murder is psychological, physical and financial strains upon the survivors.

Axiomatically, the lives of the victims are so much more than a statistic or a sensational story. Be it their song, their story, their poem, they all have a legacy. Even though it is a dark and heavy subject matter, as a society we are fascinated with the mysteries and whodunnits surrounding the ultimate crime.

I selected 16 of the 70 or so victims, whom I knew personally or was associated with a friend or a close relative of theirs, to provide a fuller account of them and their survivors.[13] Each account is different because each had differing lives and families. I can only hope this discourse will be distilled by many - lovers, haters, dreamers and dream breakers - to recognize the horror of murder and the life altering aftermath of this crime.

Eerily, many families have suffered through multiple murders. As depicted here, of the 11 victims selected, there were multiple murders within their immediate family in 5 cases.

The murders occurred in a mosaic of contexts. Among them are a grandfather and a baby, a soldier, college professor, and two brothers. They ranged in age from an infant to a 75-year old man, and size, from a 17-pound baby to a 7 foot, 330-pound man. The death of a few garnered greater than usual news coverage. But the commonality among them was that most were "ordinary." But ordinary still equates with special because of who they were to family and friends and given they were all God's children. And in any event, they all had the same identity: human being.

Everyone Has a Life Story

Everyone has a story; some more complicated than others. Before

Introduction

being victimized some had glitter, which can make their storytelling shine, and others whose life was uninteresting to most observers. Some lived life intensely; others dreamily. The dilemma is they all are not present to give their account of life. This will fill in the lacunae or other voids.

The stories generally start gladly, emerge badly and end sadly; meaning they start as pristine innocent babies and children, face challenges and then end in an unexpected death.

This book attempts to provide a face to a few of the victims within the cadre of persons whom I listed in my personal survey. It is a campaign for their legacy. It also gives a face, a story and an emotional outlet to their survivors. Additionally, it is a campaign to spotlight the issue of murder in this country and all of the issues associated with their killing. Consequently, I consciously decided that to achieve this objective I had to blend their stories, with research concerning the reasons for murder and identify the need for better strategies to mitigate murders and the pain of survivors.

For most of these victims, or that of their loved ones', real or complete stories have never been told, since their murders were "ordinary," or "usual", or their societal status was minimal. For a couple of victims herein, their deaths were part of a national cataclysmic event or triggered from a sensational set of facts which may have made their deaths and lives more public or newsworthy. However, for the others, their lives were statistical or bordering on near anonymity.

It is apparent from the accounts herein that being victimized by murder is not reserved only for bad people and vice versa - nice human beings are often the victims of very violent crimes. Indeed, most of the victims for whose life story I account or discuss would not be considered bad people by the reasonable, normal citizen. Of course, a few may have had arrests or criminal violations, but that did not fully define them. The lack of opportunity or not being able

Introduction

to cope with some of life's challenges may have more import to their life story than an arrest.

Additionally, having grown up and attended high school in New Orleans, there were far more on my victim list of 70 plus who lived in New Orleans, accounting for more than any other jurisdiction.

One of the survivors whom I interviewed, a former neighbor, and whose loved one is discussed herein, commented that I could have written the book based just on the murders which had occurred in our old New Orleans neighborhood in Treme. Or I could have written only about some of the victims who passed through the doors of the neighborhood funeral home, Labat-Charbonnet's.

So true. There were more than enough victims on my list to fill the slots for this book so that I would not have had to venture beyond the 36-square block area of the "old" Treme. As we all used to joke when we were younger, everyone from the neighborhood followed the same life path – came into the world through former Charity Hospital's maternity ward and went out through Labat-Charbonnet's in a hearse. But that would be too familiar and limited a depiction of someone's legacy, despite the color and charm of New Orleans. It also would not define the issues as broad and national in scope, which it is and deserving of national attention.

In addition, because murder usually involves victims and perpetrators who know one another, it creates strange personal dynamics. A mother in Washington, D.C., who lost one of her sons to gun violence, relates how she recently was having a conversation with a life-long friend who was discussing with her the circumstances surrounding her brother's murder 35 years ago. The friend said her mother had called her at work a few days prior to the discussion. The friend was wondering why her mother would call her at that time when she had told her mother earlier that morning that she would be attending an important meeting. When

Introduction

she answered her mother's phone call, however, her mother informed her that the police had arrested her brother's killer – after 35 years. The next part of the story was even more shocking – the killer was her brother's best friend! The friend had frequented their family home often after her brother's killing. Indeed, he had been at the home less than a month before his arrest.

The Landscape of Murder

As a social or criminal justice phenomenon, murder has possibly not drawn the level of attention it deserves recently, beyond sensationalism, because the murder rate has dropped significantly from decades ago. Many citizens may be at a contentment level or view it as an issue which will likely not affect them or their families. But it still deserves to be a huge national challenge, given that we are talking about tens of thousands of persons each year and the concomitant misery for many more survivors.

Over the last 50 years there have been about 880,000 murders in the country.[14] In a more delimited time period, between 1990 and 2014, according to the FBI, there were 447,599 murders in the United States, averaging about 17,900 a year. To put it in perspective, this latter number reflects about 200,000 more deaths than the combat deaths from World War I, Vietnam War, Korean War and the Iraq and Afghanistan wars combined.

In the same violent vein, because guns have such a dominant role in this depiction, we must also consider the prevalence of gun violence overall in assessing the issue. The difference between a gunshot victim dying and being a non-fatal surviving victim may be influenced more by luck, advanced medicine or more rapid emergency transport by EMT, than the intent of the shooter. The problem is that there are no acceptable or reliable statistics regarding the number of nonfatal gunshot victims, some of whom lived but were disabled or paralyzed. There is an absence of

Introduction

accepted numbers because there are no standards or required mechanisms to track gunshot victims.

The estimates from researchers range from 20,000 to 100,000 nonfatal gunshot victims annually.[15] The CDC reports that there were 81,034 nonfatal gunshot victims in 2014.[16] Even if relying upon a conservative or mid-figure of 50,000 annually, means that for the same 25-year period 1990 to 2014, there were about 1.25 million nonfatal gunshot victims.

Sadly, too many in that half-million figure, for murders, were young African American males or concentrated in poor, urban neighborhoods. Many had not even reached the age of 21. Far too many are receiving toe tags when they should be receiving high school or college diplomas. As Bishop Desmond Tutu proclaims, they were "struck down in the bloom of youth".

Although the chances of a young black man being murdered are 15 times greater than young white males, in the media black men are more likely to be depicted as perpetrators rather than victims, worthy of some level of sympathy. In some low-income neighborhoods, homicide may decrease the life expectancy of black men by 5 years,[17] resulting in even greater social inequality for black families.

Unquestionably, at their birth no one predicted that any of the specific victims discussed on the following pages would fall prey to murder.[18] Indeed, as you will decipher, a few would have fallen to the bottom stratum of any statistical analysis or algorithm, seeking to identify those likely to be victimized.

Although not fully reflected in this book, murder has unequal application to certain urban communities, such as Englewood and Fuller Park in Chicago, St. Roch and Central City in New Orleans, Westmont and Compton in Los Angeles, or Clifton-Berea in Baltimore. For residents in neighborhoods such as these there appears to be no such evidence of a decline in murders or shootings.

Introduction

Regrettably, murder and gunshot victims have evolved into the new normal.

While some may proclaim victory because of the decline in murders nationally over the last few decades, the numbers and rates are still far too high in a civilized society. Additionally, the United States has a higher rate of murder than many other industrialized nations.

If we consider the number of murders and nonfatal gunshot victims annually, we are considering close to 100,000 victims, in a year such as 2014. Although still not a number which reflects all deaths, if it were, this would place gunshot victims in the category with accidents, strokes and Alzheimer's for leading causes of death.

Still, the vast majority of times the victims, both fatal and nonfatal, were ordinary citizens of no particular note or notoriety. The sheer magnanimity, however, of nearly half a million lives lost through murder should shake most of our communal spirits, even if none of our loved ones are included in the morbid statistic. Thus, this discourse is about 11 of those ordinary, yet special, souls.

The Act of Murder

Murder is the consummate violation of humanity or abuse in life. "Murder" is not the only verb which can be used; also, kill, slaughter, or execute are appropriate. It not only affects the victim, but more than any other crime, it affects a schlong of survivors. Hence, the terms "ordinary" and "murder" cannot coexist in the same sentence; although most victims may be ordinary, there simply is no ordinary murder. It is the ultimate, non-reversible crime and violation of the highest moral principles. There is a reason it is categorized as a violent crime - because it is always violent, whether it be by gunshot, stabbing, beating, poison, etc.[19]

What distinguishes murder from other deaths is that it is the result of an intentional, usually cruel, act of another. It is neither a natural result or disaster, mistake nor even byproduct of recklessness.

Introduction

No one ever describes murder in delicate or equivocal terms. As Cynthia Jenkins, sister of homicide victim, Karen Jenkins, says: "Violence is awful. It's an expression and explosion of emotion on the same level of love, but in its opposite direction. It leaves devastation, destruction in its wake. It is productive though if it awakens us. It's hard to understand all of its ramifications, because it has the propensity of generating its own energy."

Sometimes, the stories of murder are bone-rattling. For example, in *State v. Carruth*, the court describes the horrifying facts regarding the murder of a 12-year-old and attempt murder of his father:

"`[Carruth] and [Brooks] transported the Bowyers [father and son] back to the road construction site, this time to the murder site. [Carruth] walked Forest F. (Butch) Bowyer away from the car and cut him on the [right side of his] neck [and he said, "that's sharp, isn't it?"] [Carruth] shortly thereafter cut Forest F. (Butch) Bowyer's throat. [Brooks] also cut Bowyer's throat. [Carruth] then sat on Forest F. (Butch) Bowyer and told him to "go to sleep." It was during this period of time that the child, [12 years old] William Brett Bowyer, asked [Carruth] and [Brooks] not to hurt his daddy. The response to the child from [Brooks] was that he needed to be concerned about himself, not his dad.*

"`The defendant, Michael David Carruth, told [Brooks] "I've done one, now you do one." At this point, [Brooks] shot the child in the head. When a gurgling sound came from the child, [Brooks] commented "the little M.F. doesn't want to die" and shot him two (2) more times in the head. The child, William Brett Bowyer, fell into a shallow grave [that Carruth and Brooks had dug earlier]. The father, Forest F. (Butch) Bowyer, was thrown on top of the child. [Carruth] and [Brooks] laughed and joked as they threw dirt on the dead child and his father, covering them in the shallow grave.'

"(C. 704-06.) After Carruth and Brooks left the scene, [Forest]

Introduction

Bowyer dug himself out of the grave and flagged down a passing motorist for assistance. He later identified both Carruth and Brooks as the perpetrators of the crimes." [20]

Under legal precepts, there are varying degrees of murder. First degree murders, which are killings that are the result of premeditation or committed in connection with a felony, are at the top of the criminal code apex. Many survivors are familiar enough about the criminal laws to comprehend the general distinctions. For many survivors, nevertheless, these are mere technicalities which are important only insofar as it affects the level of punishment. Most survivors believe that the level of justice for their loved ones demands the maximum charges and sentence.

In fact, the act of murder is a penumbra of moral or personal crimes – it results in stealing a loved one; assault on the psyche of survivors, and robbery of victims' dreams.

For many, murder not only violates nearly every moral or human principle, it also intrudes into God's business. It is reasoned that this is so because God gives life and only he may take it. Additionally, the 6th Commandment clearly forbids murder - "thou shalt not kill" - despite biblical translational challenges for war, justifiable homicide, and application of the death penalty.

In some instances, the victims were murdered even though they hoped and dreamed for a better life or were on the right path to recovery from some setbacks. There is the story, for instance, of Antonio Anderson from Baltimore who posted on Facebook a month before his killing: "Feeling blessed just turned 25 today a lot of people don't make it to see my age." Then, 2 days before his death, he again posted on Facebook: "Thank God for another day."

In others, such as infants or young children killed as a result of child abuse or caught in gang cross-fire, they were never in a position to shape their lives or prevent the killing.

Introduction

Sometimes the term "sometimes" is apt for the murderous occasion or killing. Sometimes the bullet was not meant for them – they never saw it coming, but things can go bad in a second when convulsed by violence. As the well-worn adage goes, they were in the wrong place at the wrong time. Sometimes they had entered into a zone of risk, or courage, depending on your perspective, which for them was just a way of living. Sometimes they had "wronged" another person, or even the perpetrator, who retaliated.

More sparingly and certainly more controversial, people without dark hearts may be an assailant. As Dr. Martin Luther King, reminded us "there is some good in the worst of us and some evil in the best of us." Emphatically, this does not excuse their crime, but offered to depict the general nature of people.

With equal application, the term "oftentimes" may apply to the murder or its aftermath. Often, there is a more compelling story of their lives behind the story of their murder. There are also often critical matters about them or their life's deeds which are not found in the police reports or coroner's reports or news flashes. The victims are often just anonymous statistics and the newspaper accounts look and sound too familiar.

Although it may appear naïve on my part, but what always prevails in the end is that it was not the perpetrators' decision to make – either law enforcement or the judicial system is supposed to determine an offender and punishment or, more spiritually or appropriate, God's determination on life.

Concededly, some made mistakes which are also part of their life journal. Life had become devalued or their path had been diverted and they knew their lives were at risk. Few, if any, however, expected to be murdered when they awoke the day they were killed. And who plans their life to live only to 20 or 25 years old, or younger? Although we have often heard young gangbangers or others prophesize that they don't care because life is short for them, much of such talk is unfettered braggadocio.

Introduction

All of the victims were different in their own unique way, some with amazing grace and others with *de minimis* swagger. Above all, they were someone's birth child and a spiritual descendant of God. As President Obama declared in his eulogy of Reverend Clementa Pinckney:" You don't have to be of high station to be a good man."

The effect of murder cannot be measured solely by the number of victims. The stories about each murder expands to depictions about the families or loved ones, because with each death a part of the remaining family members is taken or lost. For every victim, there are many family members, including parents, siblings and children, as well as close friends, who are affected. If hypothetically, each murder has a serious psychological effect on at least 50 family members and friends, nearly 900,000 persons are affected each year.

For the vast majority of victims discussed here, individually their deaths did not stir the national conscience. With respect to most of the victims herein, for news organization there was nothing particularly newsworthy about their killing, except for a 15 second spot on the local nightly news or a few sentences in the local newspaper. For a few, their deaths triggered unusual media coverage.

Although all ordinary people, they still deserve a place in history, even if it is only God's chronicle. The headlines regarding their killing start to look familiar. The stories may have common themes. We must ask, even if there had been a dispute or disrespect, did it warrant a death sentence?

The Elusive "Why"

Often the fight for survivors is to know the "why". Sorting out what happened may be easier than determining why it happened. It appears that the predominant questions for survivors surround why was their loved one murdered and why did the perpetrator commit such an act of violence. The questions are often intertwined, yet the

Introduction

answers may be far more complex. Normally, there are no lucid answers, with the motives and characteristics being broad and varying extensively.

There has been significant research regarding the broad question of why people kill one another. For instance, one researcher, Dr. Mattiuzzi, has advanced the typology of most murderers: (1) chronically aggressive individuals; (2) the over-controlled hostility type; (3) the hurt and resentful; (4) the traumatized; (5) the obsessive; (6) the paranoid; (7) the insane; and (8) the just plain bad & angry.[21]

One cannot help but think of what drove a person to have such a dark voided heart? Was it the result of a narrow mindset, mental disease, or negative upbringing, or has Dr. Mattiuzzi captured the critical typographies?

Our minds may even venture to a more granular analysis – what was the perpetrator thinking at the time of the murder - how did he get to the point of either so much rage and viciousness or abject apathy? Did they have dark psychological pasts? Can they be reformed?

Borrowing a term from writer Criss Jami, but using it for a different meaning, what is the "killosophy" that brought them to this reckless place? Is there a place in their soul which is so evil that any reason or morals disappear, or is the law of the streets so compelling that they felt compelled to take a life – or two. On a practical level, do they think of the time that they may have to spend in jail or was it self-hatred which drove them to kill in the first place?

At a micro level, research and scholarship in the area about why people kill has been widespread, but nowhere near complete nor scientific. A few recent studies have concluded that, from the standpoint of neuroscience, the lateral orbitofrontal cortex (OFC) section of the brain is activated when people kill. The more

Introduction

justified the killer believes about the killing the less active this section of the brain and the less guilt they feel. And more forward-looking, through video games and parental conduct and messaging, are we teaching our kids to kill?

The practical answer is elusive because what makes one kill another is as varied as the illogical justifications in the minds of the killer. The justifications for retaliation, gang or drug murders, no doubt, differ from that for most domestic killings. And serial killers fall into a wholly separate category. Likewise, there are macabre instances of murder where the killing was simply the result of a desire to know what it felt like to kill someone or as target practice.[22] Furthermore, although murder is abnormal behavior, not only the mentally ill commit murder.

Often there were precipitating factors leading to the murder; victim having angered someone, harmed a family member of a perpetrator, a debt, or drug deal gone sideways. In other instances, it happened in an instant or the moment, without warning, being in the wrong place and the wrong time or being with the 'wrong" person. Rarely, if ever, is there justification for the resulting murder. Indeed, there have been indictments against gangs or groups, which allege that multiple killings were committed not merely to establish fear and intimidation, but to enhance their social media status.[23] Federal prosecutors contend it was "killing for the sake of killing".

The Investigation Discovery channel aired a show recently dedicated to dissecting the answers to the question of why. It is entitled "The Mind of a Murderer", and narrated by a psychiatrist and trial consultant, who goes behind bars to interview murderers, all in the chase to better understand what drives people to kill. She unearths dark secrets about child abuse, rage, schizophrenia and other personal conflicts and demons. Unfortunately, it leaves significant gaps and fails to provide sufficient depth regarding the issue. Frankly, the issue is far too deep for any single analysis or

Introduction

television program to provide answers.

In his suicide note, one young killer involved in a school shooting, killing 3 and wounding 11, could not answer why: *People are not afraid to die, it's just how they die. I don't fear death, but rather the pain. But no more. I regret the foods I'll never taste, the music I'll never hear, the sites I'll never see, the accomplishments I'll never accomplish, in other words, I regret my life. Some will always ask, 'Why?' I don't know — no one will. What has been, can't be changed. I'm sorry. It ends like it began; in the middle of the night, someone might think it selfish or cowardly to take one's own life. Maybe so, but it's the only free choice I have. The way I figure, I lose either way. If I'm found not guilty, I won't survive the pain I've caused — my guilt. If I'm convicted, I won't survive the mental and physical punishment of my life in prison.*[24]

CHAPTER 1

BOMBER –HIS HEART WAS BIGGER THAN HIS STATURE

The children were all playing together on the sidewalk when one boy fell on the other boy causing the other kids to shriek – "Bomber fell on Monte." Monte got up starry eyed, like a wet dishrag. They began to laugh since it had happened so precipitously and like "splat", he was on the ground. However, it was both funny and scary to them since Bomber was much larger than Monte, although he was only a couple of years older. To them it appeared that Bomber was twice Monte's size and his frame had completely covered poor lil Monte. This difference in size and weight would carry forward for the remainder of their lives. Bomber grew to 7 feet and more than 300 pounds and Monte weighed in at about 5'7, and about 140 pounds. Bomber's name was William Simpson and Monte's was Otis Lamont Parks.

Being playmates were not Bomber and Monte's only connection; there also was an unfortunate link to broader sociological and criminal justice phenomena. Both boys were later murdered at the other end of a gun barrel, one nearly anonymously on the outskirts of the same small town where they had collided as kids, and the other prominently and making international headlines, more than 1500 miles away in Texas. Both Bomber and Monte were on the road to overcoming setbacks and difficulties in their lives when they were senselessly murdered nearly 21 years apart.

Simpson was killed in Texas, half the country away from where he was raised in the small western New York town of Olean. The town of about 20,000 is situated near the southwestern border in upstate New York. Most shocking, for the reasons described below, he did

Bomber

not die at the hands of the Ku Klux Klan in Vidor, Texas, as many expected he would. Instead, the tragedy occurred at the corner of Victoria and Royal streets in Beaumont, Texas. Bomber was only 37 at the time of his death.

Bomber started his life on April 10, 1956, in Los Angeles, California where he was born to parents Mary and William Simpson Sr. At birth, he was an average size; 22 inches and 8 ½ pounds. His mother was born in New Jersey and his father, who was born in the state of Washington, had black and Cherokee Indian ancestry. His pedigree line in terms of height was overlong – his mother was about 6'2, and his father was about 6 feet 5 inches. His older sister, Lorraine, was also tall. She was more concerned about her height and stature than he was. She would often complain to her cousins about being too big or too tall. But as this story unfolds, Bomber's size was a mere footnote to the man he became and the adversity he faced.

Simpson was brought to the small town of Olean from Los Angeles in the summer of 1961 at age 5 by his aunt, Ida Hill. She had previously visited them in California but had gone again to get William and his sister, Lorraine, this time after calamity struck the Simpson household. She brought them to Olean where she and other relatives lived.

Already, he was huge. Known to his family as "Bomber," he was 48 inches (4 ft.) tall and 60-65 pounds in kindergarten. When his cousin Delores first took him to Elementary School No. 4, they had to locate an adult desk for Bomber to sit. Bomber was easily recognizable; he was the largest child at his age in the small, friendly and quiet town where he grew up as a child. Bomber stood out not only as a result of his size, but because of his personality and smile.

The "big ol boy" who lived on Green Street and also Seneca Avenue was loved by nearly everyone, particularly his uncle Henry Hill, with both referring to one another as "my buddy". Mr. Hill also shepherded Simpson to school every day, as an elderly crossing guard. Bomber's life appeared to be ordinary. He laughed a lot, played a lot, and attended church and school functions.

Growing up, Bomber was very close to his sister Lorraine, who was 4 years older. She was tough and his protector – his guardian angel. Despite his size, he was gentle and kindhearted and, as a result, some kids picked on him. They did not do so in Lorraine's presence, however, because she loved her brother so much that she would fight for him; even if that meant a physical confrontation with a boy. She relates how one red headed bully at school, who picked on Bomber, took his hat and threw it up a tree. Bomber began to cry. Lorraine beat the kid to a pulp forcing him up the tree to retrieve the hat and once he did so beat him again. Of course, he never again teased or bullied Bomber.

Their mother often commented that the two siblings' personalities were misaligned. In her view, Bomber should have had Lorraine's personality and, vice versa, she should have had his. Where he was gentle, she was no-nonsense, and where she was mouthy and opinionated, he was reflective and quiet. William looked like and had features of his mother, but his sister "favored" her father, exhibiting some Native American facial features. Nevertheless, the two children's bond was unshakable, even if later in life it was more spiritual than physical.

Bomber attended School No. 7 Middle School and eventually enrolled at Olean High, where he was on the basketball team. During the summer, he worked as a camp counselor for youth. Not surprisingly, he was the largest student in the school and one of the tallest players in the state of New York. Of course, this did not alter his demeanor or personality. He was gentle, soft-spoken but liked to talk.

His sister relates how in one important basketball game, Bomber mistakenly ran over an opposing player knocking him to the ground, reminiscent of his crash with Monte. As she screamed for

Bomber

Bomber to play on and disregard the opposing player (reasoning that was part of the game), he leaned over to the other player, apologized for knocking him over, and helped him to his feet. She thought, "grab the ball and dunk it as hard as possible". All the while the opposing team retrieved the basketball and scored the winning basket. He had what some describe as a big-man syndrome, wherein he was afraid that he might hurt somebody. Moreover, this simply was who he was as a child, teenager and, ultimately evolved as an adult.

Many urged him to pursue a sports route. Because NBA great Bob Lanier, about the same size, had attended St. Bonaventure in Olean years earlier, just down the road from where Bomber played, some sought to compare Bomber to Lanier. These comparisons were wholly unfair and unrealistic because Bomber had not developed skills or had training nearly equivalent to Lanier. It was also an era in Western New York where basketball was hot with players such as Tom McMillen and Randy Smith, who also advanced to the NBA. His high school did not play against players of that skill level. Instead, they played the likes of Hornell, Fredonia, Depew, and Bradford. More on point, Bomber and Lanier's temperament, inner drive and personalities were different.

What's unknown is how those comparisons to Lanier affected his psyche and confidence. Similarly, his mother's distinguishing his accomplishments from those of his sister and others appear to have affected him and his self-esteem, according to his and friends.

Bomber, however, was more than an uncommonly tall basketball player in high school. He was a member of the school choir and socially conscious, being one of the first students to sign up to vote when he turned 18.

Going Astray - An Emotional Journey

When Simpson left Olean, he ventured on an emotional journey with personal trials and tribulations. He was offered a scholarship

Bomber

to play basketball at a small college, in Allentown, Pennsylvania. However, he did not stay long, transferring to a school in Indiana. Again, he did not stay long. He came back to Olean for a short stint but left again, since his sister had moved away to New York City. From there he moved around the country and continued that journey into marriage later but again for only a brief time.

Simpson was known to others outside of Olean as "Bill" or the "Gentle Giant." Those who met him consistently mentioned that he almost always smiled and was never in a bad mood. If he was depressed, they did not see it.

Somehow Bomber was indeed troubled and got lost along the way. He strayed from Olean to Piscataway and Plainfield, New Jersey, where he lived above a bar for a while and was homeless for a short time. During the period when he was homeless, he suffered frostbite or hypothermia, resulting in removal of parts of his toes. As a result, the Gentle Giant walked with a noticeable limp and sometimes used a cane.

It is not clear what caused Bomber to stray away from his family and venture hundreds of miles from where they lived. Bomber was seemingly searching for something missing in his life or escaping from some troubling family instability or dysfunction. His relationship with his mother was fragile, but certainly not the result of his actions. It is unquestioned he wanted his mother's love. His father was dead and his sister who may have been too young to help him through all of the instability had moved away. He felt alone and had to make it on his own.

Bomber disappeared into himself. Undoubtedly, later he wished he had pursued a college degree, since he certainly was smart and had academic abilities. Maybe he was pushed too hard by his mother. Rather than going that route he appeared to recoil from it. He wanted to be a free spirit where he was fluent in friendship.

There are some indications that he was seeking out relatives in other parts of the country, such as Louisiana, New Jersey, Georgia

Bomber

and Texas. Even more unclear is the effect upon him of his father William Simpson's death. However, wherever he landed he remained in communication with his mother Mary Simpson Lewis, who had remarried after his father's death, as well as with his sister.

He traveled the country, hitchhiking, bumming rides, and taking buses. He slept at homeless shelters or on the streets, and ate at the Salvation Army and other food camps. He sometimes worked odd jobs, including helping others at the shelters. He would also hang out with those who drank and smoked some. However, he was not a stereotypical homeless person. He did not wander the streets, pushing a grocery basket, or linger on corners begging for money. He sought out stable places or institutions where he could eat and sleep and contribute. Through this journey, he was philosophical, paying close attention to societal and political issues and reading whatever he could find.

Bomber and his sister Lorraine   **Bomber in snow in Olean, N.Y.**

He eventually wound up in the uptown section of New Orleans for a while, where he had some maternal relatives, and then moved on to Beaumont in the eastern part of Texas. Bomber had a series of social and life challenges while living in Beaumont. He had fallen in love and in 1991 married Willie Scott Collins, who was 7 years older than him. Their marriage was brief and did not develop into what either was searching for. He joked with one friend that he got married after a night of drinking and he was on a life of adventure.

Those who knew him on a deeper level knew he was far beyond a homeless straggler. But they questioned, how do you constrain an adventurer who was willing to risk criticism?

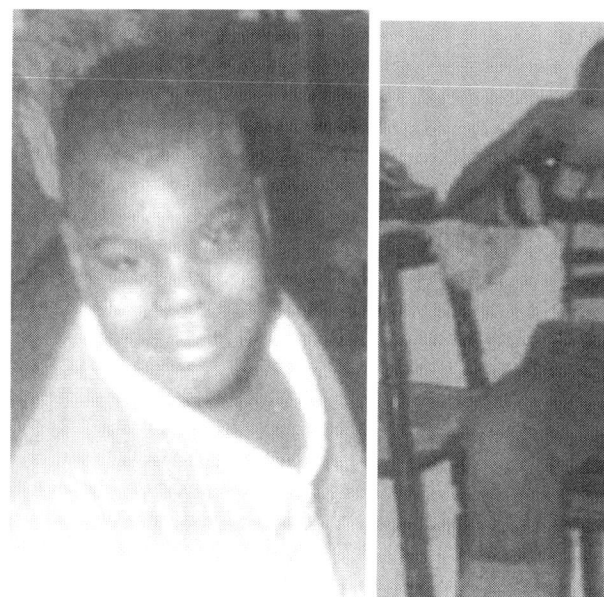

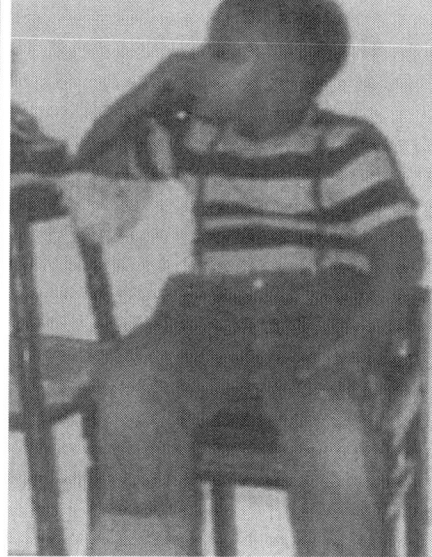

Bomber as a child on the phone

Bomber did not tell any of his family members of his marriage plans or even that it had happened. His days of seeking his mother's approval were in his rear-view mirror. He was, in short, searching for himself and for love.

This was exacerbated by health problems because he also developed diabetes. Despite suffering from diabetes, he was

Bomber

determined to have a meaningful life. He wished to have a career or job where he helped others.

However, he again became homeless. He also had lost his job after being injured while working for a construction company.

A street ministry Pastor, Kenneth Henry, from Central Baptist Church of Vidor, met him on the streets of Beaumont and invited him to live with his family in neighboring Vidor. After living with the Pastor and several families in Vidor for a few weeks, Pastor Henry then recruited Simpson to move to Vidor Village, the housing project, which was part of HUD's integration plan as a result of a government audit and lawsuit. A federal judge had found that HUD engaged in intentional discrimination against blacks. Seeking better opportunities and a fresh start, Bomber officially volunteered to integrate the public housing project in Vidor. He promised the Pastor that he would remain in the housing project for at least six months.

The Pastor also believed that it was in Bomber's best interests. Although he was big-a "Gentle Giant"- no one could recall him ever having shown any anger.

Bomber and his uncle, Henry Hill

Bomber

Even though Vidor was only 11 miles to the east of Beaumont they were worlds apart and a study in contrasts. Beaumont is an oil community situated off Interstate 10 about 90 miles east of Houston, and the county seat of Jefferson County. Surrounded by swamps, it had a prior history of racial tensions, with a riot occurring in 1943 with white and black citizens clashing. During the WWII era, blacks flocked to the city because of jobs in the shipyard industry, creating tension between the races as they competed for jobs. Fifty years later, racial tensions had eased somewhat. There were about 114,000 residents, nearly half of whom were African American, and the city celebrated Dr. Martin Luther King's day.

Simpson in L.A.

On the other hand, Vidor was an all-white logging town of about 11,000 residents, also located off of Interstate 10. The racial attitudes of some in Vidor were equivalent to what occurred in Beaumont 50 years earlier. More pointedly, it was a stronghold for the Ku Klux Klan, and a notorious "Sundown town".

Bomber

Vidor - Sundown Town

A sundown town is a purposely formed all-white segregated town which excludes other races, usually by heavy intimidation, threats and sometimes physical violence. Oftentimes, the segregation is perpetuated with the cooperation of local law enforcement and city officials who refuse to enforce laws and indirectly condone such conduct. Classic indicia of a sundown town are the presence of signage or postings at the entries to the town, warning black citizens that they are not welcome, such as *"Nigger, Don't Let The Sun Set On YOU."* The message was clear: leave town before dark or the sun setting or you would be assaulted or even killed. As the saying goes, ostracized groups (such as African-Americans, Jews, and Hispanics) should not even be allowed to breathe the air there after dark. Although there were hundreds of such communities in America, some existed only by reputation; others were real.[25]

Vidor had all of the manifestations, inwardly and outwardly, of a sundown town. The living conditions were subpar and many of its residents were poor, ensuring the type of tension and conflict that are often associated with poor communities and riddled with pick-up trucks. On the outskirts of Vidor at one time were two of the classic sundown postings: with one reading, "Niggers read this and run. If you can't read, run anyway," and another that simply said, "Nigger don't let the sun set on you in Vidor." The KKK had proclaimed, "Vidor is a white city and has remained white because of the Klan."[26] Hence, it was unquestionably a sundown town – of the worst type. On Main Street in the 1970's a bookstore boasted in bold lettering, KNIGHTS OF THE KU KLUX KLAN. Some in town philosophized that the town just happened to turn out that way- all-white!

Although prior to moving to Beaumont Bomber had probably not heard of or experienced the level of racism of a town such as Vidor, many African-Americans from the western part of Louisiana were well aware of the town's reputation. It was traditional for many traveling west to proclaim that they would "gas-up" in Lake Charles, and travel during the daylight with a basket of food, so as not to be caught in Vidor, searching for gas or food.

There was some buy-in by some, but not all, of the residents of the town of this form of racism. Another tactic to discourage blacks or Hispanics from moving to or even stopping in town was to place cards or signs in businesses broadcasting that it contributed ten percent of its earnings to the KKK. Even if not true, it reflected the sentiments of some.

The Klan's presence and actions were prominent. So were the actions of other white supremacist groups. Their tactics embodied chilling independent and creative thinking among the residents. Often mimicking a religious order, the white supremacist groups sought to capitalize on the residents' poverty, and lack of education and opportunity. Of course, they claimed the residents' misery and woes was because of alleged unfair advantages accorded to blacks, Jews and Hispanics.

Thus, there were many KKK rallies and they held fundraisers to resist the government's integration plans. Previous hearings by the U.S. House of Representatives had even established that some of the KKK members in East Texas were ministers or preachers. Importantly, some residents of the housing projects in Vidor were avowed members. One member of the group, Edith Johnson, was later convicted in federal court of harassing Simpson.

A typical rambling from these times may have sounded like that enunciated by Tony Berry in Indiana: "America, these are dark times right now. We have niggers running rampant in the street. They have taken over our major cities. We have spics, Jews, and everybody else running crazy in the United States if America, but we the white people are here to take it back. We are in dark times, but where there is total darkness, there must be some light. Passing the flame to an officer next to him, he said, "Will you take the

Bomber

desire and the concern for your race, your nation, your country and keep it to yourself, or will you pass it to a brother Klansman?"[27]

The seriousness of this level of racism in this area of East Texas was exemplified by the James Byrd Jr. murder by three white supremacists, in Jasper, Texas, on June 7, 1998, which garnered national attention.[28] Jasper, which is in an adjoining county to Vidor, was also a hot bed of racism, even though the town was about half-white and half-black. Byrd was lynched by dragging when the three murderers chained his body to a truck and dragged him along the streets, severing his right arm and head. His body was discovered in pieces, strewn along the highway, his torso on one part of the road and his head and other limbs on other parts. Even his dentures were located in a place different than his head. A pathologist testified that Mr. Byrd was alive during the majority of the time his body was dragged.

In his closing argument to the jury the state prosecutor struck out against violent racism, analogizing to a public health issue: "It's something that's a virus," he said. "It's something that's dangerous. It's something that spreads from one person to another."[29] The judge sentenced two of the defendants to death and the other to life in prison, marking the first time in Texas' judicial history that a white man had been sentenced to death for killing an African-American.

As an analog, this was the same racist and hate virus strain that existed in Vidor and East Texas years earlier. The segregation of housing in east Texas in the early 80's led some African-Americans to protest to HUD initially about discrimination in Texas public housing projects, including the one in Vidor. More than eighty percent of the housing projects in East Texas were segregated, with one official justifying the government's action as a "moral decision". In addition, HUD had issued an internal audit report which found that efforts to desegregate public housing in East Texas had failed due to inefficiency, infighting, and bureaucratic

Bomber bungling.

The Atmosphere of Racism and Segregation in Public Housing

The efforts at integration in public housing in Texas had started long before Bomber arrived in the area. Several black residents of East Texas filed a lawsuit against HUD in federal court, alleging that HUD intentionally and overtly discriminated in assigning residents to public housing, openly segregating the projects.[30] In 1986, addressing a lawsuit pending for nearly 13 years, federal judge William Wayne Justice, ordered the desegregation of public housing in 36 counties in East Texas, including Orange County where Vidor was located. On appeal by the government, the appellate court upheld Judge Justice's decision; but ordered the judge to craft a mechanism for compliance including appointing a special master.[31] However, the federal government did not enforce compliance until years later after Henry Cisneros was appointed the head of HUD.

Under Cisneros, HUD finally began its efforts to integrate Vidor Village. Many African-Americans on the waiting list for housing had declined the government's invitation to move into Vidor, having learned of the city's reputation as a sundown town. And their fears and doubts were well reasoned.

Upon learning of the plan, the Klan protested vigorously and threatened violence against the residents as well as the mayor of Vidor. But HUD proceeded with its plan. It considered the Klan's actions as "blatant resistance to desegregation".[32]

About six months prior to implementation of the plan, CNN interviewed several individuals in connection with the projected move into Vidor Village. Among those interviewed were the mayor of Vidor and its Assistant Police Chief, two residents, Ross Dennis and Edith Marie Johnson, a Catholic priest, and a Grand Dragon of the KKK. It was evident from the interviews that there were strong differences of opinion and that there would be resistance.

Bomber

Nonetheless, Bomber moved into the 74-unit public housing project along with seven other African Americans in February 1993. Prior to their residency, there had not been a black resident in Vidor for nearly 70 years. Recognizing the years of resistance to integration of housing in Vidor, HUD had moved the families in at dawn, under the cover of darkness. Bomber moved into apartment 62 located at 175 Vidor Drive. The Klan responded immediately with alleged "security patrols" around the town and housing project.

The complex was ringed by a chain-linked fence and consisted of 74 units, constructed of brick and beige vinyl. The landscaping consisted of large oak trees and loblolly pines. Some of the existing white residents extended a welcome to Bomber and the few other black residents. One remarked that their new neighbors were like everyone else, simply trying to make a living and raise their children.

One of the benefits to the existing residents from the integration plan was that the housing authority had begun to improve the conditions of the projects, which had fallen into disrepair. The white supremacist groups sought to leverage those improvements with the white residents by bellowing that the government favored blacks over them, since allegedly before the black residents arrived the authority did not care about the projects' deplorable conditions.

Soon after moving into the housing development there was trouble for Simpson and the other black residents, as well as some white residents who assisted or associated with them. There were constant threats, taunts and hateful efforts at intimidation, including a bomb threat. White supremacist groups came from as far away as Mississippi to join in the intimidation. This caused all of the black residents to leave within only a few months, with Simpson being the last black person to leave. In fact, for three black females, they left after only two weeks.

Simpson and Decuir's "incursion" into Vidor Village was not the first, nor last, attempt to integrate public housing in the nation. There had been, for example, attempts in places such as Trumball Park Homes in South Deering outside of Chicago to integrate in the 40's and 50's which had generated fierce opposition from whites who threw firebombs and bricks, and set vehicles afire. Walter White of the NAACP had remarked that the threats and racism was so strong that Mississippi had followed the African Americans who had migrated to Chicago. Nevertheless, Vidor was distinguishable because it was a sundown town, existing as such a half-century later.

Staring Down the Barrel of Racism and the KKK

About two years prior to execution of the integration plan and Bomber moving into Vidor Village, Ross Dennis had moved his family into the housing project. Dennis was white in his mid-fifties and was retired and disabled. He also suffered from asthma and emphysema. Prior to the project's integration Dennis described his life as peaceful and carefree. He socialized with the other residents, including Edith Marie Johnson, and considered her a friend. Other residents visited his apartment for coffee. He had been elected as president of the project's tenant association. This all changed dramatically when Vidor Village was integrated.

John Decuir, a disabled construction worker, and a diabetic, was the first African American to move into the housing project. Coming from Beaumont, he was aware of the town's reputation and that the Klan intended to agitate the residents of the project but was not concerned initially.

At first, there appeared to be some calm as the young white children took to Bomber, in part fascinated by his size and kindness. Indeed, awestruck by his size and warm demeanor they would come knock on his door asking him to play with them. They loved to see him, referring to him as "Big Bill", and he would swing them in his arms in the air. He loved them too.

Bomber

"Children don't see color", he later acknowledged, and having grown up among many white children and classmates, he sensed that things would calm down.

He and Decuir also became active in the project's efforts to rid the area of drugs. Some residents also welcomed Simpson and Decuir by bringing them food.

But the small flow of cordial behavior and integration transformed rapidly into ugliness. Residents chose sides of either accepting the plan or opposing it. Those who opposed it did so vehemently, passionately, and illogically. Johnson, who had served time in prison, led the opposition. She threatened to "burn the niggers out."

On the other hand, Mr. Dennis, who had been raised by an African American woman, sought to calm the tension, and reason with the residents. The opposition was emboldened by the Klan and two other white supremacist groups, the White Knights and White Camelias, who regularly appeared, handing out literature and trying to recruit members. They tried to recruit Dennis several times and, after he declined, they openly and incessantly threatened and harassed him.

Moreover, the black residents seeking work were rejected for every job to which they applied. The African American women (Brenda Lanus and Alexis Selders), who had moved there from Baton Rouge, were threatened with assault if they were out after dark. They were often referred to as "bitches" or "niggers". They contend that they were unaware of Vidor's history and reputation. They became so afraid that they would not enroll their children in school. Even the white children, who had adored Bomber, began to change, with a few donning hoods, symbolic of the KKK.

At the same time, Simpson and Dennis quickly became friends. They had coffee together and Simpson was a daily visitor to the Dennises' apartment. They would play cards and dominoes, take walks and eat meals together. They discussed every political, social

Bomber

and religious topic imaginable. Simpson also did not own a car and depended on Dennis or other white residents to transport him to obtain insulin for his diabetes or to buy food.

Simpson, Dennis and the other black residents were subjected to a daily barrage of insults, racial taunts, threats to their lives, name calling and vandalism from some of the other residents, even the younger white children. Someone once called in a bomb threat. The prime resident tormentor was Edith Marie Johnson, who lived across from Dennis.

Both Simpson and Dennis tried to look out for one another and had each other's back. Yet the risks were great and the pressure and stress incessant. Bomber stood tallest and loomed largest against the KKK. They witnessed the KKK brand of intimidation first-hand. He reportedly faced up to several Klansmen who came to his apartment door, threatening him, and he responded to them in a baritone voice seldom displayed to "get off his property". They ambled away, apparently unwilling to face the prospect of a defense from the huge man known as Bomber.

The conduct and threats were so constant, outrageous and over-the-top that both Dennis and Simpson complained to the police and local authorities. Pathetically and reminiscent of sundown town mentality, nothing was done, even though the Mayor firmly supported the integration plan. Assuredly, he thought that even life on the streets had not been as tormenting.

Both men lost weight, suffered from anxiety issues and stress and constantly had to watch each other's backs. Sometimes Simpson stayed over at Dennis' home to avoid being trapped by himself.

Government Actions and Investigations

Eventually, Simpson wrote a letter to HUD Secretary Henry Cisneros, wherein he recounted that he had "been called 'nigger' by people in Vidor more times than I can count." Additionally, raising the seriousness of the circumstances he proclaimed: "I must raise

Bomber

my voice in a cry for help. ... I fear for my own life and well-being."

Thereon, HUD conducted an investigation, brought administrative charges against Johnson and rendered a determination. HUD's administrative decision regarding Simpson's and Dennis' complaints of discrimination is telling regarding the types of harassment and intimidation they endured from one of the residents.[33] For instance, the administrative law judge found:

> 6. After Mr. Simpson moved into Vidor Village, Respondent [Edith Marie Johnson] on repeated occasions directed racial slurs and threats to him within his earshot, as well as to Mr. Dennis. Charge '][7. For example, in the Spring of 1993, Mr. Simpson was in the front yard of Mr. Dennis' residence. Respondent was standing in the street in front of her residence and stated loudly enough to be heard by them, "If that goddamn motherf---ing nigger comes into my yard, I'll kill him with my baseball bat and that goes for those goddamned motherf---ing nigger- lovers across the street." Charge ¶ 8.
>
> 7. At another time during the Spring of 1993, while Mr. Simpson was in Mr. Dennis' yard, Respondent stated loudly enough to be heard by Complainants, "Look at that nigger and those nigger-lovers. If I had a gun, I'd kill that nigger. I could just puke." Charge ¶ 9.
>
> 8. During that same time frame, Respondent stated to Complainants, "It is bad enough to live with niggers, but worse to have to live with nigger-lovers as well." Charge ¶ 10.
>
> 9. Also in the Spring of 1993, Respondent threatened another African-American tenant of Vidor Village with a bat because of that tenant's race and color.

> *Thereafter, Respondent displayed the bat on a television show, Inside Edition, and threatened to use the bat. Complainants learned that Respondent had threatened the other African—American tenant with a bat. Charge ¶ 11.*
>
> *10. In March 1993, Telegraph magazine reported that Respondent stated, "We don't want niggers here. . .we never had niggers here. . .the only way I'd say hello to a nigger is with a baseball bat." Charge ¶ 12 (emphasis in original).*
>
> *11. In July 1993, Respondent stated to a white resident at Vidor Village that she had attended a Ku Klux Klan meeting and that the Klan intended to burn down the entire complex and shoot anyone who tried to escape. Respondent intended that the white resident would repeat the statement to others. Respondent's statement was repeated to Complainants. Charge ¶ 13.*
>
> *12. In mid-July 1993, Respondent stated to a white resident of Vidor Village that she had attended a Klan meeting and that, "on a certain Wednesday, something would happen to niggers and nigger-lovers that would take care of everything." Respondent intended that the white resident would repeat the statement to others. The statement was repeated to Complainants. Charge ¶ 14*

The actions were so extreme and threatening that the Dennis' simply could not take it anymore and in August 1993, Mr. Dennis moved his family from Texas to another State. The other black residents also left. That left Bomber to face the full brunt of hate and racism – alone. While he had stood up to racism when he could, it was beyond stress; he had begun to sense danger and as a result became fearful. Concerned about Bomber's safety, Mr. Dennis telephoned him from his new home and found Simpson's voice shaky and trembling.

Bomber

Despite his size, Bomber had become nervous and afraid as a result of the persistent bombardment of taunts and threats. His requests for help from HUD were genuine and expressed doubts about the sincerity of federal and local government authorities in addressing the issues of desegregation and safety. However, his relatives were in New York, New Jersey and California, more than a thousand miles away. But now in Vidor he had only a few friends or compatriots or family; with some dangerous foes and enemies out to harm him. He was literally and figuratively alone and afraid.

According to the Texas Commission on Human Rights (TCHR), the KKK crossed the line from protest to violence when they threatened to blow up the projects and made direct threats to project residents. The Commission had to take it seriously because one of the KKK leaders had admitted to others of being involved in black church burnings. When members of the TCHR began an investigation of the Klan, they also received death threats, along with the mayor and a white minister. TCHC found that Simpson, Decuir, and the Denisses were not the only residents who were threatened by the white supremacist groups; a number of white residents who chose either to support the integration plan or were opposed to the white supremacy groups were also threatened and intimidated. Again, there was bases to be concerned because a number of those threatening citizens were convicted felons.

Simpson grew more weary each day and knew that he could not bear it much longer. As the *New York Times* reported in late August 1993: *"Bill Simpson, who in March became the second black person to move to Vidor in recent times, is also leaving. "It's gotten to the point where my nerves have been on edge," said Mr. Simpson, who at 7 feet and 300 pounds, has never been physically threatened but is tired of the harassment. "I don't want to worry who's going to do something and what they're going to do, when it's going to happen, where it's going to happen."*[34]

Simpson related to the Associated Press, and as reported by the

Bomber

Washington Post: "There are good people here, don't get me wrong," Simpson said Sunday in his last known interview, with the Associated Press, as he prepared to leave Vidor. "But it's overshadowed by the negativity, the hostility, the bigotry of this town..."I've had people who drive by and tell me they're going home to get a rope and come back and hang me. . . . "[35]

As Bomber had noted in his interview, all of the residents in Vidor were not hateful and he had become friends with several white residents, who gave him rides, brought him meals, or visited with him. Many viewed the Klan as outside agitators, who were stirring the pot of hate and they were not going to be part of it. They privately applauded the government's actions, since they believed the Klan was causing their town and many of its residents to be cast in an unfair light. In fact, some had openly rallied against the Klan with anti-Klan signs. They were concerned about the stigma and stain which this conflict would leave on their community. They were trying to overcome the legacy of Vidor as a sundown town and rid itself of the Klan.

Reverend Dennis Turberville, who had spoken out against the Klan's intimidation tactics was subjected to one of its customary intimidation tactics. KKK members placed a card at his church that read, "You have just been paid a friendly visit by the Ku Klux Klan. Don't make the next visit your worst nightmare." It had its intended effect - he became scared.

One of Simpson's friends who also lived in the projects in Vidor, Alan, said he had spent time with Simpson and respected his values and sense of community. He was aware of the Klan's presence but was not fully aware of the level or degree of hate which was reaped upon Simpson, and therefore surprised that this kind and genuine man had to leave.

However, the final straw for Simpson came when he saw five carloads of people vising Johnson at her apartment and was told the next morning that it was a meeting to plan his death. This was

Bomber

> 175 Vidor Drive
> Vidor, TX 77662
> July 26, 1993
>
> Mr. Henry Cisneros, Secretary
> Housing and Urban Development
> Washington, DC 20410-5000
>
> Dear Mr. Cisneros:
>
> Being one of only two black residents in Orange County Public Housing Authority, Vidor Site, I too must raise my voice in a cry for help. We have been promised blanket security for this site and none exists. The Ku Klux Klan has free access to this project and the full blessing of the local police to come and go as they please. This was proven to me when the Grand Dragon came to my front door for a confrontation with me while the local police looked on with the local Housing Counselor. Our newest black families refused to stay here for more than two weeks because of threats against their children by another resident. I feel that the local police are affiliated with or at least support the Klan.
>
> Mr. John DecQuir, the first black to move to Vidor has made plans to move because of the racist attitudes of a few people who live in this project and a lot of people who live outside. In the city. Personally, I fear for my own life and well being as well as the lives of the Ross Dennis family who have worked hard to further the desegregation effort. Now, we see all our work falling apart in our faces and we are in danger. As I write this letter, there are five vehicles parked at the residence of Edith Marie Johnson. They are making plans for retribution against her with the Texas Commission on Human Rights. Because of this situation, we have decided to give up the fight and try to leave Vidor. Neither of us can do any more to further the program and we are trapped by our own poverty in a situation that is very volatile. If we stay, we die; it's just that simple.
>
> *[handwritten: Sent this same letter? A Heartbreaker]*
>
> My questions are, was the desegregation of Vidor a planned failure? Is there indeed a conspiracy to keep Vidor all white? Does this conspiracy reach high into HUD and low into OCPHA? Must the Dennis Family and I die for a cause that will die with us? Will the blood of innocent victims stain your hands before this is over? Why is nothing being done to the Executive Director and his staff for allowing this to happen? Please ask yourself these questions and see if you are satisfied with the answers.
>
> We appeal to you for help and we need it quickly, before it's too late.
>
> Sincerely,
>
> *William F. Simpson*
> William T. Simpson
> Resident
>
> cc: Bill Clinton
> Shirley Lewis
> Glenn Selig
> Tom Oxford

Bomber's letter to HUD Secretary Cisneros

not the first time he was afraid and feared for his life. But now it seemed more eminent and the threat had magnified. Part of him was still telling him to stay and fight, even if he was alone.

Bomber

However, the fights which he had waged in the past may likely have been considered worthless by him, since he felt let down by government authorities at both the federal and local levels. So, why stay?

So, he cast his future toward moving back to upstate New York in the Buffalo area, intending to return to Beaumont only as a temporary refuge, since he had applied for disability benefits and planned to move once they were approved. Hence, he packed his belongings and arranged a move from Vidor Village to Beaumont on September 1.

> YOU HAVE BEEN PAID A SOCIAL VISIT BY THE KNIGHTS OF THE
> **Ku Klux Klan**
> DON'T MAKE THE NEXT VISIT A BUSINESS CALL

That day and the next, newspapers throughout the country reported about the tragedy of Bomber's planned move, with some declaring that racism had won! Not easily frightened and having endured a lot in one of his last statements to reporters, Simpson said, "I see no future here, except death." Although he may have had a premonition of his impending death, he did not fathom the "where and why" it would occur.

His Killing

It is reported that shortly after moving to Beaumont, Bomber was killed. HUD had arranged for his moving, inspected the home which he intended to rent, and transported most of his possessions to Beaumont. They had approved his rental and made the appropriate payments. One of the considerations for their approval was that the rental property was within a block from the Salvation Army, where Bomber could get food and clothes.

Bomber rented space from a private investigator and friend, LinMarie Garsee, close to downtown in an old, worn down neighborhood. He had chosen that neighborhood, in part, because of Garsee and its proximity to the library, since he enjoyed reading. However, the area still was known for drug use and prostitution.

Ms. Garsee, who had become very close to Bomber and provided necessary assistance, had driven to Vidor to get him and transport his remaining possessions. They arrived at about 1:30 p.m. The rental home was directly across the street from her home and she would be able to look in on him. She noted, however, that he only had two or three small boxes of clothes or other items, as the entirety of his personal property. He had lived unhinged for so long; it was evident that he was not into the materialistic trappings of life. Bomber needed only the necessities to sustain him.

When they arrived in Beaumont, Ms. Garsee asked Bomber whether he was hungry and he replied "yes, very". Known simply as "Bill" to her, she fixed him what he wanted; bologna and cheese sandwiches, and he ate four. They talked, as they had so often in the past, about life, family and his Christian beliefs. His instincts and experiences informed him that he could trust her.

Bomber was now back on familiar ground, having lived in the neighborhood before. Although there were drugs around and occasional violence, he would not have to look over his shoulder at every moment as he had while living in Vidor.

At about 3 p.m., he said to Garsee that he "was going to walk across the tracks to visit some friends, and then I am going to go home". To this day, Garsee believes the reference to going home, rather than coming back to the rental property, was a premonition of his death. She also knew, based upon her communications with him about his spirituality, that he was not afraid to die. She says she will never forget those last parting words.

Before he left, he met with another friend, Richard Stewart, who was one of the few people in the neighborhood who was nearly as large as Bomber. He was nearly 7 feet tall and before Simpson left for Vidor, amusingly for two large men, they used to tow around town in a small red car. He gave Simpson about five or six dollars so that he could get a drink, because Bomber had not received his disability check. Beaming and smiling, as usual, Bomber headed across the railroad tracks.

It was a typical summer day in "Boremont", a nickname which the city had garnered because of its laid-back style and lack of excitement. This would be Simpson's first day of "freedom" in quite a while, since he had been confined to his apartment in Vidor. What he wanted most was a drink and time to relax, given all the pent-up anxiety and stress of living in Vidor.

That evening Simpson stepped out into the steamy air of Beaumont and met an old friend, Lydia Faye Washington. They went to get some beer and were walking down the street, along with Washington's daughter, Ada. As they walked, a car, with three black males, began to circle the block several times and yelled out something to Simpson and Washington. They figured that this was just typical loud-talk in the hood. Bomber was not looking for trouble; his nature was to avoid conflict.

But this was a tough neighborhood in Beaumont, and arguments and "woofing" was not uncommon. The thought that they might be harmed was not even evident when two of the three young men got out of the car with their faces covered and confronted them, demanding their money. According to Ada, they said something to the effect of "lay it down", referring to emptying their pockets. Ada

Bomber

told her mother to "just do what they say". Simpson initially pointed out that he "only had $2.15."

Ms. LinMarie Garsee

At this point it is evident that Simpson had endured enough. He had just left a situation of incessant racism and here it was some young robbers were demanding that he turn over all of his money, the pittance that he had. According to court testimony Bomber then refused. "Do what you got to do to me," he said, "but I'm not going to give you anything." The shooter then shot him several times with a Tec 9 automatic weapon. Loud explosive bangs exploded from the gun, an assault weapon popular among gangs, and which had been used in mass shootings because of its large capacity.

After grabbing for her purse, an assailant also shot Washington several times, hitting her in her leg, which later had to be amputated, and shortened her life span.

After suffering several gunshots, Simpson tried to run but did not get far because of his injuries and his gimp leg. He fell face forward, bleeding profusely. Because he was still moving, the assailant walked over to him and shot him again. Simpson died about an hour later at Beaumont's Baptist Hospital. He had been shot 5 times – 1 in the right ankle, 2 to the left calf, 1 to the left thigh, and 1 gunshot to the left chest.

Ironically, one of the last words which Simpson spoke to

Bomber

Washington before they were assaulted was how he was finally home and did not have to worry about looking over his shoulder any longer.

His death was reported both nationally and internationally. Only about 12 to 14 hours after leaving the racially infested town of Vidor he was violently murdered in cold blood in Beaumont more than a thousand miles from his birthplace and 1500 miles from his hometown! His hat and some of his belongings were still on the bed, in the clapboard rental home, which he had not ever slept in.

The next day young kids milled around the outline which police CSI had drawn at the scene in the street where Bomber's body fell. Although some of the kids were aware of what had happened, most were unlikely cognizant of what preceded his death in Vidor and its significance historically.

Garsee, only a few years older than Simpson, cried continuously when she learned of his killing. She had received a telephone call from a local newspaper reporter near midnight asking her what she could tell them about his murder. "His murder", she thought, stunned, she did not know he had been killed. She was confused and bewildered, and not believing what she was hearing. When she did focus, she thought back to earlier when she saw the face she had always known – a smiling, laughing, joking, gentle giant.

Before that, she reasoned that even though he had a wandering soul and wanted to explore life, he had finally found contentment in being free of the harassment. He was happy. However, his sense of contentment, similar to other aspects of his life, was momentary.

His murderers were identified as three young gang members, including two who were cousins. Initially, police suspected a young man named Michael Wayne Zeno as the killer, based upon the statements of some witnesses, but later determined that the killers were others. Nine months later three black youths were charged with his death: David Jerome Brown 17, and his cousin,

Bomber

Benjamin Milton Brown 16, and Kamaal Leday 18, all of Beaumont. David and Kamaal were charged first. Benjamin was charged a month later. They were all charged with capital murder as a result of a botched robbery. It was alleged that both of the Brown cousins got out of the car with masks on to commit a robbery and Leday was the driver.

Both Jerome and Benjamin admitted involvement in the crime. Jerome Brown confessed to police that he shot Washington and Simpson. He sought to justify his actions, however, by contending that Washington owed him about $200 which she was refusing to pay and that when he demanded his money, she reached for something in her purse and he began to shoot at her. He further stated that she ran toward Simpson and that he accidentally shot Simpson several times. He implied that Simpson had accidentally got into the line of fire.

Benjamin said that Jerome pulled the trigger but that he had not expected Jerome to kill anyone. He led investigators to the weapon and it was recovered. Leday stated that he was merely giving Jerome and Benjamin a ride home and was unaware that Jerome intended to shoot anyone, although he was aware that Jerome was in possession of a Tec-9 weapon, which Jerome had shown him that night at a party.

Possessing a weapon of that caliber and of such destructive force was about building "street-cred"; and that weapon could be used for varied purposes, including robbery and murder.

Police were initially stumped because of conflicting statements from witnesses, even though the city had offered a reward for arrest of the killers. Police eventually were able to resolve Bomber's killing while investigating another homicide. It was revealed to them that the Browns and a third individual had pooled their money and purchased the Tec-9 from a pawnshop about 6 weeks before the murder. Witnesses disputed Jerome's version of the facts, with one who knew him positively identifying him from the scene and others who stated that the Browns had discussed with them their roles in Simpson's murder.

Although all three were charged, after deliberating about two hours, a jury only convicted David Jerome Brown, the shooter, who received a life sentence. Benjamin Milton Brown was acquitted, and the prosecution did not proceed with respect to Leday. Under a public health analog, Bomber's slaying was still the result of a dangerous hate virus, but of a different strain and possibly dissimilar causative factors, i.e., racial self-hate. Suddenly, the narrative with respect to Bomber had changed, with the negative perspective being altered from Vidor to Beaumont.

Emotions of Family and Friends

Mary Simpson Lewis discussed how she planned to bury her baby boy in Rowland Heights, California. She had talked to him shortly before his death and they had discussed an upcoming visit by him. She also noted that despite his size and life failings, her son had a big heart.

His struggles and death were chronicled in the *New York Times* and the *Washington Post* and *People, Jet* and *Time* magazines and several books. The FBI investigated his death and did not find any link to the town of Vidor or the racism he had endured in the sundown town. Ironically, Nelson Mandela had accepted the Nobel Peace prize that same year. As his mother said to the *Nashville Tennessean* in September 1993: "Don't hate anybody. Not even the man who killed my baby my little boy. Try to make a difference. Reach out and touch a life so it won't happen again."

Lorraine, the only remaining direct family member and a practicing social worker and therapist, says Bomber's death is still raw and painful but she is healing. With both force and forgiveness, in confronting the racism and hate, she says: "I seemed to be forced to consider the cognitive impairment and hardened hearts of all responsible for my brother's death, and I too, like my mother, needed to make the painful decision to forgive because that's all these people knew. This unconscionable and deadly "virus" was the air they breathed and food they ate from the womb. That's what kept them alive. It was their oxygen. They were ignorant, and hate and fear was their educator and school master."

Although Lorraine had received several letters and phone calls from Bomber, she had not seen him for nearly twenty years. Not uncommonly, she felt a level of responsibility for his death, because he had identified indicia, or red flags, that he had some struggles and his life may be at risk. She felt she should have acted on her instincts and gone to pick him up from East Texas. She also felt guilty for not calling him more.

But she hesitated because his letters were usually positive and filled with spirituality and biblical verses. Her role as protector never ended and she now feels it is still important to protect his image, even though in the end Bomber stood up for himself in the face of adversity when many others would have "cut and run."

Additionally, like several others, she has not dismissed the idea that her brother's death was master-minded by persons other than the three teens who were indicted. She felt that somehow, even if unspecified, the level of hate was so strong in East Texas that she logically concluded that the racism and hate had not stopped but instead ended his life.

Her thoughts of others being responsible for Bomber's murder were echoed by Gary Bledsoe, then Texas NAACP leader and an enforcement lawyer with the state's attorney's office. In a letter to Attorney General Janet Reno, he stated he thought Simpson's murder was tied to what had occurred in Vidor. Of course, the KKK opposed any such investigation or inquiry.

There were several ironies to Simpson's death. Although he had grown up in a predominantly white town, with mostly white friends, and attended predominantly white schools and churches, he faced daunting racism from some whites in Texas. Equally compelling, he died at the hands of other black men. Even though he was 7 feet and more than 330 pounds, this did not prevent teenagers with a gun from confronting, seeking to rob, and ultimately killing him. However, for the gentle and kind kid from Seneca Avenue in Olean, it was ultimately his heart and bravery that persevered and made life better for others.

Aftermath

Bomber's death became larger than his life because it brought to the forefront many troubling issues in this country, some of which we believed as a society had significantly changed – "sundown" towns, racism and segregation in housing, and others we hoped would change - intra-racial violence.

His death ballooned beyond a personal story or tragedy, and entered a discursive arena concerning racism and segregation and sultry "sundown towns". It is ironic how a troubled, once homeless, man, who enjoyed a drink, could stand up to the ugliness of such racism. As Ms. Garsee recalled, despite his circumstances, Bomber was very articulate and could explain his positions forcefully and logically.

It also demonstrated that living in a "sundown town" had not converted all, or even most, of the white residents into bigots. Bomber's white friends in Vidor and Beaumont, such as Dennis, Alan and LinMarie, were "hit hard" by his murder. They had all embraced him as a true friend, and assisted and sought to protect him, regardless of his race, size or social status.

At the same time, his murder focused attention upon issues such as black on black crime and the emergence of younger murderous perpetrators. It was also during one of the most tumultuous periods for murder nationally, marking his death among the many senseless murders that were happening in the country.

Bomber

Mr. Simpson's story garnered attention throughout the country, and indeed, other sections of the world because of its tragic nature, what he had endured in Vidor and what many believed were the dangers he had escaped when he left the racist town. After his killing, of course, there was finger-pointing and criticism about who was ultimately responsible for Bomber's killing.[36] Was it the racial hate-baters in Vidor, or the government for failing to protect him in the face of such hostility; the young robber who pulled the trigger; or each were factors combined in a strange symbiotic way?

It spawned a number of changes, with the pro-integration Mayor resigning, a high-profile murder trial of his killer, the Texas Supreme Court being called upon to resolve issues regarding the KKK releasing its membership lists, additional critical audits of the housing authority, the forced resignation of the head of Orange County's housing authority, a revised blueprint for integration in Vidor, and an FBI investigation into Bomber's killing. President Bill Clinton referenced the troubles in Vidor on at least three occasions in speeches in 1994, declaring, "We ended an ugly chapter in discrimination in Vidor, Texas."

The state government also became more aggressive in combatting the Klan. Texas officials obtained an injunction against the Klan, prohibiting them from intimidating residents, from demonstrating at the project entrance, and from impeding access to or egress from the project.[37] It also prevented the Klan from circumventing the injunction when it applied to adopt a part of the highway which ran adjacent to the projects, allegedly as part of the state's adopt-a-highway program.[38]

A year after Simpson's murder, on October 14, 1994, the TCHR issued charges against the Knights of the Ku Klux Klan, Texas Realm and White Camelias of the KKK, and various members of these groups, which had become aligned in their resistance and threats of violence in Vidor. It was brought on behalf of the THRC Commissioner, Mayor Woods, Decuir, Simpson, Joyce and Ross

Bomber

Dennis, and various other residents of Vidor Village (black and white), and a minister, all of whom had been threatened or intimidated by these groups and its members. The THRC's findings and charges, which focused upon the KKK groups and its members, were far more specific, daunting, and overwhelming than HUD's administrative decision.

The THRC found, among other things, that the KKK had engaged in rallies, cross burnings, offered white children $50 to beat up any black kids who moved into the complex, and told residents that they had dynamite which they intended to use to blow up the housing project. In interviews with the print or other media the KKK repeated statements of how they intended to retaliate against anyone who supported integration of the projects. One white supremacist owned a gun range where he had targets named "Official Runnin Nigger target" and "Federal Nigger Huntin license."

The KKK was engaged in drive-bys where they would brandish their weapons, donned hoods and uniforms, and threatened residents. The residents feared for their lives and their families. KKK members would often brag about their intimidation of project residents.

The following are some of THRC's specific findings:

100. On one occasion, Mr. Dennis and his wife, Joyce, observed the White Camelia's school bus at a nearby service station because of curiosity. During this time, Mr. Dennis heard one person, state:

> *There will never be niggers moved into Vidor, or if there is, we will burn the housing project down so they won't have any place to live. (emphasis added).*

101. When Mr. Dennis asked what would happen to the White tenants of the project, the Klan member said, "they will have to burn too". The response caused Mr. Dennis to fear for his and his family's safety...

Bomber

103. Mr. Dennis saw a school bus painted gray with a sign that said, "White Camelia, Ku Klux Klan." When Mr. Dennis stepped up to look inside, they saw a military style rifle rack full of semi-automatic weapons which Mr. Dennis believed to be M-16's.

64. At another of the rallies sponsored by the Knights of the Ku Klux Klan, -Texas Realm, Saturday February 21, 1993 <u>The Beaumont Enterprise</u> reported the following exchange regarding John Decuir, the first black man to move into the Vidor public housing project:

Michael Lowe: "Vidor is a town of 11,000 people and one Black criminal."

Audience Member: "We'll take care of him!".[39]

In 1995 and 2000, the federal district court also issued additional judgments, requiring HUD to undertake desegregation measures and to promote housing mobility, where residents could choose where they wanted to live.[40]

Whether or not Bomber intended to advance housing and civil rights, he did so and consequently is a brief illuminating light in civil rights history. Prior to his murder the federal and local government's initial actions were subpar. His killing embarrassed them into more direct and meaningful action.

The government doubled down on its efforts to end discrimination in housing in Vidor. It recruited additional African-American families to live in Vidor Village, providing additional security, at a cost of one-half a million dollars. Shortly thereafter, one of the black mothers who had moved into Vidor Village commented how she felt safe in the projects. Donise Jackson described her welcoming: "They just come up to me and ask me, 'Are you one of the ladies who moved out here?' and I tell them yeah, and they just, you know, some of them hug me. Some of them shake my hand and greet me. It's really not something I thought would take

Bomber

place."[41]

The federal government also sued Mr. Simpson's primary tormenter, Edith Marie Johnson, in a federal administrative action, brought criminal charges against her, and recruited additional black families to live in Vidor Village. For the first time in its history, HUD assumed the functions of a local housing authority when it took over the Orange County Housing Authority in Vidor, Texas, finding that the county had failed to alleviate the racially hostile atmosphere.

Additionally, the federal government indicted a few Ku Klux Klan members who had threatened Reverend Turberville. They pleaded guilty to several charges, including violating federal housing laws, being an accessory after the fact for lying to a federal grand jury investigating the case, and obstructing justice for harassing a witness during an investigation.

Moreover, the Texas Commission on Human Rights subpoenaed the membership lists of the KKK and White Camelia Knights to determine who may have harassed the black residents of Vidor. When they refused, both groups were fined and one of their members jailed. THRC also obtained injunctions against both groups, barring them from the housing project. In another twist of irony, the lawyer selected to defend one of the white supremacist members was a black attorney from Houston, named Anthony Griffin. Mr. Griffin successfully blocked the release of membership lists.[42]

One noteworthy event was that the ominous town entry signs for outsiders have since come down.

Still, despite the efforts, some of it was a little late and not enough. Ms. Johnson never paid the fine, the criminal penalty was insubstantial and she never served a day of jail time. Similarly, none of the Turberville defendants served any jail time and some went on to be charged with further hate-related crimes. Poignantly, the KKK continued its hate activities, with some of the same members who had harassed and threatened Simpson and others, appearing at a rally on the courthouse steps in support of the killers of James Byrd a few years later. And according to census records as of 2000 only 8 African Americans resided in Vidor. In HUD's subsequent attempts at integration, despite 10 available units at the all-white housing project in Vidor, none of the approximately 50 blacks on the county housing authority's waiting list was willing to move into the complex. Still, HUD cited its actions and efforts in Vidor as a success.

The polarization was not limited to Bomber and time in Vidor was brief. Similar to Bomber, the DecQuirs' and Dennis' homecoming, Donise Jackson's welcoming was short-lived. Within four months she was preparing to leave after a man threatened her and her children in a grocery store parking lot. "He had a knife, and he said he wanted to kill me and my nigger babies," Jackson said. An 18-year-old is awaiting trial on a misdemeanor charge of making a terroristic threat."[43] Most of the other families could not find jobs. Thus, there still was significant sociological debris, despite the government's efforts.

Simpson's Legacy

Bomber never set out to be a civil rights crusader or advance the fight against racism. He had lived comfortably with all races wherever he resided. He was simply trying to find a place to live when he went to Vidor and similarly seeking safe refuge when he returned to Beaumont. Unconsciously, he became a pivotal figure in housing civil rights in the deep South.

This does not mean that Bomber did not sense the importance of his actions or was oblivious to political and social issues. All facts are to the contrary; despite the lack of funds and homelessness, he discussed a wide range of topics with family and friends, including politics and social issues. He was also a very religious person and well-read. Of course, in Vidor he was forced to discuss the issues with Dennis, his lawyer Tom Oxford, and family about hate and racism.

In contrast to many other victims of senseless murders, his killers did not know him and, unusually, his murder was written about nationally and the subject of several documentaries and included in some books. He was run out of a town, where he was merely seeking peace, and into the arms of mindless, violent criminals. According to Lydia Washington, who had suffered the gunshot wound to her leg, before the shooting he had told her how happy he was to be back in Beaumont and escape the racism and tension in Vidor. Also, in an interview a few hours before his murder, he said "load had been lifted off his shoulders" by moving back to Beaumont. However, in the end, indirectly and directly, a cocktail of racism and street violence killed him.

His family, friends and the public then had to face the harder questions about the lingering doubts about why he was killed, what the federal government would do next to integrate Vidor, and how would the community heal.

Bomber's sister, Lorraine, posited that she did not believe that the young gang members were solely responsible for her brother's death. Whether as a result of an arranged murder or otherwise, she says many persons other than David Jerome Brown, who is imprisoned, were responsible for Bomber's murder. "All of those responsible were never made to account for their actions!"

Although the likelihood of the KKK being involved in Simpson's murder appears implausible, there was at least some reasonable

Bomber

basis for such a theory of involvement. The THRC's investigation provided some fuel to this theory. It found that at one Klan gathering in November 1993, one KKK member revealed to others that he had helped set up the "hit" on Simpson. Thus, when Gary Bledsoe, and attorney Tom Oxford requested a federal investigation, it was not considered untenable. However, eventually there was nothing to substantiate this claim and it may have been another attempt by the KKK to cause fear in the community for anyone who supported integration. The FBI's investigation did not substantiate KKK involvement in Simpson's murder.

Present highway sign designating Vidor & Beaumont (photo/A. Goodly)

In that sense, there was still a cloud over Bomber's killing wherein some believed that justice still did not prevail, since those who had harassed and issued death threats were not jailed. At least one family member felt that Bomber's death resulted in a peculiar sense of karma or justice, when informed that many of those who were involved in harassing Bomber and others died early in life or also met untimely deaths.

Bomber

Aside from the senseless loss of Simpson's life, his murder is a lesson in both the ineffectiveness of the government at times and the power it has to combat discrimination and hate. As well, it is testimony to the hate of others based upon ignorance, and unfocused anger by some.

Despite its groundbreaking efforts, the government failed to protect Simpson from violence and intimidation in Vidor Village. Second, while some may applaud the prosecutors' efforts regarding Johnson and the Turberville defendants, their sentences of 40 hours community service, and minor court costs, respectively, were woefully inadequate. The only meaningful event related to Johnson was that she moved out of the complex in January 1994, when HUD sought to integrate the housing projects again.

In the end, Bomber was exceedingly brave. In his quiet way, he stood up for what he believed. He was the last to leave Vidor. He stood up to the Klan directly and fought against his primary tormentors using legal tactics. He stood up to young robbers, when possibly he shouldn't have.

His actions defy the reasoning and logic of many sociologists. Here was a person who was essentially homeless, demonstrating that with a big heart you can help others, even though he was financially destitute. Additionally, Bomber had a level of personal integrity and intuition to recognize that not all, or even most, of the white residents of Vidor were racists, as reflected in his interview with *the New York Times*. Through all of his troubles, he also maintained a strong level of spirituality, seeking to lead a life that reflected Christianity. In fact, the few conversations he had with his sister before his death were laced with references to scripture and the Bible.

According to some who knew him, Bomber never sought notoriety or to be a civil rights protester. Nevertheless, he was cast into a role

Bomber

of hero and he accepted it, until he lacked adequate support and the system failed him.

Many in society have benefitted from his spilled blood. Vidor now has a slightly more diverse population, in some part, because of Bomber's sacrifices. The government improved its administrative processes in housing, again, in part, because of his efforts. Bomber's life also depicts how humanitarianism can trump hate, racism and ignorance.

Bomber and his cousin Gloria

Lorraine echoed how proud she is of her brother's efforts and how, consistent with his personality, he carried a mantle of a person with a big heart. However, he just wanted his square of peace.

One of Lorraine's life lessons from her brother's killing was not merely confronting grief, but the collateral issue of forgiveness. At first, she was angry and felt alone with no one to talk with. Although a certified licensed social worker, consistently addressing the personal issues of others, and having had other

Bomber

personal challenges, Lorraine applied her teachings and clinical experience to herself.

Aside from turning to her faith in God, she engaged in a mindset of being more forgiving. Lorraine reasoned that her brother would have wanted her to forgive those whom had wronged him. It also made her stronger in confronting issues related to racism and discrimination.

She tells the story about how she now lives near where the KKK originated, and one day recently was being closely tailgated by a pick-up truck with a plate bearing a confederate flag. The truck also had a monkey with a noose around its neck. The truck appeared to be driven in a threatening manner, close on her rear bumper. Lorraine refused to be intimidated, however, and did not budge from her lane on the highway. After the pick-up passed her, she reminisced briefly about her brother's problems with the Klan. Then within minutes, along the same road, she saw that two white police officers appeared to have stopped a young black man on the side of the road. She feared that there would be some police abuse, but as she got closer, she saw that one of the officers was changing the tire on the car of the driver.

With intuition, similar to that of her brother, she says that although she believes the pick-up truck driver reflected the hate in some circles, she hopes it is indicative of the minority of citizens in the country, and that the police officers along the road that day and others are more reflective of the majority of citizens.

A sad postscript to Bomber's life story is that the calamity which caused him to relocate from L.A. at age 5 was that his natural father, with the same name, had also been brutally murdered in L.A! When police arrived at the scene, they found him bleeding profusely on the front porch of his home.

By all accounts, Bomber and Lorraine loved their father, although

Bomber

he was murdered when Bomber was only 5. She says that her father's murder had a profound impact on her life, whereas Bomber appeared more reserved about discussing its effects on him. Now, both father and son had been murdered in the primes of their lives at ages 38 and 37, respectively. Lorraine reports that she is still searching for the meaning of the senseless deaths of her father and brother.

Bomber and father William Simpson   Lorraine and her father

MONTE

Remember "lil Monte"? Twenty-one years later, in August 2014, Bomber's playmate, Monte, was also senselessly murdered. Similar to Simpson, Monte had moved away from Olean and lived in New Jersey for about 15 years before returning to Olean. When he returned to Olean, he left his mother and others back in New Jersey. But he still had family in the Olean area and wished to

Bomber

escape some of the tensions and temptations in Jersey.

When Bomber was slain in 1993, Parks was back in town. Parks was killed, execution-style, in 2014 at the age of 54. The killing occurred off Route 16 in the Town of Allegany, near Olean. He was killed at a location overlooking the town, which was considered a scenic view to the town in the valley below, and often visited by tourists and naturists. Monte's killers rolled his body down the overlook, but fortunately it did not descend all the way down the mountainside. Some scenic viewers discovered Monte's body as they were hiking, trying to enjoy the view.

An alleged friend, Gary Maull, 30, shot Parks while he was on his knees, because Monte supposedly owed him money and he mistakenly assumed Parks had begun working with law enforcement authorities against him in a drug case, according to police. Maull had directed Hall to pick up Monte and drive him, Maull, and another witness to the scenic view, where the shooting occurred. Although there was conflicting testimony at trial regarding whether a fourth person was present, it was established sufficiently for the jury that Maull had shot Monte. Hall and Maull then placed gloves on and shoved Monte's body over the overlook, down an embankment.

Monte had become a bit player in the drug scene in Olean. As the prosecutor declared at trial: "The problem with addicts who also sell was Mr. (Parks) was using more of the drugs than he was selling. ... This is what cost him his life," [prosecutor] Rieman said. "According to most accounts you will hear in the courtroom, Lamont owed the defendant a couple hundred bucks. That's what he lost his life for. In addition, the defendant killed him because he believed he was a snitch (in another court case against Maull)."[44] As a consequence, he shot Monte in the face with a .38 caliber revolver from a distance of no greater than 3 feet.

Bomber

As described at Maull's trial, Monte struggled with drugs throughout his adult life. Not surprisingly, this affected most aspects of his life, including relationships with family and friends, employment, and health. More tragic, it rendered him a victim in

the cruel drug world, albeit one cocooned in a small town.

The town had suffered through one horrific incident 40 years earlier, in December 1974, a few months after Bomber graduated from Olean High School. A student at the school had placed the school and town in the national spotlight when, from a 3rd story classroom, he shot and killed 3 people and injured 11 others. Since then, the town had averaged less than1 murder annually, with for instance, only 1 murder between 1999 and 2008.

Although small it had one element which is common to urban areas as well as small towns-drugs. There have been various studies which have linked victim substance use and homicide victimization at high levels. In most areas, drug-related homicides are usually territorial disputes, dealer robberies, or the result of drug-related debts. Although statistics on drug-related homicides are elusive, because it has been difficult to define what is drug-related, reliable research has estimated that drug homicides constituted between 25 to 50 percent of the murders. Monte's killing fell into this category.

As the case regarding Monte's murder proceeded to trial, the effects, both emotionally and physically, were devastating to his family. His sister Paris, struggling with emotions and spirituality, appeared at the court proceedings as the rock of the family. His mother, who had traveled from New Jersey, was nervous, anxious and afraid, and had curled into a ball as the pretrial ran its course, Then, she was hospitalized shortly before the trial began with a stroke and was unable to attend.

During the course of the trial, hospital personnel telephoned Paris

Bomber

and informed her to rush to the hospital because her mother was "not going to make it." They said that she was bleeding from the eyes ("crying blood"), due to kidney problems. In fact, her kidneys were failing, as she was cramping, confused, and short of breath.

Maull was convicted on charges of second-degree murder, tampering with physical evidence, second-degree criminal possession of a weapon, bail jumping and third-degree assault, and ordered to serve a sentence of 34 years to life.

Another alleged friend, Thomas C. "Turtle" Hall, then 54, of Olean, who identified Monte to others as his "best friend", was also involved in Monte's murder. He was the person who helped dispose of his body. He was also convicted, via guilty plea, of second-degree criminal facilitation, for admittedly helping Maull try to hide Monte's body. Hall was sentenced to a 7½-to-15-year prison term.

Monte (pictured above) was survived by his mother Donna L. Clemons; his father, Otis Goodwin; his uncle, Walt Peterson, three children, Brandon and Brittani Clemons, and Ezra Johnson; a sister, the Rev. Paris D. Maine, and a brother, Orman W. "Topper" Clemons.

Monte's mother, Donna Clemmons, died about a month after the trial, before Maull and Hall were sentenced. Parks' family proclaimed that Monte's murder and killers had killed her too, although indirectly. She had taken sick upon learning of his murder and never recovered.

Similarly, Hall's mother had taken ill as a result of the killing. After his arrest and jailing, he had telephoned his mother in New Jersey to let her know that he was jailed. When she asked him why he was arrested and he informed her that it was for Monte's murder, she also suffered a stroke.

The stroke nearly took her life.

Monte had struggled with his ancestral identity, since he had been isolated from his biological father, and longed for that fatherly link. When it did not happen, he turned to drugs and crime. Despite these troubles, he was intelligent and often held full time, engaging, jobs for employers such as GE and RCA. He had not only acquired some marketable job skills; he also had the type of personality where he could talk his way into a job.

He also had a lot of friends and was known for his generosity. But drugs had taken over his life and you could see the ravages of drug abuse in his face. His sister says that he usually refused to have his picture taken because he did not want others to see how drugs had destroyed his body and aged him.

There was an element of perplexity, however, to Monte's murder which did not exist in Bomber's. Bomber did not know his killers, nor had he ever met or interacted with them. To the contrary, Monte knew his killers, and they were considered friends or associates. Living in a small town, most people knew one another and their lives were intertwined. This means that the family of the killers were intertwined with Parks', with Monte's sister, Paris Maine, being the Pastor of the church, which all three families attended.

Moreover, Maull and Hall played on Paris' church's basketball team. Pastor Maine and her family, unsurprisingly, at times also ran into the family members of the killers at the supermarket, mall and other places.

Closing Argument

It is ironic that two young men who were playmates from such a small non-violent town would meet similar violent fates, such as that which beset Bomber and Monte. While they were of dissimilar stature, they had other traits in common. Both had big hearts. They had suffered through calamity and, at some point, had substance abuse issues of differing degrees, that distanced them from their families somewhat. Both had "lost" their fathers, one through murder, the other through parental conflict and distancing. Both had precipitative discussions with others about becoming closer to family. Importantly, both were struggling to overcome those troubles. It is also undisputed about their levels of intelligence and giving spirits. Analyzing every strand of their stories makes it unmistakable that neither deserved to be killed, and their murders clearly left devastation within their families.

Bomber's murder sparked important conversations about both race and murder, but those discussions were short lived. Although most survivors of these men have endured past their emotional peaks, it is clear that both Bomber and Monte were facing crises and hardships far greater than their loved ones understood. Even though the nation's murder spikes are usually driven by violence in major cities, Bomber's and Monte's murders also show that homicides affect citizens from communities which are not usually troubled by murders and violence. In the wake of their deaths, it can be reasoned that their deaths expose the breath of illicit drugs, violence and murder and less so the overwhelming power and reach of poverty.

CHAPTER 2

MY BODY TELLS ME – IT'S ALL ABOUT THE 11'S

It was June 10, 1992. To the vast majority of Big Easy residents there was nothing unusual about this day or early the next morning, Thursday, June 11 - until the single, life-altering, gunshot which pierced the air striking 19-year-old Claude Anthony Doucet, Jr. in the forehead. He did not die immediately, was loaded by medics into an ambulance and rushed to the hospital, and initially listed as being in stable condition. However, he never left the hospital. His lifeless body lingered for another four months in Charity Hospital in New Orleans before he passed away from the gunshot wound.

The tragedy

Claude was at his girlfriend's apartment in the 3700 block of North Dorgenois Street in the infamous Florida Housing projects in New Orleans. There was a loud banging knock at his girlfriend's back door about 1:20 a.m., with two unknown young black men asking for Claude. Cautiously, she did not open the door or let them into her home. Because Claude was lying across the bed, she awakened him and told him that two guys were at the door asking for him. "Claude, they want to talk with you," she exclaimed in a worried voice. He decided to go out into the hallway and speak with them. There was no rustling or commotion. However, within moments she heard a loud crack. It was the tragic gunshot that altered her life as well as many others.

His girlfriend says she ran into the hallway, saw that he had been shot in the head, and immediately called the police. His assailants had made their getaway, in ghost-like fashion, as calmly as when they had arrived.

According to the police when they arrived, Claude was sitting in the dimly lit hallway with a single gunshot wound to the forehead, which had occurred at close range. Police crouched next to him to observe the wound and assess how much he could communicate.

The mystery related to gunshot wounds is that the surface may be very different than what was occurring internally. In this instance the EMTs saw the entry wound but could not determine the extent of the damage, but reckoned that it was probably severe, in that he had been shot in the head. They sought to communicate with him in a whispered fashion.

The scene was a rather dark hallway in a three story architecturally typical project building in the city. They were brick and concrete structures, all appearing the same except that there were also two-story structures. To each building there were front and back entrances with doors to each apartment. The buildings were adjoined with long concrete sidewalks with grass courtyards which had not been landscaped or treated for years, and sparse vegetation or trees. Although the maintenance crew did a fairly good job of maintaining the property, the landscaping was at times studded with some cigarette butts, wrapper bags from McDonald's, and soda cans.

All told, it was not an atypical crime scene in the Big Easy. A gunshot victim in one of the city's housing projects, in the cover of nightfall, and execution-style. It was modern-day Al Caponism, with all of the vestiges of cold-bloodedness and message-sending. The assailants had probably exited from the rear staircase of the building, as though they had wings.

It all happened in a matter of minutes with the fatal act initiated in a mere millisecond. He was lucky only in the sense that most gunshots to the mass of the head or brain usually kill their victim

My Body Tells Me

in a fraction of a second and his wound was to the forehead.[45] He not only was not killed immediately but survived for four months in the hospital, and the crime was initially categorized as an aggravated assault.

Of course, neither the police nor EMT technicians could determine the full extent of the gunshot wound. On impact, a gunshot typically causes two holes, or medically speaking cavities, in the body, with one from the outside appearing as a narrow or thin hole, but inside there is a larger hole, as tissue is thrust away from the wound. This certainly appeared to be what resulted in Claude's case. The damage on the inside was larger and terrible, since it had hit a vital organ in which the tissue does not expand; his brain.

On October 11, 1992, Claude passed away while still hospitalized, and the police then formally categorized or listed his death as a homicide.

Earlier that morning of June 10, Claude had talked with his mom, Cynthia Doucet, on the telephone about how he was changing his life and intended to dedicate his life to Jehovah. As if sensing that his life was in danger, he said he had cut his hair, ditched the earring which he wore, and was moving back home from his apartment, vowing that he was "through with the foolishness". He echoed that "no one cares about you out here", referring to the streets. As she had responded on several other occasions, she said to him, "if you want love, get it from your family."

Although his parents were preparing to attend a conference in Biloxi the next day, his mother said "why don't you come and spend the night here with us." Claude demurred, saying "I'm going over to visit a friend", who lived in the Florida Housing projects. She assumed it was a girlfriend. He asked her to pick him up the next morning at his apartment. Although she had never met this girlfriend there was no specific reason to be worried at that time.

My Body Tells Me

Although Claude had always been family oriented and loving to his parents, about a year before, when they saw him going astray, staying out late, and festering with the wrong crowd they demanded that he leave the household, until he was willing to obey their rules. They thought this was the best way to love their son at the time. Of course, if he changed and was willing to comply, they would gladly welcome him back home.

Frustrated that he was wasting his talent, his mother looked him in the eye and told him, "I can tell you what to do in life but I can not do it for you". "You must want to do it for the right reason," she emphasized. At the same time, he had rationalized that he could make it on his own. These "make-sense" pleas were rejected because, similar to many others his age, he was immature and not as wise as he surmised. As a result, he found an apartment not far from his family's home and got a job.

However, Claude's chance at change or altering his life, which he had vowed to his mother, was taken from him when the bullet punctuated the night. Later that morning was supposed to be his transformation to a normal, more risk aversive life. His parents wanted to trust that he had learned some of life's hard lessons early enough, even though he was only 19. Aren't most lives, and true success stories, comprised of people who have been given second chances?

After the shooting, Cynthia beat herself up continuously for not insisting that Claude stay with them that night before being killed. Although she can say with no degree of assurance why her son was killed, she later recognized that her discussion with him was a sign of his life being at risk. His life had been threatened before by drug dealers but he smoothly talked his way out of harm - at least that's what he thought.

It also was not necessarily one of those "wrong place wrong time"

My Body Tells Me

situations. He had not ventured into a neighborhood with which he was not familiar or known at least peripherally. He was asleep at his girlfriend's apartment and intended to be back at his apartment in the morning. However, she happened to live in one of the notorious housing projects in the city's lower 9th Ward - the Florida housing projects - in a city where all of the housing projects were known for violence and inordinate numbers of murders. Each project was a world of its own, with a hard code of conduct, which some residents exercised.[46] Then, HUD had labeled the housing authority in the city (then with nearly 13,500 units) as the "most troubled".

Although it was near midnight when the shooting occurred there was not an assemblage of people who emerged from other apartments. Was it because they didn't care, simply immune to the violence, or did not want to be involved because of fear? As in many other cases, no witnesses emerged, even though it was highly likely some existed. The projects went on mute. This is a chronic problem in inner city neighborhoods facing rampant violence and murders. As the old saying goes, if they knew they lived on Fear Avenue or Retaliatory Boulevard. Even without Facebook or other social media then, word undoubtedly spread among his "friends" about what had happened and, more importantly, who had committed the killing. That is usually the way it goes.

While police were not sure of the motive for the murder, it had some of the signs of a contract killing. It could have been drug-related, since it also did not happen during the course of a dispute, argument, or domestic matter. The rumor on the streets was that there was a contract on his life after he physically beat a drug dealer in a fight. The two men who had come looking for him on the night of his shooting could hardly pronounce his name, as though they had never met him. The single shot to the head was the signature of a possible execution.

My Body Tells Me

If the hallway could talk, it would scream in pain about a brutal gunshot to the head of an innocent young African-American man, with a full life ahead of him. His shooting had happened in one of the unsafe projects of the city, where so many young men before him and since him have lost their lives, almost always to senseless gunshot violence. The hallway would also exclaim that the single gunshot, lasting a millisecond, would echo in the hearts of his family for a lifetime.

The Family's Reaction

The dreaded telephone call to the Doucet household came from his girlfriend's mother at about 2 in the morning, saying Claude had been shot. His mother's initial reaction was shock and disbelief, but she was pleased that he was still alive. She was already wide-awake, having woke up about a half an hour earlier with a splitting, foreboding headache at the region of her forehead, eerily occurring near the same time of the shooting, and place of Claude's gunshot spot – the forehead. It was as though she was operating under a vision and spirituality beyond the others around her. Thus, before the phone rang, she knew something was wrong.

Nevertheless, her husband immediately got dressed and suggested that she stay home since he would "take care of it." Although Cynthia was strong mentally, emotionally and in her faith, Claude Sr. thought this was part of his protective responsibilities, as a father and husband, to shelter her from the evidence of violence. This time it had hit home. Though he did not know what to expect when he got there, he got in his car and raced to Charity Hospital's emergency room.

Claude had been rushed into the emergency room, where a team of medical personnel, donned in blue and green cotton hospital scrubs, sought to diagnose his injuries and assess whether he was, in emergency room parlance, "salvageable." They figured he was

My Body Tells Me

but did not know how long he would live. Thus, they performed surgery. Charity had seen many gunshot victims in its day and was considered one of the best trauma centers, even if that title was driven by having treated so many gunshot victims. That year it would treat about 2,500 gunshot victims, with amazing results – about 6 out of 7 patients survived. Emergency room doctors at the hospital noted, worryingly, that they treated more gunshot victims than military doctors in combat zones.

The Doucet family is very religious, placing faith in their God to get them through this tumultuous event. Indeed, their armor is their God. In light of their faith, despite the pain, they have not been chronicled into a funeral mood.

It is not even proper to term it an "event", however, because it altered the remainder of the family's life eternally. It caused his parents and sister to have many private interviews with themselves, searching for answers.

For his parents, their most tormenting emotion was experienced because of the killing's effect on their daughter, Dana, his younger sister. She was quiet and reserved so it was hard to gauge her emotions. According to her mother, she was so devastated she said Dana did not want to be around other people. With time, she was able to meld back into social circles but trusted only a few people outside of her family. Later she acknowledged that although the pain was great, she simply could not cry.

When asked today how she feels, nearly 25 years later, she is strong and allows, albeit hesitatingly, and having to reflect on such, that it "changed her life". But she is able to cope. "It does not seem like it's been 25 years or anything close to that," she adds.

Dana sat with her daughter, now 18, pointed to her and said "Chip would have been in the center of her life. He would have played with her as a child, because he was a big kid himself, and protected her later as a student in high school".

Claude was a "good son" who generally did not give his mother any trouble in the home. He was colorful with an engaging, megawatt personality. Even though his mother considered some of his friends as dangerous, she did not sense at the time that he was in danger. She noted he had one serious and deadly vice that bothered her, something that many young men in the Big Easy were afflicted with - the desire to have quick money and being untruthful regarding where he was obtaining more money than his minimum-wage salary provided.

Cynthia had grown up and lived most of her childhood in the city's Sixth Ward or Treme neighborhood. Though urban, it had the feel of a small town, because everyone seemed to know one another, or certainly someone in their family or circle of friends. It was also a location which others throughout the city frequented, because of its night life and closeness to the French Quarter and Canal Street, the primary shopping venue. There was a commerce of drugs and sale of "hot" items. Nevertheless, she had not been lured into the party lifestyle associated with her "hood". What she wanted most out of life was a family- husband and children, living a traditional life. She was a nurturer and wanted to be someone's mom!

The neighborhood was full of characters with unique nicknames – "Piece of Meat", "Tot Taylor", "Rock the Boat", "Precite", "Slick", "Blood", "Kenny Boy", and "Bo Monkey". Most of them were talented and entertaining, but sometimes on the other side of the law. She was surrounded with a large immediate family of eight brothers and sisters, and a more extended family of other step-brothers and step-sisters. More critically, she had a mother who was so stern and intent on protecting them that she felt she was possibly abusive.

Nevertheless, living in the Treme she could not escape all of life's negativity. There were fights and shootings and drugs. Killings in the neighborhood seemed to stem from "dope", domestic-related, or arguments. There were no drive-bys, few automatic weapon assaults, or gang violence. Clearly, she knew what it was like to see families destroyed by drugs or violence.

Claude Sr., exhibiting the protective frame of a strong father, says that he would have elected himself to be murdered rather than his young son. With reasoning common to parents who have lost children to murder or calamity, he thought about what he could have done differently to protect him; his only son. It is not as though he had not had many discussions with his son, preaching about the dangers of the "streets". He says he "still feels the effects of his son's murder" and "has his moments." He acknowledges that the grief and pain were mixed with emotions of revenge or retaliation, since he had grown up in the same violent streets.

At least one of Cynthia's sisters was judgmental, inferring how something so tragic could happen to a family so steeped in their faith. Rather than washing their hands of their God, the tragedy brought the family even closer. They courageously dealt with the psychological aftermath.

Claude Doucet, Sr. and Cynthia Legohn had attended John McDonough High School together, marrying soon after graduation. He went to work as a trucker and Cynthia worked at a restaurant. Elation is an understatement for their feelings when their son Claude was born on November, 11, 1972 in New Orleans at Charity Hospital. What Cynthia always wanted was coming through-being a mom.

The family then moved to Chicago for several years, but returned to the area in 1981. So, Claude's early years were spent in the Windy City. When they returned, they did not live much different than those in their neighborhood; however, they held steady to their

My Body Tells Me

religious beliefs.

According to his mother, Claude was "always talking and moving." It was as though he came out of the womb babbling. He would talk with anyone with patience to listen – family, friends and strangers. She says he inherited this from his grandmother Laverne (her mother), not her, since she was quiet. She commented that "he never met a stranger". For this reason, she would often tell him to give himself a break and be quiet. He also used his appetite for chatter to schmooze and communicate his way out of trouble. Because he was so engaging people liked him and were drawn to him. "He was just a joy", she says.

The only personality trait that matched his talking was adventure and curiosity. He brought home all the bugs and creepy crawlers, such as frogs, he found in the neighborhood and grilled his parents about all of the science and anatomy related to each.

He had a special relationship with his younger sister, with the typical sibling aggravation, where she would complain to their mother about him picking at her. But her love for him was unfading, even when he conned money from her.

There was another personality trait which he wore openly on his sleeve – that is being protective of his mother and sister. He usually wore a smile and joked, except when someone, friend or foe, showed any interest in either of them. He would turn serious, look determined in their direction, and tell the person to back off. Because his mother looked like she was his sister as he attended high school, for protective reasons he requested that only his father come to school for parental matters. He simply did not want anyone saying anything flirtatious to her.

In retrospect, his sister views him as a man-child - brawny, strong and courageous, but also giggly and filed with jokes. Even when he conned money from her, he would repay her indirectly with gifts and fast food. However diverse was his personality traits, or more appropriately ability to adapt from living room to street corner, she still misses him immensely.

Holding On

Claude's existence in the hospital was somewhere between modest recovery and an obituary, leaning far closer to death. The chance of survival was probably less than 5 percent. However, there was probably no better trauma center in the state than Charity Hospital to deal with his injuries, since for decades it had seen several gunshot victims arrive at its doors in ambulances every day of the week. Despite having lost its accreditation a few years before based upon fire code violations and struggling through inadequate funding, the hospital was still revered for its ability to threat trauma victims and unusual diseases.[47] Chartered in 1736, but several rebuilding's later, it was the safety net for most of the city's impoverished residents.

As the weeks, then months, following the shooting passed, the immediate family was programmed into a ritual of work-hospital-home, with many nights a struggle emotionally and physically to get home. It pained some of his aunts and uncles so much that they could not bear the misery of visiting him. The bullet had struck Claude's pituitary gland and lodged in his brain stem. It had caused instant blindness and his mother remembers the massive swelling of his face.

The pituitary gland is located between the eyes behind the nose and is considered the master gland because it controls hormones and other hormone glands. It is close to the optic nerve. Injury often affects growth, blood pressure and reproduction. It also helps maintain mental faculties.

In the early 1990's research was expanding concerning traumatic brain injuries (TBI), with the country's military experiences in

My Body Tells Me

combat serving as the catalyst for better treatment. Doctors analyzed Claude under an ICU scoring system to determine matters such as speech, painful stimulation, orientation to person, place and date; and, undoubtedly, he had a severe TBI score.

According to the doctors, removal of the bullet from the brain would have caused instant death. Although a few doctors' prognosis was grim, thinking he would die within a few days, others were more hopeful and performed surgery to remove certain bullet and bone fragments and clean the area of dead brain tissue.

Claude, as a 2-year-old

When he came out of surgery he was still swollen and bandaged. He was still fidgety and fighting and had to be strapped down. He was on a ventilator, but his eyes were open. His biggest complaint – guess - was that it hurt him to talk; his favorite hobby.

Ironically, the physician who performed the surgery, Dr. Bragg, was the son of a friend of Cynthia's mom.

Once wheeled into a hospital ward, the family took in the scene, smells and sounds of the hospital room, with tubes, machines and hospital bed, and other patients around, and could only wonder how long he would be there and, if so, in what condition. Was there a rush to judgment by the doctors in predicting the outcome?

Nevertheless, the next day was Day 1 of a new life for Claude, as well as his family, with some prognoses being in the category of "hopeless". His doctors told the family they would not know more until after several days and further testing. As of then, even if he survived, they said they didn't think he would ever be able to live at home and would more than likely be institutionalized. It would be too much work for them.

Charity Hospital, courtesy National Park Service

Built in 1939, at one time Charity was the second largest hospital in the country; serving more than 100,000 patients annually. By 1992, it had all the architectural vestiges of an old hospital - mostly standard light cream tiled walls, a bunch of concrete and mortar, steel chairs, crowded waiting areas, as well as cramped patient rooms, with medical equipment lining the halls.

My Body Tells Me

There would not only be medical but psychological services in the milieu of functions which were necessary as part of his care. Untold then was that the family would be the primary provider of psychological care and seeing a talkative, independent and engaging young man transform into a dependent person in a declining condition. Regardless of how long he would be in the hospital and the scope of services, they were committed to being supportive of him and his needs.

Chip was an exceptional patient according to his doctors. His huge smile was still emboldened on his face but gone was some of his swagger. If he was in fear of not making it, however, there was no evidence of such on his face or in his voice. He had as much hope as anyone in the building.

He pined for the opportunity to enjoy the fresh air outside the bleached environment of the hospital walls and hearing the suffering around him. Even though he had family visitors most days, there still was so much missing that most people take for granted. Just to have all of the basic human senses would have been a blessing.

Because his family had been informed that he was blind they purchased a radio for him, but he insisted that he preferred a television because he could indeed see. Although doubtful of his claim, his mother brought him a television for his hospital room.

He amazed his mother one day on a visit to see him when he asked what she was wearing and she said a jumpsuit, and he retorted that he knew and that it was "red", though she had more than one jumpsuit in several colors. Medical personnel related similar depictions, and his lead physician indicated that they wanted to study Claude because he had performed in an exceptional manner to their treatment.

They also discovered that he was not like many of their other

My Body Tells Me

gunshot victims. They found that he was intelligent and had an unusual optimism. When the hospital checked his work history for a disability assessment, they found that he had worked all available quarters for purposes of qualifying for Social Security.

While the medical prospects for Chip were grim, the family pinned their hopes on their God and Chip's optimism. From an objective medical perspective, regrettably, there was experience and researched basis for a grim prognosis.

According to the American Association of Neurological Surgeons (AANS), "[g]gunshot wound head trauma is fatal about 90 percent of the time, with many victims dying before arriving at the hospital." Unsurprisingly, they are the most lethal of all firearm injuries. While there are multiple factors which determine the extent of damage caused by a gunshot wound, AANS reports that "a bullet wound going through the right frontal lobe tip toward the forehead and well above the base of the skull is likely to cause relatively mild clinical damage because it passes through no vital brain tissue or vascular structures. However, a similar bullet passing downward from the left frontal lobe tip toward the temporal lobe and brainstem is likely to be devastating because it passes through eloquent brain tissue and is likely to injure important vascular structures inside the head."[48]

There were a slew of doctors, nurses and interns, with their own microscopic view of prognosis for Claude, mixing good news with bad. They were often relying upon standardized medical timelines.

Although the family was hopeful, Claude's belief was even greater. The gunshot had not destroyed the real Claude. He believed he was going to win, and his spirit was indomitable.

The family was very appreciative of the staff at Charity hospital. On one occasion, however, when a doctor was insensitive to Claude and also openly negative to him about his prognosis,

My Body Tells Me

without blinking, Cynthia was all over him. "Never tell him that type of news".

Without their faith, the Doucet family would have succumbed to hopelessness. They did not.

Did he Die Multiple Times?

At some point his health began to decline, and he was put on a trachea and feeding tube. Once a fit and toned young man, his weight had plummeted to about 85 pounds. He then slipped into a deep coma, which lasted about 2 or 3 weeks.

A coma was not unexpected in light of the trauma and swelling which Claude had suffered. The swelling was to the brain itself and could eventually cause the brain mass to push down on that part of the brain stem, that's responsible for arousal and awareness.

But the family was still confident because they recalled that when he was first brought to the emergency room after the shooting, most doctors did not believe he would last through the day. They had underestimated him. Then after performing the initial surgery some estimated that he would only live a few days. Again, they had underestimated him. So, this time, after the coma, when doctors said he was not going to make it much longer, they were still somewhat skeptical. He was such a fighter!

There was another event, while he was comatose, when nurses were alerted by the machines to which he was connected going off in his room. The machine's beeping was an indication of consciousness. One of his aunts was vising at the time and the nurse asked her what had happened. His aunt Alma, who would visit nearly every day, responded that she was talking to him, as she usually did, and his body seemed to twitch and acknowledge what she was saying. Surprising to the nurse for a patient in a coma, his aunt said she kept repeating his nickname of "Chip", which the nurses were not aware, whereas the nurses had referred to him only as "Claude". Alma said that "Chip" was reserved only for close friends and family, and he must have heard her and felt secure enough that his body responded.

Recent medical research has found that one of the most effective tools to assist coma patients with recovering their consciousness is for someone with whom they are familiar starting a conversation with them. And according to similar studies, 30 to 40 percent of patients who are believed to be in a state of full unconsciousness retain some level of consciousness.

That supposed "final day" came in September and the hospital called the family and said that he had passed away and a family member was necessary to identify his body. When Mr. and Mrs. Doucet arrived at the hospital, personnel could not locate him or his chart. They finally located his body in the morgue, which was attached to the hospital.

The Doucet's walked the long dreary hall at the bottom of the hospital to the morgue, where his body lay among other victims of violence, old age or health infirmities, such as cancer and heart attacks. He had not been placed in a cooler yet.

Miraculously, he was not dead, indeed. They had removed the breathing equipment when they declared him dead, but he was still breathing on his own, while lying in the morgue. They were stunned that he was still alive, though they had already declared him medically dead. He was not. Chip was still fighting.

Because hearing is thought to be the last sense thought to go in the dying process, had he heard the doctor declare him dead? Had Claude, the ultimate smooth talker, cheated death and talked his way back to life?

Hospital personnel promptly transported him from the morgue

My Body Tells Me

back to a hospital ward, where he continued to breathe on his own, although laboriously. Was this an example of a medical miracle?

He certainly had refused to give up.

How Claude had cheated death was both a medical puzzle and somewhat mystical. He had battled brilliantly and was too alive in his own way to die.

Doctors asked Claude's parents' permission to write about his medical case as part of their research, which the parents kindly permitted. According to some of them, this was a medical miracle! Doctors and nurses looked at one another and shook their heads; baffled. Otherwise, they could not explain what had happened. For some unexplained reason, spiritually, he was given an additional breath of life.

More recent research and technology allow clinicians to detect consciousness in people believed to be brain dead and exhibiting no outward signs of awareness. Advanced medicine has also more recently established that in rare instances a person believed to be brain dead may recover brain function.

Claude lived for another couple of weeks. But, on the morning of October 11, the hospital called again and said he had passed away. This time it was real. Far beyond the doctors' initial prognosis, his body had finally shut down.

His mother recalls that the previous day he had complained about being very cold, despite having several blankets. He begged her to stay, but she said she would see him in the morning because she had to go home to cook something for his dad and help Dana with her homework. She felt bad that she had to leave him since she had not often said "no" to him while he had been hospitalized.

As she left, she saw a tear roll down his face. This was her final memory of his mature, but still baby-like, face. In that moment,

My Body Tells Me

sadly he was again the same infant born to Claude and Cynthia. As she reached the hallway, a tear also rolled down her cheek.

Particularly, during his hospitalization, Claude's eyes spoke for him. They were usually bright and full of life, despite his physical limitations and pain. That night his eyes were dimmed.

Claude officially passed away on October 11, 1992. Given what had occurred several weeks earlier, Dana, of course, had to ask, "are they sure he is dead?"

His story of cheating death would be legion in this storied hospital in New Orleans, where so many city residents had come through its doors and whose staff was chocked full of stories of medical miracles. In his 4 months stay, the hospital had compiled at least 4 thick folders of records.

His body was cremated and his ashes were temporarily held by his grandmother, then his aunt, who placed his urn near the stereo because he loved music.

And then there were the photos. Whether taken as he posed or impromptu, whether as a child or young man, Chip was usually smiling or cheery. His last four months, hospitalized, were a depiction of another side of him.

When Doucet family members were asked whether it would have been better for him to expire on the night of the gunshot or go through 4 months of hospitalization and suffering they all replied, without hesitation, that the additional four months were preferred. Although they saw him in pain and deteriorate, and life sapped from his body slowly, they still could hug him, kiss him, communicate and hope for a medical transformation.

Dana conceded, however, her views changed once Chip reached a vegetative state; she then wanted to see him out of his misery. She also knew that there would be unforeseeable maladies which would affect everyone in the family. But her focus was that Claude could never bear mentally a vegetative state which was so distant from his personality.

Of course, it would have been nice to see him "blinged-up" in earrings and gold jewelry, although such was an artificial life or facade.

When doctors said that if he lived longer, the family would have to change his diapers and it would be a burden to care for him constantly, his mother responded strongly and matter-of-factly, "that is what I had to do when he was a baby". "That is what I had to do when he came into this world and what I would have done to keep him in the world".

Doctors also told her that he would probably suffer chronic, severe headaches. Cynthia was not discouraged! They also said he would suffer from a depressed mood. Without hesitation, Cynthia expressed that she was still not disheartened.

As noted, Dana's perspective was somewhat different. Based on a quality of life assessment, she was able to let go once he reached the stage where it was clear that under even the best of circumstances, he would not live anywhere near a normal life. For her, Claude's personality was far too strong to be confined to a vegetative existence. Not only would she not want to see him live such a life; she was convinced he would not want to live such a restrained existence.

Led Astray

For some reason, Claude started to be led astray when he turned 15. As a result, he had some minor scrapes with the law, having been arrested for car theft with two of his buddies in an adjoining parish. When he appeared before the judge in Jefferson Parish, the judge released him, sensing that he was no true threat to society,

My Body Tells Me

and telling him that the criminal life was not for him.

His parents had read him the same sermon more than fifty times.

They implored him to take a look at who he was becoming. Nonetheless, there were further indications, however, that he was doing some illegal things to obtain funds. Because he would not obey the rules of their home, they demanded that he find another place to live.

When his parents would confront him about his vices and their suspicions that he was doing something illegal, such as selling drugs, he would flash his wide, engaging smile and simply deny all suspicions and allegations. He did not want to admit to anything because he did not want the truth to hurt them. He was loquacious and charming and used it to his benefit at times.

As much as he liked to control the environment which he was in, by being the jokester and story teller, he appeared to not recognize that he had conceded control of his life to the streets and the code of those who ruled there. It was a whole different world, consistent with what his parents had expounded upon.

He was in the streets but not of the streets. When his mother would refer to him as "Chip" in the earshot of certain rough friends, he would remind her to call him Claude, since those friends were not entitled to know his intimate family nickname.

In an open conversation with his parents he once told them that he knew they loved him and had done all they could to raise him. "It was not you or dad," he said; "I wanted to do what I wanted to do". He also knew that he had gone astray. His mother thought to herself that he simply did not recognize that "it is not a nice world out there." Her heart was telling her that "he would have to learn the hard way and would never learn anything if she let him do as he desired". Although she did not wish to be as strict as her mother was with her and her siblings, she also knew that lack of discipline could only lead to bad things.

No Smiles

Having grown up in another of the city's housing projects - the St. Bernard project - Claude Sr. had several discussions with his son about the dangers of the streets and some of the young men Claude was hanging with. He explained that Claude was not of the foundation or character to compete with drug dealers and hard-core criminals. "See son, those guys don't smile", suggesting that their lives were so messed up, they had little to live for. Recognizing the dichotomy, Claude Sr. warned his son, "You are not going to last in those streets." "And even if you show love, the streets don't love you back".

It was a lesson which Claude Jr. possibly learned in the most difficult way – with his life. Profoundly, Claude Sr. recognized that while different people dibbed and dabbed in criminal activity in the city, like other aspects of life or business, there are different levels of risk taking. Thus, there are those who are malicious, with bad intentions, and others who are focused on trying to make a fast buck.

Claude Sr. had essentially escaped the trappings of the "bad neighborhood" and negative influences through spirituality and athletics. He became a star running back at John Mc Donough, being voted on some all-city football teams. Going forward there was little time for nonsense since he had a wife and family to support.

Claude Jr.'s way of life, however, was not uncommon. There were, and still are, many young African-American men who existed under the same "code" or rules, which are informal rules that govern interpersonal conduct, including violence. "In the street culture, especially among young people, respect is viewed as almost an external entity that is hard-won but easily lost, and so must constantly be guarded."[49] They were talented and had strong family upbringings and as a result were respectful of their parents, yet street-wise and tough, constantly aware that the code of the streets was never to let anyone disrespect, "use", or "punk" you.

The code and this constant fight for respect also drove their style of dress in clothes, jewelry and the like. So, for them, they had one personality for the home and family and another for their friends and the streets.

At the risk of oversimplification, deep down some people have dark hearts and others have good hearts. Moreover, the unwritten rules of the "streets" demand your life for certain transgressions. In other words, under the code, life was cheap. And Claude simply was not of the malicious ilk and instead had a support system upon which to build a future. He figured a lil extra money allowed him to buy some of the clothes and jewelry that fit the dress styles of others in the neighborhood.

It was rumored that Claude had disagreements and physical confrontations with drug dealers where he had beat them up physically. It was further rumored that he had talked his way out of a "hit on his life". He put those disagreements to the side, but allegedly they did not. After his death, some of his friends related how Claude dabbled in selling drugs "here and there" and probably had another "hit" on his life by drug dealers.

So, was his killing about a drug debt, revenge, or jealousy? It was never clear. What was undisputed was that he had been shown love by his family, had parental direction, and had not suffered poverty.

But when Claude vowed to his mother to cut his hair, ditch the earring, and stop hanging with certain friends, indirectly, he would be abandoning the code which had driven his life into nonsensical conflicts. Did ditching the code also affect the artificial shield which kept him and other young men on alert for danger? It's a tougher decision than many imagine because of the peer pressure and potential of losing the friends and artificial "status" that may have taken a few years of conflict and swagger to build.

Parents, such as the Doucets', often question whether their children will be followers or independent decision-makers. Although there were certainly manifestations of Chip as being his own person, there were also signs that he was a follower, in the sense that he wanted a piece of the fast life, and would take the types of risks associated with such lifestyle.

The Real Chip

Dabbling in selling weed and interpersonal conflict with drug dealers was hardly a full or accurate depiction of Claude. He was colorful and engaging. Friends relished being in his company. By all accounts, Claude was a good person, who loved family, friends and animals. "Chip" as he was known to his family and friends, was special, well-liked and exhibited distinctive human qualities. He was close to his mother Cynthia, father Claude Sr., and younger sister Dana.

Dana noted that she and Claude were polar opposites. Where she was quiet and reserved, he was bubbly and effervescent. She talked to few people and had few friends, and he talked with everyone and was loved by all. He wanted to be the center of attention, well dressed, with several girlfriends. Dana would have rather blended into the corner. She rooted for the good guys and Claude rooted for the bad guys.

As his mother described him, "he was very friendly and loved by all. He was 6'2, 185 pounds, muscled, wore sized 12 shoes, and still growing." He was also intelligent and a good student where he had attended his parent's alma mater, "John Mac". Despite the transgressions with the theft of a car and hanging with some unsavory friends, he was an obedient and respectful son. Academically, he was far ahead of most of his classmates. He excelled in difficult subjects such as math and chemistry, and also scored high on standardized tests. Claude's academic achievements were outstanding enough that he was offered an academic scholarship to Texas A&M, which he never fulfilled because he failed to graduate due to missing too many days from school.

His mother tells the story about her meeting an elderly woman at a bus stop in New Orleans, wherein the stranger told her about a young man from the neighborhood who helped her bring in groceries and perform other help around her home. Suddenly, Chip appeared near the bus stop and the elderly woman pointed and said, "that's him", asking Cynthia "do you want to meet him?" Holding back, Cynthia chuckled and said proudly "I think I know him well." That type of activity and his love of people more clearly defined the real Claude. She had often watched as he connected with strangers. She would laugh at his brazenness.

In some ways, Claude, Jr. already had it all. He was handsome, intelligent and athletic. His personal stat sheet ranked high- he had lots of girlfriends, was proficient in most sports, and had achieved certificates as an honor roll student on many occasions.

Attempting to ensure completeness about his character and personality, however, his mother says "on the other hand, he liked money", implying that he had imperfections as we all do, and was a "follower". Undoubtedly, the latter contributed to a lifestyle or associations with others more dangerous than himself which led to his murder.

Claude's murder was not of the variety we read about in *People's* or *Reader's Digest* magazines, in the sense that it had happened to an ordinary person. Nonetheless, Claude was a special person to many. Considering the human population, however, Claude was ordinary; as is more than 99.9 percent of the world's population. But then in God's eyes we are either *all* ordinary or *all* special, depending upon your perspective or level of spirituality. More importantly, we are defined by our family, friends, loved ones, and spiritual Supreme Being, regardless of how the rest of the world may judge us. In any event, he was taken from his loved ones far too soon.

Having grown up in a loving home in the 7th ward of the city to a close-knit family, Claude was respectful, kind and God-fearing in the home. His family values emanated from his parents and sister Dana.

Violence in the projects

In 1992 there were ten housing projects in New Orleans, comprising more than 12,250 units and tens of thousands of residents. The city was at the high end of city rankings for the percentage of residents living in public housing units.

The Florida housing development, which was the smallest of the projects, was constructed during World War II, between 1941 and 1946, as housing for veterans and to help families made homeless because of the Depression. It sat on an 18-acre tract of land bounded by Florida Avenue, Dorgenois, Congress, Law and Gallier streets. Its layout employed traditional architectural principles for housing developments in the South. It was rebuilt in 1953 with nearly 80 percent of the population living at or below the poverty level and 98 percent of its residents were black. At its height, there were 47 two-and three-story brick buildings with about 734 units and more than 2,500 residents. It has since been razed.

One of the development's early residents was Ruby Bridges, the courageous young black girl who desegregated the 9th Ward's

My Body Tells Me

William Frantz school. She was one of the first African Americans to attend an integrated public school in New Orleans. She was one of four young black girls at the epicenter of the integration school crisis in the city.[50]

At age 6, Bridges attended the formerly all-white elementary school, flanked by federal agents and a cacophony of taunts and threats by an angry mob. She was the only black student in the school and because of the threats and venomous climate ate her lunch in her classroom every day. She is featured in the famed Norman Rockwell painting of her fateful opening day at Frantz, titled "The Problem We All Live With," and now hanging outside the Oval Office in the White House.

Claude, cousin Herbert, and a friend in the neighborhood

However, by the early 1990's the Florida had fallen into serious disrepair, and violence and gunplay was normal. This was also the hard early 1990's when dope and violence ruled the city. The 5-year period 1990 to 1994 represents the largest number of murders ever in the city – 1,762- for a 5-year period. There were 279 murders throughout the city in 1992, staining it with the highest metropolitan murder rate in the entire country (55.2); it exploded to 395 in 1993, again the highest rate in the country at 80.3, per 100,000 residents.

The murder clearance rate for 1992 was 41.2 percent (115), and 34.4 percent (136) for 1993. Claude's murder was only two years before 1994 when the city suffered the highest numbers and murder rate ever for the Big Easy, with 421 killings, at a rate of 85.8.

Additionally, during this period homicide victims were becoming younger and Claude fell into the most vulnerable age and ethnic category: a black male between 18 and 24.

Claude and his sister, Dana

Importantly, during this period less than forty percent of the murders were solved or "cleared". Killers often were never arrested or roamed free. It was not as though they did not have a clue about what happened or even possibly who were the perpetrators. Resolution or clearance has been tied to a number of factors such as the status and race of the victims, location of the murder, and more compelling, could they find credible witnesses to make a story stick.[51] Consequently, the police's failure to solve

My Body Tells Me

Claude's murder then was not atypical. Moreover, it occurred in a neighborhood setting where some police were later found to have conspired with drug dealers and killers.

And nearly one-third of the 421 murders (145) in 1994, occurred in NOPD's Fifth District, which outdistanced every other district. Poignantly, that year there were 52 murders in three of the largest housing projects - the Desire, Calliope and Florida in 1994. The Florida led the way where there were an astounding 26 murders, thus directly victimizing nearly one of every 100 residents. Thereafter the police established a sub-station in the projects.

A court decision describes two of those murders in 1994:

On July 10, 1994, at around 2:30 a.m., in the 3700 block of North Dorgenois in the Florida Housing Project, Edward Elbert "little Wynn" Wynn was shot several times by two assailants. The autopsy revealed that the victim had eighteen gunshot wounds entering from the front and back and from the base of his neck, down his torso and through his extremities. Although the toxicology report indicated a high level of alcohol and the presence of cocaine, the cause of death was from the gunshot wounds.

On July 16, 1994, at around 9:30 a.m., in the 3800 block of North Dorgenois in the Florida Housing Project, William Henry "Peewee" Jones was shot several times by two assailants. The autopsy revealed that the victim had fifteen gunshot wounds entering from the front and back. The toxicology report from this autopsy likewise revealed a high level of alcohol and the presence of cocaine, but the cause of death was from the gunshot wounds, several of which would have been immediately fatal.

State v. Nelson, (La. 4th Cir. 1997).

Two young men were convicted of these murders and sentenced to life in prison, where they remain today.

Thus, Claude's death was not the only homicide victimization in, or resident from, the Florida. The aforementioned murders, which the court describes, occurred in the same Florida project block or the next block from Claude's. A similar slaying occurred a month later in 1992 when two men approached a 27-year-old man and shot him several times. Another one of those other victims was Ruby Bridges' youngest brother, Milton, who was murdered in the development in November 1992, only about a month after Claude died. Only 30 years old when he was murdered, he left four young daughters who ended up living briefly with Bridges (then married as Hall) and her family.

Those daughters were students at the Frantz school, which Bridges had integrated more than 30 years earlier and had volunteered at since her graduation.

In addition, during this same period, the Florida was infested with crooked cops who worked from the project and were involved in drug running, protecting drug dealers and intimidation. Several of them were later convicted by federal prosecutors of a murder which occurred in October, 1994, while still on the police force, with the leader having ordered a "hit" on a citizen who had reported police brutality. During his trial, it was brought out that although the Florida was the smallest of the city's ten projects, it had the most murders in 1994 (23), which decreased after the arrest of the NOPD officers. That lead police officer was sentenced to death and is currently on death row in a federal penitentiary in Terre Haute, Indiana.

Aftermath and Deja vu

Now that Claude is gone, his mother says "it is like part of me is missing and I won't be myself until I get him back." She also says that through his murder she recognized that "fathers love their children as much as mothers do," acknowledging that she saw the

My Body Tells Me

struggles of her husband in dealing with such a great loss of a child. Whereas she can talk about Chip's murder and listen to a tape recording of his voice, his father simply cannot.

One of the more perplexing phenomena was Dana's transformation from Claude's death. He had been her protector, provided jokes and entertainment, and always there for her. She believes her life spiraled downward later as a result of decisions she made triggered by Claude's killing. She began to root for the "bad guys". Years later she also wound up choosing a young man in her life, unconsciously to replace the loss of Claude. Although he initially appeared to have Claude-like personality and qualities, in the end he did not, by any measure. Nearly everything that could go wrong went wrong. They separated while she was 4 months pregnant and only 20 years old.

The magnanimity of the issue of violence and murder beyond Claude's killing is not lost on the Doucet family, with Cynthia saying that "it's amazing the number of people who go through this, so I end up talking about it on a regular basis, maybe every other month." Psychologists and other mental health experts often discuss the benefits of talking with others who have had similar life tragedies or seen up close the effects of human cruelty.

Support groups have now become common and most city governments utilize victim professionals to assist families. Undoubtedly, these spirited and cathartic discussions by Claude's mother provide some psychological relief, secondary only to her reliance upon her religious bonds and continuing strength of family and close friends.

Tragedy struck Cynthia Doucet's family again, nearly 14 years later in July 2006 when her nephew, and Claude's cousin, was killed by his companion, leaving behind a young son and daughter. The children were left with the complexity of their father having

My Body Tells Me

been murdered and their mother jailed for the killing. Similarly, Herbert Spurlock, Jr., 32, was her sister Karin Legohn's only biological son.

Cynthia was able to respond hurriedly to her sister's house when she learned of her nephew's shooting. The oldest male child had called the police and exclaimed "my mommy just shot my daddy." He had been shot once in the chest. She relates that "feelings of déjà vu" overcame her and she suffered through "an out of body experience." The nephew's companion was trying to leave the scene after the shooting but was captured by others before she could leave.

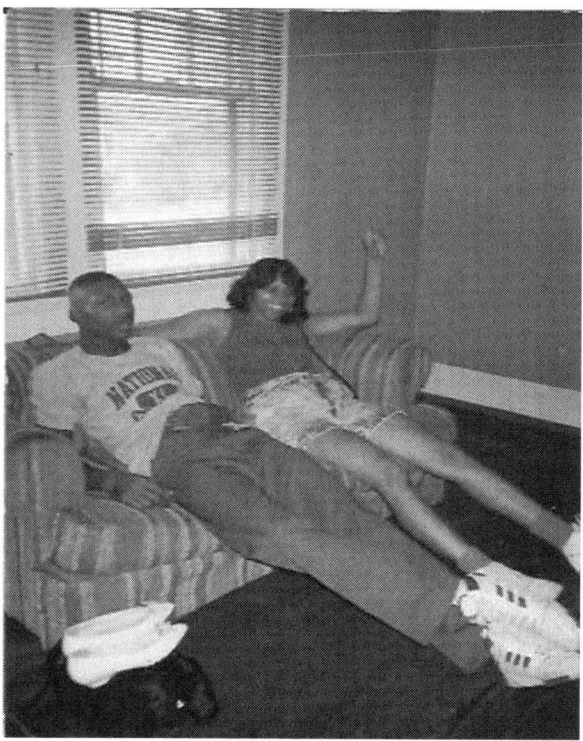

Claude and his mom, Cynthia Doucet

Cynthia's protective familial instincts, however, were to keep her sister Karin calm and not allow her to view her son being transported in a body bag from the home by the medical examiner's office. She reached out a protective hand and coaxed her from the front door of the home. She had been over that psychological cliff with her son's killing and fought to avoid some of the pain for her sister. For her the good thing was that the perpetrator of her nephew's murder was caught – it was sad however, that it was his companion, someone she knew and had shared time with.

Still, it reflected one of the more cruel ramifications of one parent killing the other - minor children left with grandparents or others, with one parent dead and the other imprisoned.

Claude's killers were never caught, arrested or prosecuted. Hence, executioners were on the loose. Whoever killed him wound up on the non-clearance side of the ledger. No motive has been revealed and his murder is probably not even among the cold cases; if so, it is ice cold. For the Doucet's, they were just as hungry for justice as other families and did not care about clearance or murder solved rates.

In fact, there has not been any contact from the police with Claude's parents since that tragic week in June 1992. From the government's perspective, his life became "another statistic" or another unsolved killing of a black man. The identities of the perpetrators were never even known or revealed. But it is clear that in the "streets" others know who the killers were, as is the case in many unsolved homicides. There was a significant likelihood they were in Claude's age range, since then nationally nearly 40 percent of known firearm homicide offenders may have been between the ages of 15 and 20 years old.[52]

Deep down, Cynthia believes that some of his friends know who killed her son, and that there were those who offered condolences who have the answers to all their questions. They were not talking then and are not talking now.

One wonders whether in the then existing climate of violence the killers killed again or were themselves murdered, since retaliation was rampant in the city. It is also befuddling about whether the killers even thought about the serious consequences of murder in Louisiana, where although many perpetrators are never caught, most of those who are convicted take a one-way ride to prison never to return to society.

When asked her views on guns and violence, Mrs. Doucet says she has always hated guns, and that life has become so cheapened.

Although there may be no Hollywood or spellbinding feature to the story about Claude's killing, to his family it is far beyond cinematic; it is wrought with devastation and tattered lives. Relying upon their faith they believe that they will "see him again right here on earth", in a resurrection.

This year, Claude would have been 43 years old. For some families, the date or anniversary of the murder may loom larger, like a cloud, each time it approaches. When Claude's mother was asked about how she remembers the date or anniversary of when it occurred, she said mysteriously or spiritually, "my body tells me". Thinking deeper about the critical timelines she noted the number associated with Claude's life events – number 11 - birthday, November 11, shooting, June 11, and death, October 11.

Karin and Herbert

Karin's reaction to her son's murder in July 2006, was different than Cynthia's, yet not unusual or atypical. Nearly every level of betrayal, emotions, and consternation existed in connection with her son's murder.

Whereas, Cynthia had been nearly speechless upon learning of

My Body Tells Me

Claude's shooting, with her hand over her mouth and a calm demeanor, Karin was enraged and fiery. Her emotions were evoked in loud screams and foot stomping. Knowing the killer, she wanted to "hurt her". "Why would she do this, when I had been like a mother to her", Karin thought.

Herbert had lived at home with his mother, girlfriend, and two minor children. His girlfriend had lived with Karin and Herbert, since she was about 16 years old, even though she was not related by blood or marriage. Karin just had it in her heart to help and take care of her, after her grandmother, with whom she lived, passed away. She helped her through high school and entering college. His girlfriend had killed Herbert as he was preparing and signing cards for his girlfriend's birthday.

She and Herbert began a relationship and existed as part of the larger family. For all practical purposes, Karin had raised the killer, as though she were her flesh and blood.

Herbert's death initially left Karin angry and hostile, feeling betrayed. She says, "I was mad with God for a long time. Although they said He takes the best, He did not have to take the best of the best."

Karin's instincts were driven to "an eye for an eye; tooth for a tooth" perspective. If she had acted on her instincts of revenge, it would have been easy for her, she felt, to have been in St. Gabriel's [the women's prison facility where the killer was imprisoned] for murder. "She [the killer] took something I cannot replace." Only prayer and faith in God brought her out of that phase of grief; though she "still has her moments of anger," but has no thoughts of revenge.

"You don't get over losing your only child, especially if he is a good one" Karin says. And he was a good son! "All he did was work and take care of his family", she eulogizes. "His family was his life." She further explained: "he was not a street person; he was a homebody". He helped everyone in the neighborhood. He stayed at home so much that his son nicknamed him "Homey". When friends would ask him to go out for a drink, Herbert would usually refuse, preferring to have a drink at home. Some commented that he was like a father and mother, because even though he worked a construction job, he would come home and do laundry, clean the house, help with homework, and attend school functions.

Herbert's killing was surprising and befuddling. There were no indications of infidelity or anger on his part toward his girlfriend. He simply appeared happy and content with a family lifestyle and never complained. Herbert sacrificed personal material possessions so that she or his children would have a better lifestyle.

On her birthday, his girlfriend arrived home after consuming drugs and drinking. She called him into the bathroom, and without warning, shot Herbert.

Karin was instantaneously converted from a grandmother to a mother, a task and responsibility which was unexpected and required extreme sacrifice. Opening a different chapter in her life, she was not sure, at first, how she would deal with the variety of issues which accompanied that responsibility.

Some of the initial concerns was negotiating the currents surrounding what she would do regarding listing the killer in Herbert's obituary as his companion, and the children visiting their mother, who was in jail pending a trial. With some reluctance, she listed his companion in the obituary, but left the decision of the children's contact and visiting with their mother to them. Karin's brother, Darrin, volunteered to transport them to the prison, if and when they desired to visit their mother.

Her granddaughter's comment one day reflected the tragedy, conflict and trauma which the murder had inflicted upon the

My Body Tells Me

children. Troubled, she initially responded to questions about visiting her mother by stating, "when she killed my daddy, she killed my best friend".

Next, came the criminal proceeding, which Karin attended. She was an employee of the local civil court and, thus, well familiar with the justice system. What she had expelled from her mind in terms of "street justice" would now occur in the judicial system, where Herbert's killer was claiming insanity because she had allegedly been hearing voices. Where Karin had been enraged, she had calmed and simply wanted to fight on her son's behalf.

The day of reckoning was upon her as the court considered a guilty plea, and the court would consider Karin's opinion before accepting such a plea and the applicable sentence. She knew the process. Nonetheless, internally, there was a fight between lingering anger and level-headedness. The equation of what was right and just under the circumstances had to factor in how it would affect the children. She knew that she had to nudge her personal feelings and animosity to the side.

During the plea phase of the criminal proceeding, the judge pointed to Karin, and at the same time turned to the defendant and emphasized to the defendant: "this lady [Karin] gave you a gift". "You were facing life in prison without parole, and possibly the death penalty". Karin had agreed to the reduced plea deal because she knew her son loved his girlfriend and she wanted to avoid further emotional damage to her grandchildren.

However, the children have struggled to comprehend the killing. It is difficult to understand why their father was murdered so cruelly. What had he done?

Fortunately, Herbert's son (Herbert III) has excelled in private school (with a GPA of 4.01) and now attends Tulane University in New Orleans, the recipient of a Ron Brown academic scholarship,

My Body Tells Me

and is on the dean's list. In connection with his Ron Brown scholarship, the program noted that he had "been a mentor to young African-American males who come from the same background as he and share the same passion to break the cycle of violence and imprisonment that exists in New Orleans."[53]

More recently, Herbert's daughter also graduated from a private parochial high school in the city. Her response differed from that of her brother.

Herbert Spurlock III with his grandmothers

At her graduation Herbert's daughter, Tre'Breha Youngblood, added a surprising twist and revelation regarding her father's murder. In a four-page unsolicited memoir/poem, entitled "Momma", which she had her aunt Lucille read to the crowd gathered to celebrate her high school graduation, she set out some of her thoughts and pain regarding that tragic day. She revealed that after her mother shot her dad, she turned the gun on her and her brother, Herbert III. Her brother shielded her from harm, placing his body between his sister and the gun. Although she heard the "click" of the gun her mother was holding, it failed to fire.

In the memoir, she explicitly compares her mother to Grendel's

103

My Body Tells Me

mother ("monster-woman") in the English poem *Beowulf*. She added further in that memoir:

My parents met in high school. Soon after, the very shy, only child, fell in love with the outgoing, charismatic she-wolf. Not belonging to any of the cliques in high school, he had no one to warn him of her two personalities. ...Being so blinded by love, never could he have for-seen that the love of his life would take his live.... My perfect world had been shattered.

Had her mother also intended to kill her children? Her description of what had transpired was not inconsistent with the reporting of the police officers, their examination of the weapon and that the car which the mother had packed only included her clothes and personal items, but none for the children. In a mysterious way, some believed that it was spiritual intervention which had saved their lives. More compelling, Tre'Breha had lived with these additional facts and the associated pain for more than eleven years, having to let go of another turn to the story which had been imprisoned within her.

More critically, it evidences that she still is in great pain and grief more than a decade later. In the memoir, she acknowledges that she is still healing, confirming that grief is a process, not an event. She was grateful, however, to her brother, grandmothers, and other family for being her protection and safety net.

Similarly, to date, since his funeral, Karin has been unable to visit the gravesite of her son. She knows she would be an emotional wreck if she did. She also becomes fidgety on the date of his killing, his birthday and other holidays.

She says she is not sure about how she mustered the psychological resources to survive, but she did. Her passion is now linked to the development of her grandchildren.

My Body Tells Me

Lucille and Ashton

During the course of the writing of this chapter, another of Karin's and Cynthia's nephews was killed. Ashton Collins (AKA "Twin"), with a twin brother, had been a track star of Olympic stature, at the University of Texas, had also modeled, and was an aspiring rapper. He was killed at age 32, after he was shot 5 times and another man injured, in East Austin, Texas. They had to prepare to attend another funeral and console another sister, Lucille.

Lucille was, and still is, simply devastated. A reflective Lucille could only mutter nervous musings at times. Still in an emotional cloud, constantly crying, and at times unable to eat or sleep, she has been unable to discuss her son's murder. Her eyes were telling them; however, how unbelievable Ashton's killing was.

Although Ashton and his twin brother had been in some serious legal trouble recently, lived care-free, and had an undeniable penchant for gambling and flashing money, there were no signs that his life had been threatened. His life had at one time been so promising - a star track athlete, with Olympics aspirations and matching abilities in the 400 meters and relays. Ashton had been selected as an All-American in track three times, held the Texas Longhorn record for the 400 meters for 13 years, and anchored the men's 4 x 100 meters relay team.

As a rapper, "Twin" (*Twin outa Da Six*) had produced several rap videos. Some of his rap songs feature tributes to his old New Orleans neighborhood of the Sixth Ward, but was also laced with rough lyrics and depictions of trap houses, guns, drugs and money. In one Ashton raps, psychically, that he will "not be lending out his trust no more…. I got trust issues." Ashton was allegedly killed later by someone he trusted.

His obituary was freighted with a listing of numerous friends and family, without references to Claude and Lil Herbert, as they were among the predeceased. However, words were not big enough, or reflect sufficient specificity, to describe the pain of his mother.

Lucille had faced the tragedy of gunshot violence before in 2002. Ashton's father had died of gunshot wounds in New Orleans in September of that year.

Numerology or Coincidence

Ashton's killing occurred, unnervingly, on the 11th of August, 2016. Again, it was not lost on Ms. Doucet that the number 11 resurfaced in connection with the latest tragedy, even though she is neither a numerologist nor holds any belief in the paranormal.

But what do you call too many coincidences? Is this mere superstition or circumstances that are capable of assigning meanings to certain numbers? It seemed to mean something generally to the family, but they were unsure of its meaning.

Ashton Collins

Similar to astrology, numerology, which roughly falls into the general category of astrology and cosmic wanderings, is a belief in linking a number and a coinciding event. For instance, astrologists

My Body Tells Me

have studied whether a horoscope or birthdate can be used to determine the likelihood of a person becoming a serial killer.[54] Although not as popular as people following astrological and Zodiac signs, which are linked to their dates of birth, numerology has been around for centuries. For each number there are positive and negative attributes. In fact, a few people consider themselves forensic numerologists, possessing the ability to decode and solve murders using numbers.

Others believe that the secrets to life and death are hidden in numbers. Those numbers may be tied to certain life triggers, but most prominently a person's date of birth. These numbers allegedly establish your blueprint for life and what is considered a life path number.[55]

If there is a belief in numerology it can be both positive and negative. In numerology, 11 is considered a Master number, connected to intuition, and represents leadership and the greatest spiritual perception. It is the highest number used in decoding the mystery held in numbers. It is also associated with a wanderer or free-spirit.

It is also significant that it repeats the same number, i.e., two "1's".

Numerologists claim that it links the darkness to light and the mortal to the immortal. On the other hand, its alleged negative characteristics are stress, conflict and scattering. If it is perceived ominously, it also reflects "K" in the Roman alphabet, which some ascribe to "killed" or "killing". Another numerologist contends that an eleven person has various realms and in passing from darkness to light is considered a "High Priest.[56]

From a binary numerical indicator, it has an interesting characteristic. For instance, applied in a 6-digit manner provides the following result – what is considered a palindrome: 111111 x 111111 = 12345654321. Interestingly, the combined life path numbers, based upon their dates of birth (inclusive of month and day), for Claude (11/11/72 - 4), Herbert (8/22/73 - 3) and Ashton (2/18/84 - 4) was none other than 11! More mysterious, the fathers of all three murdered sons were born on the 11th day of a given month. And for some numerologists and paranormalists, Ashton's twin status was another indication of the number 11- 1 for him and 1 for his twin brother.

And, surely, in craps, it is a winning number!

Of course, skeptics contend that if you search hard enough you can find some commonality in numbers between any two human beings or groups of humans. Others contend that given the limited number of numerals that exist, repetitions are inevitable and based on mere superstition.

The family, however, never applied such numerical significance to the tragedies, other than to note the common dates. The unusual and unplanned tragedies were enough. Whether others would ascribe greater significance to the numbers is an open question. And if considered, by some, it would only mystically be considered in the fabric of a city with historical ideas of voodoo, fortune tellers and mystical spirits.

Conclusion

In the end, three sisters have now lost sons to gun violence; for two of them, it was their only sons. Their reactions were all individually unique, with Lucille being most reserved, but the pain and grief was palpable for all of them.[57] They had seen violence growing up in the Treme, but never imagined that it would hit so close to home and so often.

On the other hand, each son lived a different life. Although each murder was distinguishable and unrelated, and sparked by differing reasons or motivations, it is as though the stories merged, with all

My Body Tells Me

three sisters sharing unspeakable pain, and an unanswered question of "why". Involuntarily, they had all been drawn into a cycle of violence and death for which they had not chosen, and there were no logical answers, except spiritually.

Ms. Doucet and daughter, Dana

The three sisters' losses, singularly or combined, have been immeasurable; however, they still have one another. When Karin (slightly older than Cynthia) and Lucille (slightly younger) heard about the shooting of Claude, on that still muggy early morning in June 1992, it was unimaginable that a life could be taken so intentionally and cruelly. As they comforted Cynthia, they could not fathom that their lives would similarly be altered. Their stories, however, provides a valuable lesson for the rest of us – you have to have strength, emotionally, spiritually and communally, to get through such a tragic occurrence as the murder of a son, because the grief is everlasting and can strike at any time.[58]

CHAPTER 3

KILLING OF THE MEDIATOR FOR CONFLICT RESOLUTION AND NON-VIOLENCE

The newspaper obituary and internet described her funeral services: *Visitation for Dr. Karen Jenkins begins at 11 am at Holy Name Catholic Church in Omaha, followed by the funeral mass. Preceded in death by parents, Clark and Catherine Jenkins; brother, Jimmy Jenkins. Survived by brothers and sisters, Cynthia Jenkins, Ken Jenkins, Bobbie Evans, Earlie Braggs, Lynn Jenkins; nieces; nephews; great-nephews; aunts; uncles; extended family; friends; students; colleagues.*

Born in Cleveland, Ohio, before moving to Omaha, Karen was the youngest of 7 children of Clark and Catherine Jenkins. She had a relatively ordinary, but not easy life. There was some family dysfunction and she suffered some minor health issues. But she overcame it all.

Her academic and social achievements were anything but ordinary or typical. Highly educated, she had graduated from Holy Name High School, received a bachelor's degree in Journalism and Broadcasting from Creighton University and a Master's of Arts degree from the University of Nebraska at Omaha in 1997. In 2007, she earned a doctorate in conflict analysis and resolution from Nova Southeastern University in Fort Lauderdale, Florida. She had also traveled to many countries throughout the world personally, as a volunteer, or working, including Nigeria, Haiti, Northern Ireland, and Italy.

In 2010 she was living in Omaha, in America's heartland. It was a

The Mediator

city acclaimed by some as a nice place to live and raise a family. Two years before, in 2008, *Kiplinger's Personal Finance* magazine listed the city as the nation's third best city to live, work and play. *Forbes* similarly identified it as the "best-bang-for-the buck" city in the country in 2009, with a moderate pace of life.

Even though in the early 1990's Omaha's criminal landscape began to transform with the influx of gang violence, it still was noted as a city in which one could raise a family. For instance, the number of murders tripled from 11 in 1990 to 35 in 1991. Still, its murder rate was remained relatively low, usually less than 10 per 100,000 residents.

We refer to Dr. Karen Jenkins as "Dr. Jenkins," "Karen," or "Karen Jenkins," because she embodied all of them. The doctorate side was brainy and thoughtful; the Karen side was affectionate, adventurous, and unassuming, and at times silly; and the Karen Jenkins side was a family person and alter ego of her sister Cynthia.

Missing

At age 48, on Monday, October 18, 2010, Dr. Jenkins was considered as missing, because that Sunday, October 17 was the last day she was seen or heard from. Her older sister, Cynthia Jenkins, called Omaha police after she had not heard from her for two days. The sisters spoke several times a day, every day, and she had not heard from her either Sunday or Monday and she could not reach her by landline or cellphone.

Even though Karen was a rather busy person, she would always stay in contact with family and friends. She owned several businesses which were located in the vicinity of 40th and Ames in North Omaha. There was a constellation of entities - a nightclub on Ames Street, as well as a building next door where she rented apartments and a barbershop. The barbershop was situated on the corner and the apartments were located behind and above it, with

The Mediator

entrances on 40th Street. The beauty salon was adjacent to the apartment entrance and a car detail shop was closer to the parking lot of the bar.

The only sign of her presence in the area on Sunday was that her car was parked in the back lot of the bar, Hank's Place, which was not opened and being renovated.

Consistent with what others knew to be her itinerary, the presence of her car at the bar suggested that Jenkins stopped by the bar, located at 3922 Ames Avenue, on Sunday morning to inspect the renovations. There were several other things she was supposed to do that day; pick up her brother Ken to do some house repairs, pick up a check from Big Jim's Barbershop, which is in the building next door, and return home to watch the football game with her brother.

There was one thing on her itinerary for that morning which her family and friends were not aware that led to her brutal killing! She was scheduled to meet with someone unknown to her – yet a killer. She was there for business; he was not.

Saturday night Karen had spent the evening with Cynthia and her sister's son, Cris, and another great nephew, Devin. They had baked cookies and watched the University of Nebraska football game. They were avid Cornhusker fans.

She had spoken with her brother Ken on Sunday morning with respect to a plumbing issue she had at one of the rental units. According to him, he said his sister seemed okay and there was no indication that anything was amiss. A resident in the neighborhood reported that he had seen her Sunday morning talking to a man in the vicinity of 40th and Ames Avenue; a man whom he had not seen before.

Police later confirmed the presence of her car in the back parking

The Mediator

lot. A surveillance video from a near-by business had shown her in the parking lot shortly before she disappeared. But other than that, she was nowhere to be found. Her cell phone and credit cards were not in the car, but also had not been utilized since before the period when she had went missing.

When she did not show up to teach her speech class at Metropolitan Community College in Omaha, scheduled for 4 p.m. the following day, the concerns of her family escalated. On Sunday night Cynthia had telephoned one of Karen's closest friends, Darryl Lewis, because of her concern, and he recommended that she contact the police immediately.

Further retracing her steps were signs of what she failed to do. As noted, she did not show up to teach class on Monday evening. Nor did she appear to pick up the rent from the barbershop which she owned, which was highly unusual.

Cynthia called police on Monday night and an officer came to the bar and took a report. However, the reporting officer politely informed Cynthia that adults normally return within a few days and it's usually family members who solve the mystery. Police formally established a missing person investigation on Tuesday night.

The family did not wait, however, for the official police investigation to establish a search team. Why wait? So, on Monday teams of family and friends scoured the North Omaha neighborhood near where she lived, had grown up, and had a couple of businesses. Included were Sue, her husband John and their sons; one of her best friends, Wendy, and "sister" Lindsey, and niece Lisa, and Professor Chiwengo. Additionally, from Creighton, was Ricardo Ariza, the director for the Center of Multicultural Affairs, and Michele Millard, one of Karen's friends for more than a decade.

The Mediator

They concentrated in the area of 40th and Ames, the last location in which she was seen, with searchers using the bar as the staging and assembly location.

There were 20 to 30 family members and volunteers. They broke off into groups and went door to door talking to residents and distributing fliers with her photograph and basic identifying information.

They walked up and down the five blocks west of 40th Street and Ames Avenue. Their search methods were investigative and information gathering. In the process, they stopped nearly everyone they saw, searched alleys and behind buildings and occasionally looked inside open garages. They made special note of abandoned houses and walked around them also.

The neighborhood residents were friendly and receptive and many offered their prayers and well wishes for her safe return, even though some did not know her.

They also searched other neighborhoods more scantily, looking for her on a daily basis, all without success. Days passed, then nearly a week, and she was still not found. The signs and the resultant feelings of family members were becoming ominous and discouraging.

A few days after her body was found, Cynthia diarized, in 82 pages, the critical days while she was missing and when her body was located. Like having an inside look at an NFL playbook or a CIA file, the diary is unembellished and saturated with raw emotions, but at the same time insightful, profound and quotable, which I have taken advantage of here.

In that diary, she describes what transpired before she contacted police on October 18:

Cris [her son] and I had gone down to OOIC to clean their kitchen

The Mediator

for a state inspection. As we were cleaning, around 6 or so Cris asked me if I'd talked to Karen. I said no and he said he'd been trying to reach her all day because he needed the snake to clean out his sink. He said he'd talk to Kenneth [her brother] and he'd said that Karen didn't pick him and Johnnie [ ] up for work that morning. I thought that was unusual, why wouldn't she pick them up. They'd been working on the bathrooms in the bar, so what could she be up to that she hadn't done that without calling to say she had something else going on. After we finished up, we went home.

Cris went to his house and I walked around mine for a few minutes, tried to call her but there was no answer, so I called Cris and told him that I was going to go look for Karen.

I went to her house, but it was dark. I tried the lock on the backdoor, but it was good. As her car wasn't in the driveway, I figured maybe she was down at one of the rent houses that she'd had some plumbing problems, so I went down there to 25th street, but her car wasn't there either and it was also dark. So, I figured maybe she was at the bar.

When I got there, her car was there, so I went to the door, but it was dark inside. I wasn't sure what else to do, so I went home. I figured that maybe she was out for dinner or something with a friend, maybe Lindsey or Wendy[family friends].

I called Wendy, but she didn't answer. I called Lindsey, he didn't answer. So, I called Chiwengo [friend and college professor] and talked with Pascal[ ]. I wondered if he'd seen her as they usually had their French lessons on Sunday, but perhaps they changed it to Monday. He said no, they'd been off their lessons for a while as she had so much work going on. He asked why I was looking and I told him that Karen was missing. He didn't think much of it and said, "Oh, ok."

The Mediator

Chiwengo called me back a few minutes later and said "What do you mean Karen is missing?" and I told her that I couldn't find her. Lindsey called me back and he said he hadn't seen Karen and she hadn't returned any of his calls since Saturday evening. I told him I found her car up at the bar. He thought that was really strange, too. So, we decided to meet up there. Wendy called back and I told her what was going on. I called Cris and he and I went back to the bar.

We met Lindsey up there and we looked around the bar. He noticed that the gate wasn't even locked. It was pulled shut from the inside by a red insulated wire that used to keep the gate closed when you didn't want anyone to think it was open. I think Cris was checking her car to see if all of the doors were locked. They were, but I had my key to her car, so he opened it and found the fanny pack that she kept the keys to all of the properties. I don't know; some points of what happened when are a bit jumbled now. At some point, we went in the bar and looked around. Wendy arrived and we all kind of searched through the place.

Lindsey was standing by the door when someone knocked and I was toward the inside, so I didn't see the person, but I heard the voice, she said, "Is Miss Cynthia in there?" Lindsey told her "No." He didn't understand what she said I think. People knock and ask all kinds of questions, so I figured he just wasn't trying to deal with anyone and just wanted to get rid of her. I recognized the voice as Monique, so I tried to run out to ask her. I ran out and called her name, but she was nowhere to be seen in any direction. I went back in the bar.

Lindsey and I decided to go upstairs. I didn't have the keys and Lindsey didn't either, so he said we should ask the tenants if they'd seen her. Or rather, he asked that first, but as we didn't have the keys we thought we'd ring the doorbell, but we didn't know whether the bells worked or not. They didn't but I could see that Monique, one of her tenants, light was on so I yelled her name. She came down and opened the door. We asked her if she'd seen Karen, but she said she hadn't but, she knows she was there around 3:30 because her car was there when she was on her way to catch her bus to her community service site.

We then went to Biscuit's door[a tenant]. Levon, his girlfriend answered, said she'd have to wake him up. He came to the door and half answered questions, perhaps because he was still half sleep. He said he'd seen her car out there Monday morning, but he thought that it was gone when he came back, but then it was back there again when he returned.

For family members, the week of waiting was excruciating. They were in a psychological limbo – they feared the worst but were optimistic that she was alive. The prospect of the former, however, loomed larger because it would be uncharacteristic for her to walk away and tell no one. Her absence would haunt the family until she was found.

Police initially operated from the assumption that her absence was voluntary and there was no need to look for her. This is standard protocol for law enforcement where the missing person is an adult who is mentally competent. And according to the FBI, nearly 700,000 people were reported as missing that year. The vast majority were found or returned home. Despite these huge numbers, Karen's missing was still abnormal and for Ken and the rest of the family those numbers would not have mattered.

OPD did not wait too long before they dismissed that assumption, since something sinister seemed to be afoot. They all sensed that something was terribly wrong.

Initially, there were not many leads. She was not into a criminal lifestyle or had any known enemies. And they did not have a crime scene or body to perform any tests or gather forensic evidence.

The Mediator

The police questioned friends and family and persons with whom she had contact. They also interviewed those associated with the night club, barbershop and detail shop, her apartment tenants, as well as checked homes adjacent to and within several blocks of the apartment building.

Family and friends were a slight step ahead because they had not employed the same assumptions of police and began a search a day earlier on Monday October 18. It simply was not like Karen to not call her sister Cynthia or communicate with her close friends.

The level of anxiety of family and friends was high on the anxiety gauge, but the level of determination to find her was even higher.

As noted, a network of searchers and supporters mobilized. Posts were also made on various internet websites designed to track missing persons.

One such site, Jason's Project, posted the following:

Project Jason Profile:
Name: **Karen Jenkins**
Date of Birth: 03/04/1962
Date Missing: 10/18/2010
Age at time of disappearance: 48
City Missing From: Omaha
State Missing From: Nebraska
Gender: Female
Race: Black
Height: 5 ft 5 in
Weight: 135 lbs
Hair Color: Black
Eye Color: Brown
Identifying Characteristics: Her left leg is shorter than the right, which causes her to walk with a distinct limp.
Jewelry: Unknown
Circumstances of Disappearance: Karen was last seen around 1030am in the area of 40th and Ames Ave. She was checking on a

The Mediator

building which was in the process of being remodeled. Her vehicle was left at the building, but her cell phone and purse have not been located.
Investigative Agency: Omaha Police Department
Agency Phone: (402) 444-5818
Investigative Case #: 51167 Y
Case submitted by the Omaha Police Department

Her alma mater, Creighton, was at the forefront of supporters, with staff helping distribute fliers. In addition, it offered their collective prayers while she was missing:

Prayers are requested for **Karen Jenkins**, *who has been missing since Sunday. Karen graduated from Creighton and taught at the Werner Institute for about a year. As reported on last night's news, she went to check on a property that she owns on Sunday morning and has not been seen or heard from since. Her car was found in the parking lot of the property. Her sister,* **Cynthia Jenkins**, *also graduated from Creighton and has worked in the Counseling Center, Psychology Department and in Multicultural Affairs.*

Please keep Karen Jenkins and her family in your prayers as they search for clues in the hopes to find Karen very soon.[59]

Similarly, friends who could not assist in the search full time still offered their prayers, such as Mia: "My heart weeps for you. I am so sorry. I'll send lots of love and prayers out to the Universe to help find your sister. Mia."

In initiating its search, Omaha police gathered the customary data which is obtained in most missing persons investigations: e.g., driver's license number; Social security number; a recent photograph of Karen; a description of the clothing she was believed to be wearing at the time of disappearance; information regarding her cellphone and email; description of her car; the name and location of her employer; and persons with whom she had daily or

The Mediator

regular contact.

Searching for precipitating factors or motive, the police, as is custom, searched her home. Would there be evidence of foul play or conduct on her part which would motivate someone to kill her? They found absolutely nothing untoward, no drugs, weapons, suicide notes, etc.; instead they found a home filled with spiritual and uplifting books.

A Body Found

Finally, a body was found on Saturday, October 24, at about 3 p.m., under an abandoned house across the street from Hank's, but slightly north of Ames. The large fenced-in gray and white 2-story home had been abandoned for quite a while and had been besieged by overgrown vegetation and mold.

A father and son, who were not members of the family or police search teams, and just happened to be coming from the candy store, and were on their way home, crossed down the alley between a house and the church. They noticed her legs sticking from underneath a burned-out, gray and white abandoned home on 40th Street. They screamed out when they saw her and everyone came running to the spot.

The then unidentified victim had been murdered. However, it would require further forensic analysis and an autopsy to determine if the body was that of Dr. Jenkins.

The phone call from police came to Cynthia at about 3 p.m. on that Saturday. That morning she had decided to check Fontenelle Park in Omaha, which was known as a place where killers would dump bodies. She was driving, heading towards the area of the bar along with a few searchers, after having searched the park, when she received the call. Omaha police informed her that a body had been found by some strangers underneath an abandoned home in the

The Mediator

4500 block of 40th Street.

Other family and friends were already in the vicinity as part of the search teams, having started their search about 2 p.m. that day. Confusingly, both the volunteers and police had searched that area and house previously during the week, on separate occasions. This suggested or implied that the body had recently been moved there.

As Ken Jenkins told reporters: "I don't understand how she would suddenly appear there," he said. "How does someone see that from (the sidewalk) and nobody saw that before?" He said "it's possible" someone moved the body to the abandoned house."[60]

Similarly, a family friend recalled: "That area was so out in the open, the police had been around there and Karen's family had been in that vicinity looking, and it was a very visible spot".[61]

Their suspicions were later confirmed by the police investigation when one of the killers described the sequence of events. Karen's murder had not occurred where her body was found. Instead it had occurred in one of her rental apartments across the street. He said he and his accomplice had kept the body in the vacant apartment on 40th Street where the murder occurred, for several days, before moving it to the abandoned home across the street, in the dark of night.

The family was visibly upset and distraught when they rushed to the abandoned house. The police had already taped off the crime scene or area where the body was located, and were compiling physical evidence, taking photos, and began searching for witnesses.

The house, on a slightly inclined lot, not far from the intersection of 40th and Ames, was surrounded by some overgrown vegetation and was bordered by a large parking lot to a church, near the intersection. In fact, the search team had searched around the home

The Mediator

a few days before the discovery.

The bright orange crime barriers, emblazoned *Police Line Do Not Cross*, was intended to provide a level of privacy and dignity to the body. It was also intended to preserve the integrity of the scene and allow investigators to work in a sphere unimpeded. Persons crossing the plastic barriers can unknowingly leave evidence behind or take evidence from the scene.

For the Jenkins family, it had a more ominous symbolism – was Karen on the other side of the tape, confirming a nightmarish end to the week? And if it was her body, had she suffered through the elements of the weather?

Spectators and citizens gathered around the site, gawking as police evaluated the scene and removed the body. One man just sat on the curb crying and wiping his brow. Why would someone kill her, he mused? Unknown to family and spectators at the time, but who was milling among the crowd? One of the killers!

Indeed, the killer participated, on a limited basis, as part of the search team. As Karen's brother, Ken, later recalled, after the subsequent police arrests, he saw one of Karen's tenants among the crowd, allegedly trying to find her sister. He also had commented to another family member that he speculated the killer was in the crowd.

There was not an official confirmation on that Saturday that the body was Karen, but family and friends did not need such official confirmation. The scene at the abandoned gray home was all they needed. It confirmed their fears. All of the manifestations, including body chemistry from all involved, including family, friends and police officers, were that it was undoubtedly her.

When it was confirmed, Karen's cause of death was listed as strangulation, asphyxiation and a throat bone fracture, all consistent with what prosecutors later presented to the jury about the manner of death. In short, she had been strangled to death.

The news of her murder had immediate emotional impact. Upon learning of her death, her childhood friend, Wendy, for instance, drove through red lights to get to Karen's family. When she got home that night, however, Wendy was cast into a deep depression. She sat on the edge of her couch, hardly slept and did not eat for several days. She hardly moved until Cynthia called her and said she had to eat and sleep.

Search for Her Killers

Instinctively, with confirmation of her death as a murder, the family asked of themselves the next logical questions: who killed her and why? With Cynthia and Ken leading the effort, they turned their attention and energies to answering these questions. The answers would take a few months to materialize but they were shocking and further evidence of the senselessness of many murders.

Additionally, there was an atmosphere of fear in the city until the killer was identified and captured. The fear of Cynthia and other family and friends was palpable. Exhibiting raw emotion, in her diary Cynthia discussed this foreboding feeling of fear: *"In any case, I'm nowhere near as scared as I was the day after we found Karen's body. I saw killers and death at every turn. I was even terrified that morning to start my car. For some reason, I envisioned someone putting a car bomb in it. Not that I had any reason to believe that, I just had a fear someone might be out to kill me, too. We just didn't know why Karen was dead, so any reason or theory seemed plausible to a small degree at least. I went out to my car and hesitated opening the door. I finally got myself together enough to open it."*

The North Omaha neighborhood where the murder occurred was

The Mediator

becoming littered with crime, with shootings and robberies. The murders in the neighborhood, however, were usually comprised of young male perpetrators and victims. But a senseless murder, such as Karen's, was not endemic to the area and could have happened anywhere in the city.

Karen's murder was the 29th of the year for the city. It was unusual in that most of the murder victims in the city were 20-25-year-old black males. Some were gang related and others derived from arguments or disputes. Karen's killing did not fit the profile of either.

There were 35 murders in the city by year's end. The average age of victims was 27 years old, predominantly black males, and there were only three victims 48 or older. OPD reported that half of the murders were gang related. Only one-third of the murders were solved or cleared during the year.[62]

Nor did Karen's murder fit any common national profile for victims. According to FBI data, victims were typically African American males between 17-29 who were killed by gunfire. Less than 2 percent of the homicide victims were females between the ages of 45 and 49. And 37.5 of female victims were killed by their husbands or boyfriends after an argument, and hardly ever by a male who was a stranger. Thus, Karen was a most unlikely candidate for murder.

If a data analytics algorithm had been configured at the beginning of the year, upon the basis of risk analysis of the likelihood of being murdered, Dr. Jenkins' name would have been near the bottom or lower stratum of the list.

Karen had even discussed with the manager of the barbershop the need to always be vigilant about safety, with Jenkins usually locking the door behind her when she was in the bar alone. The discussions undoubtedly anticipated danger from strangers.

The Mediator

After extensive investigation, there was no question about who killed her or why they killed her. Still it did not make sense, at least not to a rational mind. And there was no clue that her murder was impending. She had not been threatened, been in any argument or dispute which was noteworthy, or done wrong to anyone. There simply was no known danger to protect against!

Except that she was a landlord, and in a position to affect others' lives in an indirect way. Not generally considered a dangerous business, her murder demonstrates that it could be when a tenant is illogical, unreasonable, evil, or possibly suffering from some mental deficiencies.

In relatively short order for this type of killing, OPD was able to determine and identify the killer. Indeed, there were two killers! Proudly, Omaha Police highlighted their resolution of Karen's murder in their 2010 Annual Report as one of the significant accomplishments of the city's homicide unit.

The Killers

Prosecutors charged a brother and sister two months later with first degree murder and use of a deadly weapon in connection with Karen's murder. They were Monique Lee, 27, and her younger brother Gary Lee, 19. They were arrested on December 29 at their home in the 3400 block of Sahler Street in Omaha.

The presiding judge denied bond for both of them. Both defendants pled not guilty at their initial appearances. A month later, they waived their rights to a preliminary hearing.

One of the killers was known to the family - Monique. The case represented the cruelest betrayal of trust and kindness. Monique had been in Karen's and Cynthia's homes, braided Cynthia's hair, and the recipient of their kindness and generosity. When Karen rented Monique the apartment, considering her financial

The Mediator

circumstances and minor children, Karen had allowed her to live there at a discounted amount. She had also offered her the opportunity in the past to work off the amounts owed by doing charity work. That did not suffice for Monique.

Monique had previously betrayed them by stealing from them. After Cynthia determined that Monique had stolen money from her, she informed Karen that she could not be trusted. Nonetheless, they continued to help her. Ironically, Monique once told the sisters that she wanted to go to school to major in Criminal Justice and one day be a Probation Officer.

Despite her calm nature, Karen had her irritable moments and cursed occasionally. In fact, Cynthia conceded that if a person betrayed her sister, Karen would often forgive them, but at times her patience would be worn away. Monique had fallen into the latter category; her stealing, lying and failing to pay a reduced rent was enough. She had to be evicted!

A couple of weeks prior to the murder (on October 3), Dr. Jenkins had caused Monique Lee to be served with eviction papers since she owed more than $600. The summons listed October 15 as the hearing date. When the constable served her with the summons, she reacted angrily, even though Karen had helped her out in the past and had given her more than an adequate opportunity to pay her rent. However, because tenants often react angrily under these circumstances, there was no reason for the constable to be alarmed.

The eviction was ordered to occur by October 15, a few days before Karen's disappearance. Notably, Monique had been evicted 9 times within the period 2003 to 2010. But Monique stayed in the apartment beyond the October 15 eviction date; indeed, beyond the date of discovery of the body, across the street.

As noted above, Monique was among the crowd of spectators when Karen's body was found and eerily her brother Ken was right when

The Mediator

he speculated that the killer was amongst them. And Monique's younger sibling, Gary Lee, was the person on Karen's itinerary for Sunday morning, of which family and friends were not aware.

After Karen's death Cynthia moved forward with the eviction and Cynthia's nerves were on edge as she went through the process of evicting Monique, still not knowing that she was Karen's killer. She had to call a locksmith to change the locks, but had allowed her back in to get some personal possessions. Monique tried to convince her that she had paid Karen and said she did not even know about the eviction hearing. At that moment, she knew Monique was lying because the constable had previously informed Cynthia how he had served Monique personally.

The investigation had determined that the scheme by the sister-brother duo was simple, yet devious and deadly. According to Douglas County prosecutors, Monique Lee was one of the tenants in one of the apartments which Jenkins owned, located next to the bar. She and her younger brother, Gary Lee, devised a scheme to lure Jenkins to the building to kill her. Gary posed as a prospective tenant who wanted to rent an apartment from Jenkins.

Telephone records showed that Karen's last call was not to her brother but from Gary Lee at about 10:30 a.m. on Sunday morning. He was the person waiting for Karen and probably the man which one witness revealed he saw her with that morning. Further call records show that Gary called or texted his sister Monique, at 10:31 a.m. Monique, who was ordered to have vacated the premises 2 days before, but defiantly had not, was lurking upstairs in the building for criminal and vicious purposes.

Prosecutors knew that Monique had already rented an upstairs apartment from Jenkins but was in the process of being evicted. A vacant unit for rent next to hers was where the plot was carried out. From the evidence established during the investigation the motive was apparently Monique's anger at being evicted. Although admitting to others about killing Dr. Jenkins, Monique would later deny that as being the motive for her actions.

Monique was initially deceptive with detectives telling them that she had not seen Jenkins for quite some time. She also alibied herself away from the scene, claiming that on Sunday she was at the Siena Francis House, doing community service work all day. Detectives interviewed her for several hours and have commented that she was much more comfortable lying than she was in telling the truth.

Continuing in that same vein, and unsurprisingly, she later changed that story, telling detectives she was at home all day. Before trial she told her sister even another story and at trial an even further fascinating depiction of what occurred.

She perpetrated this scheme of not knowing and feigned concern throughout the investigation and search for Karen's body. On a few occasions, she approached Cynthia during the search and inquired, "Miss Cynthia, how is the search going, I sure hope you find her". Cynthia did not know that she was speaking to the killer, who knew precisely where her beloved sister was.

There was not much doubt for the government about who was responsible for Karen's murder. County Attorney Don Kleine said, "The evidence shows that Mr. Lee was responsible in luring Ms. Jenkins to that apartment upstairs where he assisted his sister in causing the death of Ms. Jenkins by strangulation."[63]

Cynthia the Investigator

After discovery of the body, Cynthia was determined to find the killer or killers. "Determined" is an often-used phrase but in this instance, it had more force and validity. She used the main resource that she had - passion. With determination, coupled with instincts, fight and intelligence, she fought on.

Without donning a badge or uniform, Cynthia converted to being an unofficial homicide investigator. Although possessing a doctorate she was bereft of any law enforcement training, or even paying any attention to the various cop and forensic shows on television, she set out determined to identify the killer. Relying upon basic visceral instincts, knowledge of Karen and her friends and habits and customs, and putting together all information which she knew or had been provided, she devoted nearly all of her waking hours to her search or thinking about what to do next.

During the investigative journey, those hours expanded because she found it difficult to sleep. She could not turn off the protective impulses and she was pouring every ounce of herself into the biggest project in her life.

After Karen went missing, life had come to a halt as Cynthia had previously lived it. Initially her mission was finding her sister, then it became finding a killer.

What used to be days of varied and diverse tasks as well as activities tied to her grandson, Rocky, became nearly singularly focused on tracking a killer. Joe Kenda, nicknamed on television as the homicide tracker, could not have put together the evidence much better than she did, even though she was without resources and police powers. Like a high stakes pool or chess game, she had most of the angles and moves covered.

Her mind was stuck on many questions: why did they decide to kill her? Did she try to escape? Did she put up a fight? Did they keep her drugged up so that she would not fight back?

Cynthia's investigative plan included a Native American medicine man and a psychic, rechecking spots in the neighborhood, going on

The Mediator

the search with a police handler and cadaver dog, and checking phone records from Karen's cell phone. She sometimes played out the theories with close friends.

Portions of her diary vividly depict the investigative hunt and how she was on the heels of the killers, whether she knew it or not at the time. It was like a variation of the game some grew up playing as a child – "hide and seek." In that game, one child is "it" and hides an item, with the objective being for the other kids to find it. The closer you got to the hidden item, "it" would say you are getting "hot" or "hotter" if you were closer or you are "in the kitchen" when you were right in the locale of the hidden item. Or you are getting "cold" or "colder", the farther away you were from the hidden item. She was often very hot or near the kitchen but was not sure or did not know it until after the arrests.

During the investigative period, Cynthia stayed in constant contact with investigators, telephoning or emailing them. She would provide detailed hunches, leads or tips, which they acknowledged as evidence of good instincts and helpful. Consistent with custom and protocol they were supportive but responded that they could not divulge any details, so as not to blow their investigation. The OPD would tell her that it was a process but they were getting hot or narrowing the field, and in one instance saying "we are inching closer".

Her instincts had led her to request use of a police trained dog at the stage in the investigation prior to the finding of Karen's body. Police instead brought in a cadaver dog after her body's discovery.

Unsurprisingly, there were some potential suspects in her mind, which she discussed with police, that were dead ends. But her thought process was not far off that of a trained homicide investigator - exhaust reasonable leads and eliminate suspects.

The Mediator

Cynthia's investigative mission was not without its challenges. The strain of each day was making it more difficult for her to focus on anything else. She was struggling with not knowing more. Her frustration was evident as she commented: *It causes me pain on so many levels not to have particulars about the case. I fought for my sister all of my life and protected her in every way I could when I could. And, not being able to do anything. I couldn't find her, I couldn't save her and now not being able to figure out who killed her, is tearing a hole in my soul. If I knew more, I could consider more, offer other suggestions.*

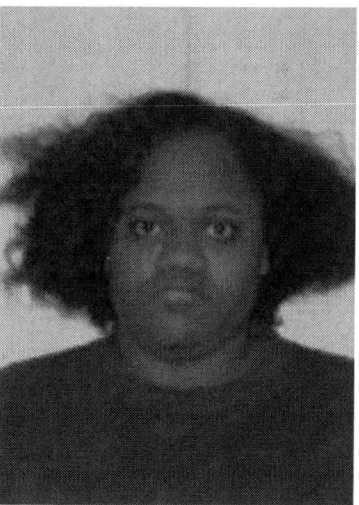

Gary Lee, courtesy of NDCS **Monique Lee, courtesy of NDCS**

Despite fighting through the frustration of not finding or knowing more Cynthia stayed the course. She was certainly "hot" with respect to Monique, thinking that she may be the killer or associated with the killer. She alerted police to her hunch about Monique.

She informed them about when Monique had come to the door of the bar on Monday night while she and Lindsey were there and asked, "Is that Miss Cynthia"? After Lindsey rebuffed her,

The Mediator

Monique quickly disappeared into the night. When she rushed to the door Monique was gone. She wanted to ask her if she had seen Karen.

She also was not surprised that the cadaver dog had alerted to Monique's garbage can, (the dogs signal their alert by eye contact, barking or lying down) but according to the dog's handler that was because it had probably smelled dead food products. What the handler did not fully explain was that the forensic science associated with cadaver dogs was not simple, because it required them to differentiate between the odors emitted by humans and other mammals and the various chemical changes in the odors. Nevertheless, she informed them that Monique was her "second best guess of who done it".

But Cynthia underestimated the pathology of the killer. She had also used the logic of what a reasonable, sane person would do, not the mind of a killer whose thought process often defies the rules or customs of logic. She thought: *It just doesn't entirely make sense to me that Monique would have done something to her just because she was being evicted. How would that help her more than a month...buying time through murder? That just seems absurd, but then people don't always think that far. She did seem genuinely shocked to be evicted though. I'm not saying Monique did anything at all other than being a thief and a deadbeat, but she's close enough to the ground that she probably knows something, some little bit.*

Cynthia had also keyed in on Gary Lee's phone call to Karen that Sunday morning. She questioned whether it was Monique calling Karen and talking for 5 minutes. The telephone call would have come after the initial eviction court date a few days before and it wasn't Karen's nature to talk about a legal matter once she had taken a tenant to court.

As she thought through the facts and gathered reactions, she did not recognize until after the arrest that her hunches and leads and spiritual impressions were so close or "hot". She was winning the game of hide-and-seek and didn't know it. Reading her diary was like replaying a game of hide-and-seek. I could mark the diary pages, "hot", "hotter," and nearly "in the kitchen."

In the end, she was right in the strangest way. Monique was both the killer and the person associated with the other killer, Gary. After the arrests, the Jenkins family now refocused again, this time from searching for her killers to seeking to ensure justice prevailed on their sister's behalf. Additionally, they were seeking answers to probing questions, predominately why she had been killed.

Prosecution and Trial

The prosecution started out jointly, charging the sibling duo with first degree murder and weapons offenses. However, it quickly began to proceed along two different lanes – one for Monique and another for Gary. Only one defendant went to trial, Monique, while in October 2011, Gary accepted a plea deal in exchange for his testimony against his sister.

In a pretrial interview with a television news reporter after pleading guilty, Gary said he did not know about the eviction or any plan to kill Professor Jenkins. "I didn't know anything until the last minute", he said. "I could have walked out, but it was already too late", he countered when asked about his participation in holding Karen's legs as his sister killed her. "It was hell for me ... I wanted the family to be at peace", he elaborates, apparently related to why he pled guilty.[64]

The trial and prosecution were essentially consumed with three issues - who committed the murder, the motivation or reason, and whether Monique had the mental capacity to commit the crime - i.e., was she insane at the time. The trial was not easy, however,

The Mediator

since there were two trials.

The first trial, which commenced on April 30, 2012, had ended in a mistrial after a medical expert changed his testimony. There, the state's expert expanded his testimony beyond what he had concluded in his written report. The mistrial had come near the end of the trial and had caused a level of frustration and exasperation among family and friends in attendance.

There was almost another mistrial during the second trial three months later, when Gary Lee tried to change his story on the witness stand. Lee testified that he had murdered Jenkins alone, and then refused to answer any more questions. This was entirely inconsistent with what he had told prosecutors as part of his plea deal, as well as what he had said in an interview with an Omaha television station. Although the prosecutor moved for a mistrial on the grounds that Lee's testimony violated his plea deal, the court ruled that the case should proceed.

The second trial had commenced in August 2012 in Courtroom No. 5 in Omaha. The Jenkins family was present everyday not only because they wanted justice but also wanted answers. They struggled with why someone would kill their sister when all of her life she had not hurt anyone and spent much of her life on a mission to help others. As a person skilled in conflict, had she known there was a conflict, she undoubtedly would have resolved it.

Nonetheless, they were torn between grief and anxiety to hear the evidence. Relying upon the testimony of Gary, statements provided to investigators by both defendants, and scientific evidence, prosecutors showed that Monique wanted to kill Karen because she had caused her to be served with eviction papers. Further, Gary lured Jenkins into an apartment which Dr. Jenkins owned on 40th Street near Ames, under the pretense of wanting to rent the vacant apartment. After Karen and Gary entered the vacant apartment,

The Mediator

Monique Lee snuck up behind her and struck Karen first, then began to strangle her with a vacuum cleaner cord. When Karen began to resist and fight for her life, she solicited her brother Gary Lee to hold her legs down, which he did.

The testimony showed that after strangling Karen, the two siblings put super glue in her nostrils and stuffed tissue down her throat, all as part of an effort, apparently to quiet her and ensure she could not breathe. Super glue! How and where had they dreamed up such a grotesque means of torture and death? They put so much super glue in her nose that it became glued to her upper lip.

Although there was some haziness about the days after the murder, the siblings apparently kept Jenkins' body in the building at 4503 N. 40th St. for several days, and may have moved it more than once, before disposing of it at an abandoned house across the street. They also continued to live in the apartment even after the body was found across the street.

The facts are similarly fuzzy regarding whether Monique and Gary killed Karen on the Sunday she went missing or whether she lived after the initial attack and was tortured and died slowly over the course of those days. Monique's sister, Deshawndra, later revealed, after the trial began, that Monique's minor daughter had told Deshawndra that she saw the body of a lady in the closet in Monique's apartment.

Moreover, Cynthia believes that the body was placed at the abandoned home sometimes after Tuesday, since the search team had searched outside the home on that day. Thus, the child's revelation was consistent with her belief that Karen may not have been killed on Sunday, but was tortured for a few days, and her body removed to the lot around the time her body was discovered.

This revelation by the child was not as critical to the prosecution since they believed there was sufficient evidence concerning the cause of death-strangulation, the approximate time of death, and the identity of the perpetrators.

For the family survivors that revelation added to the horror of the situation because they could only wonder about the pain Karen endured and for how long she may have suffered.

'I strangled her,' Lee says in telephone call from jail

The most damning evidence with regards to Monique Lee came from the defendant herself. At trial prosecutors played tapes of several jailhouse telephone communications which she had with her sister. It is standard in most local jails for jailers to record the telephone calls which inmates make with others, and later use incriminating statements contained therein in their upcoming criminal trials. Incredibly, many defendants themselves often prove to be the most damaging witnesses to their alleged innocence. This occurred in the prosecution against Monique.

In one of those phone calls to her sister, DeShawndra Lee Boatman, shortly after her arrest in December 2010, either not knowing or caring about the jail taping system, Monique admitted to killing Karen.

"I admit, I did it," she said at one point.

When her sister pressed her regarding how it had occurred, and promising not to tell their mom, Monique described how she killed Karen, struggling with use of the terms choked and strangled:

"C'mon, Monique, just tell me," Boatman said. *"I won't tell nobody. I won't tell mom. ... Did you drug her?"*

"I didn't drug her," Lee said, sniffling. *"I choked ... I strangled her. I strangled her, Shawndra."* ....

She also described Gary's role: *"Gary watched,"* she exclaimed.

"He just stood there and watched. And he held her down."

The Mediator

However, she expressed frustration about Gary and how he was cooperating with prosecutors, and letting all of the weight fall upon her. *"Gary throw all this (expletive) on me,"* she said to her sister. *"You mean to tell me, I been letting you live in my house and then you going to throw this (expletive) on me? ... This is my blood."* ....

Fantastically, she denied that she had killed Karen because of the eviction process, and that instead it was the result of some mysterious person threatening the lives of her kids.

"I admit, I did it," she says. *"It wasn't based off of what everybody thinks it is. My kids was being threatened."*...

The theme of her kids was also evident as she inquired about them. The acute pains of incarceration and separation kicked in.

"Have they asked about me? ... I need to hear them." Not only did her sister report that they were fine, she alibied to the children about her absence: *"They're fine. I just told 'em 'Mom has to take a vacation."* It appeared to become better when her sister put Monique's daughters on the phone in one of the phone calls.

Hearing her voice, Monique said: *"Hi, baby. Hey, baby,"*... *"You take care of your little brother, OK? I love you."*

At one point it was clear that she was finally concerned about the consequences of her actions, when the issue came up between her and Deshawndra about what her penalty would be: *"They probably are going to try to give you life,"* ... *"They might give you 20 years"*, Boatman speculated. *"Well, 20 is a lot better than life,"* Monique responded.

In the end, she expressed what some may consider remorse, and others may opine is merely sorry for herself: *"If I could change this, Shawndra, I swear to God I would. I can't stand being away from my babies."*

Monique's lawyers raised insanity as a defense, suggesting that she had a long history of mental illness and had stopped using her medication. Under such defense the defendant must overcome the assumption that she is sane and prove that she did not understand that her conduct was wrong, or could not control his or her actions even if she understood the act was wrong. The prosecution acknowledged that she had some mental health issues, but established that she still understood the difference between right and wrong.

She and her brother had a chaotic upbringing, growing up as foster children before they were adopted. One of the precipitating factors was that their natural mother had become addicted to crack. There were numerous other children in the foster home, with some neighbors estimating as many as ten other children lived in the home, in a strict environment.

During childhood, she had been diagnosed as bipolar and suffered from schizophrenia. During her youth, she had exhibited some disturbing signs and bizarre behavior. Other siblings testified that she and another brother had sexually assaulted her younger brother and she also tried to poison her mother by soaking her food in WD-40 motor oil. This was part of her defense related to her state of mind.

They also sought to portray a positive side. Monique was raising one of her sister's kids because the sister was strung out on drugs. Additionally, Monique testified that a mysterious person nicknamed "Black" had told her to kill Karen, threatening to take her kids if she did not comply. Why "Black" would want Karen killed was equally elusive. According to prosecutors, "Black" was a fictional character and merely Monique's way of seeking to shun responsibility for a premeditated murder.

Each side presented different versions or conclusions regarding Monique's state of mind at the time of the killing. The two experts had often squared off against one another, with one usually representing criminal defendants and the other as an expert for the government. Of course, they would usually disagree.

An Omaha psychiatrist, Dr. Bruce Gutnik, who had practiced psychiatry for nearly 40 years, testified that Lee was insane and incapable of understanding her actions at the time. As is customary in these instances, he had, among other things, delved into her childhood, adulthood, medication and substance use history, competency-related abilities, and conducted a mental health status exam. He was seeking to assess both her mental state at the time of the crime and ability to stand trial. He opined that her legal insanity was the product of a lengthy history of mental illness and an extraordinarily rough childhood.

On the other hand, Dr. Y. Scott Moore, who had graduated medical school in 1957, but had become board certified in psychiatry in 1979, testified on behalf of the prosecution. At the time of trial, he worked as a forensic psychiatrist at the Lincoln Regional Center. He had conducted a similar analysis to Dr. Gutnik, but strongly disagreed with his findings. He testified that Lee could distinguish right from wrong at the time of the killing.

The legal standard in an insanity plea required more than whether Monique was suffering from a mental illness at the time of the murder. The more important assessment was whether she knew right from wrong. Did she know what the consequences would be from her actions?

These clinical mental health assessments, nevertheless, could not wipe out the previous testimony which conveyed a type of horror and torture believed to exist only on television. There had been testimony about a beating, and strangling, and super glue, and ditching of the body under an abandoned building.

The trial had especially awkward moments for the Jenkins family.

The Mediator

First, there were the issues of how do you face and deal with killers whom you know and one of them had been in your company? Cynthia recalled that her emotions were numb to that aspect since she did not hate Monique or Gary, but at the same time did not feel anything for them. When the prosecutor had asked during her trial testimony how she felt about Monique, she firmly testified that she "did not hate her."

What was even more unsettling was the court's configuration where, as witnesses, Cynthia and her brother Ken had to literally come within inches of Monique to access the witness stand. Still Monique looked away, avoiding any eye contact.

In some ways, this was a moment which Cynthia both looked forward to and dreaded. She would be able to, at least indirectly, confront the persons who had killed her sister. On the other hand, having to relive her symbiotic relationship with her sister would not be easy.

The uncomfortable moments did not end there. Each day as the Jenkins' sat through the trial so did the natural and foster parents of Monique and Gary. They were pleasant and offered their sorrow and condolences to the Jenkins family. They even tried to physically embrace the Jenkins', which were uneasy moments.

Cynthia recalled that she had met Monique's foster mother when she had come to assist Monique move her belongings from the apartment after the eviction order. During the process, she apologized to Ken for all of the stress which Monique had caused. Even then, before knowing that Monique had killed her sister, she was unsure of how she should react. But it struck her later that possibly the apology was subconscious for the ensuing horrible news about Karen's killing or, less likely, had she known then that Karen was dead?

With all of the evidence and after several hours of deliberation, the

The Mediator

jury unanimously rejected Monique's insanity defense and convicted her of first-degree murder and the weapons offense. Their service ended with an affirmation of their names and as well as their verdict.

In attendance at the trial, Karen's nephew, Cris, exclaimed that he was "hoping for the best" and the jury had delivered such with a conviction.

At the sentencing phase, Cynthia told the judge "Monique's pretty much killed me, too, ...I can't take care of my family the way I used to. I can't forgive her. I can't find any hope. I can't find any answers.... What did she (Monique) have to gain for what she did? It's a mystery."

Thereafter, the judge sentenced Monique to life in prison. At that point, all eyes in the courtroom were on her. Again, she was at the center of attention; just in a more dreadful, depressing way, or proverbially "at the other end of the stick."

After sentencing, as she was being led out of the courtroom, shackled and in leg irons, she momentarily intersected with the Jenkins family. But there was no interaction as Lee glared at the floor.

Under his plea, Gary was convicted of second-degree murder and sentenced to 65 to 100 years in prison. He is eligible for parole in 32 1/2 years (about 2044).

With some dramatic flair, he offered the following apology to family members, saying he was young, made a mistake, and had lied.

"To the family, I apologize. To the court, I apologize. I'm a young man. I'm 21 years old. When this happened, I was 19. I've been through a lot growing up. As I sit here, hearing testimony, all I can say is I apologize. I'm young. I made a mistake. My sister misled

The Mediator

me. Yes, I lied. Yes, I tried to cover things up. I'm young. I'm a father. My son is one year old. I know I'm doing time. All I ask is for you, judge, to be lenient. I've had it rough. I take full responsibility and I apologize. But I deserve a second chance. Sorry family, I'm sorry."

The Jenkins family had attended the trial hoping to salvage a better understanding of the "why", surrounding Karen's murder, and what really happened. Although satisfied with the convictions, there still were no understandable explanations for the family. To this day, the "why" is still elusive. Did Monique truly believe that she could avoid eviction by killing her landlord, or was she simply so angry and out of control that getting caught did not matter?

Within 2 months of incarceration, Monique Lee died in prison. On January 17, 2013, she complained to prison authorities of not feeling well and was being monitored by nursing staff in the infirmary at the Women's prison at York. At about 7 a.m. she collapsed and was taken by ambulance to the local hospital where she was pronounced dead an hour later. The cause of death was not disclosed, but speculation was that she had committed suicide or had an aneurysm.

Any hopes of discovering the "why", and all of the facts, or making sense of the murder, faded with Monique's death. Although none of the family appeared to have celebrated her death, some felt that in light of the manner in which she died, she had not had to atone fully for her crime.

Her Life, Honor and Legacy

Karen was the baby in the family, the youngest of seven children in the Jenkins household. She was athletic and played most sports. As a child, she was shy and quiet. But she emerged in life to be confident and strong. She was an explorer and liked photography,

The Mediator

karate, traveling and camping. Her close friends as she attended elementary and high school, such as Wendy, described her as

"smart", a lot of fun, and "always searching". The crucial search question was for "why we are here"?

The family had grown up in historical North Omaha near 37th and Maple Streets, which is now considered the Malcolm X neighborhood. The Muslim minister and human rights activist had grown up a few blocks away, decades earlier, and a historical marker identifies a foundation in his name. The spacy neighborhood, with abundant trees, now boasts a recently constructed school named for Dr. Martin Luther King.

Both she and Cynthia had attended Creighton University in the city's center. Creighton is a private Roman Catholic college, with about 8,000 students. It is usually ranked among the best colleges in the Midwest. They were local girls who had overcome obstacles and were grounded in the community.

In college, she had won awards for her debating skills, having debated topics such as disarmament and militarism. Although she lived at home while attending college, she also attended lectures on campus and social events, and she participated in activities sponsored by the Center of Multicultural Affairs.

Jenkins worked for Creighton on three occasions, most recently during the 2007-08 school year at the Werner Institute for Negotiation and Dispute Resolution. She also worked for a time with the Carter Center in Georgia, founded by former President Jimmy Carter, where, ironically, she focused on conflict resolution within families.

Additionally, Karen worked with family violence issues. She traveled to Haiti and Nigeria. She had hoped to one day go to the Congo, to help young girls who had been raped and abused.

The Mediator

Karen as student at Creighton, with permission of Creighton University

Dr. Jenkins' conflict resolution skills were obviously passed along to her other family members. In responding to her death, there was not only grief but some anger. Such reaction is normal and understandable. The anger was born of the belief that her death was senseless. Even the trial did not clear up why she was killed in any logical, sensical way.

Although, bonded throughout the criminal process, there was some disagreement among friends and family regarding the criminal charges against the siblings. Passionate about justice and seeking to find logic for illogical actions of others, most of the family members stressed that they were not raised to retaliate. Although a few friends expressed that the siblings should get the death penalty, most family members were more measured in their approach. Consequently, they related that they did not hate the murderous siblings and were content with the charges and ultimate sentence which the judge imposed.

The ambivalence of feelings was exemplified by Ken. Even though he felt that the killers' actions deserved a death sentence, Ken told the *Omaha World Herald*: "You can't hate," ... "If you hate, you can't pick the pieces up, can't move on. If you hate, you become them."[65]

Cynthia broke down emotionally upon news of the death of Monique and was also stifled by ambivalence and ambiguous emotions. The police telephoned her that day while she was at work on her way to a meeting on campus and the world just swirled as she walked. Still grieving and in shock, it was a devastating blow on so many levels. "She's not going to do her time? She's done the ultimate time? I'll never find out what really happened? Maybe if she'd lived we could have found out more about what really happened. We'll never know? She took her own life? Why?"

Another family friend was less ambivalent, stating that he harbored hate towards the defendants. As a lawyer, he had even inquired of the prosecutor why the siblings had not been prosecuted as capital defendants, and subjected to the death penalty. He considered Monique's death a further injustice, since she did not even have to serve the life sentence which was meted out to her.

In consideration of these emotions and positions, it bears mentioning that abandonment of hate is different from forgiveness and even more distinct from unfettered forgiveness. Although the family was willing to put hate and anger aside, which took strength and courage, they were not willing to forgive or absolve the siblings for their violence against such an innocent soul. This was not a death which was the result of a mistake or even recklessness. Instead, it was murder of the highest degree - premeditated and tortuous.

The Mediator

At that point, and still, they could not make any sense of the brutal murder. And they recognized that forgiveness was more than a nod or temporary gesture; it constituted a conviction.

Nearly everyone mentioned Karen's positive approach to life and how caring a person she was. She cared about people other than herself. She was optimistic and strong. Most importantly, she was happy and spread her joy to others.

"If you looked at all the books on her bedside, they dealt with spiritual issues, and what can we do to help each other," said her nephew Cris Jenkins.[66] This was also corroborated by the results of the police officers' search of her home.

Just as you could not find a person to utter an unkind word about Karen, similarly you could find no one who would say that Karen was ever unkind to others.

Metropolitan Community College issued a statement about Dr. Jenkins through the Dean of Communications and Humanities, Susann Suprenant:

"On behalf of Metropolitan Community College, I would like to extend our sincere condolences to Karen's family and friends during this time of grief. Although she was a new faculty member, Karen's experience and community involvement greatly benefited the College and our students. Her loss will be keenly felt by faculty, staff, and students."[67]

Her legacy was also honored by Creighton. Some of the school's staff were members of the search team. And Creighton University honored her with a prayer service on Monday, November 1, in St. John's Church on campus. A memorial fund was also established at Creighton Federal Credit Union for supporting Karen's conflict resolution work with families in the community and women in the Congo.

The Mediator

Dr. Jenkins' life and ceremonies in death were communal. She did not merely teach at a community college she taught a community. Her death triggered a campaign against violence in Omaha. The Omaha Police Officers Association referred to her as "a jewel" of the community.

Her life was also remembered or dedicated in books concerning violence and conflict (*Critical Issues in Peace and Conflict Studies: Theory, Practice, and Pedagogy* (2011) *and Violence: Analysis, Intervention, and Prevention* (2012)), which the authors dedicated to her: e.g., "We dedicate this book to our friend and colleague, Dr. Karen Jenkins. Karen was a professor of conflict analysis and resolution at Metro Community College in South Omaha, Nebraska. On October 17, 2010, Dr. Jenkins was abducted and brutally murdered."

There were also community prayers, and vigils held at several locations in the community, honoring her life, including one at the abandoned house where her body was found. Consistent with Karen's life, these groupings were across all denominational, ethnic and racial lines.

Dr. Karen Joyce Jenkins lived her principles and values. One of the higher compliments we may pay a person is to reveal how they actually lived what they believed. We often talk about morals and principles and values, but for many of us our lives don't even approach our discourse or protestations. She learned early in life who she was and what she wanted and went after it.

"She knew the end of the world was not in Omaha," Darryl Lewis revealed. "There was a big world out there, and she was seeking to find what her part would be."[68]

Karen's values shaped her actions. It was those values and love of mankind that took her to foreign place such as Northern Ireland and Nigeria to work on resolving conflicts. It was also those values

The Mediator

which offered a helping hand to a person who eventually took her life.

Of course, Karen did not fathom that she would die young, and certainly not be murdered. She knew how to resolve conflict and had studied and wrote about the topic on many occasions. Ironically, her Master's thesis at the University of Nebraska at Omaha was entitled: *How African American women handle conflict in the workplace: An assessment of the impact of race, gender and class (May 1997).*[69] It addressed five conflict-handling styles and an assumption that in the workplace conflict is a "mutual activity". She had sought that method of resolution with Monique, seeking to "diffuse the emotional energy", phraseology from her thesis, to a point of exasperation. Obviously, Monique had not been similarly trained or disciplined in such methods. Instead, she resorted to an ageless phenomenon of resolution by killing, which history informs us has never worked to resolve conflict.

Karen, and Darryl Lewis

The Pains of a Sister

The description of Karen's life and legacy is also a story of Cynthia. They were so close they were like twins. Both had become

The Mediator

highly decorated educationally, receiving doctorates in their respective fields. They had an inseparable bond – Cynthia was Karen's protector or guardian angel. Cynthia clearly expected Karen to outlive her since her lifestyle was a bit less risky than her older sister. Whereas Karen would not get in trouble and had a two-drink limit, Cynthia had her fights and did not have a drink limit. Nonetheless, their spirit and beliefs were intertwined and Cynthia was similarly devoted to helping the community.

They had attended college together, conversed every day, traveled together and plotted out life together. They had similar spiritual outlooks and had vowed to be together through eternity. As Darryl commented: they were symbiotic twins, attached at the hip. So, when the unthinkable happened Cynthia's life was shattered.

Cynthia, who works as a Counselor, providing social services and treatment, has had years of experience addressing the grief and pain of others. In her diary, Cynthia confronts her pain, her grief, and her torment. Bearing her soul, she said "she fell into an abyss which she still has not crawled from." After her sister's killing her emotional pendulum was swinging between crazy and sane.

It began to affect her communications with those around her. She said "It's real hard for me to connect with people these days. I find it hard to look anyone in the eye. I know they're concerned, but it is getting harder everyday because I can't really find anything to talk about." Friends wanted to take her to lunch or dinner or just to get away, but she would usually refuse. She was bewildered by thinking there were too many things to do and then "where would I go? I don't even like leaving the house."

Once she did pivot back to anything resembling normal, she has attempted to fulfill the responsibilities of her younger sister. She now manages the rental properties and manages the bar.

The Mediator

Karen's killing, however, changed her perspective on death. She pondered the meaning of death and how it occurs. "In some way though I feel a bit less scared of death itself. It's like you just blink out and you're gone. I mean Karen's just gone and I don't know why. I know she was murdered, but I don't have a clue as to why someone would take her life like that. How could she have possibly provoked that kind of rage in someone? She was the sweetest of all mom's kids or most folks. What did she walk into that day?"

For a while, she recalls, she was angry with God. "Why had he allowed Karen to be taken?" She said that she had already lost her mother to cancer prematurely and her father in a car accident? It was simply too much. She had to learn to compartmentalize her feelings in order to work and accomplish daily chores.

Karen and Cynthia, at Cynthia's receipt of her graduate degree

She explains further: *I spend a lot of time in memory though. A lot of time trying to feel her. I know I'm still dazed. It's like a bomb has gone off. Have you ever been around a really loud sound, like right at the point of an explosion? There's a moment when you're absolutely stunned by the sound for a minute, just by it happening,*

The Mediator

its magnitude being something you've never experienced before, and it's like the sound or something hits your body and everything in you is knocked out for a brief second. I remember as a little girl being right near an M80 or something going off and you hear it and feel it and it knocks the shit out of you even though it doesn't hurt you. But, you're deaf for awhile after it and it takes a moment to get yourself together. I'm stuck in there somewhere...the sound from the world has not quite come back yet.

Cynthia clung to the life and memories of her sister, rendering it difficult to accept that she was really dead. She tried to convince herself that Karen was simply on a trip somewhere and would be back.

I have this faint sense that I'll never look at death in the same way again. There is a sacred thing about the death of a sister. I imagine there are sacred elements to every type of relationship as each is established on specific grounds. A mother produces a child from her body and that's a sacred element to human life for without one there wouldn't be the other. With twins, you both share the same womb and you travel the same road for a long time together. With a sister, especially one close in age, it's almost like a twin thing, but you're born separately and that person can thus become your best friend or your worse one.

Six Years Later

Karen's life was not "ordinary" from the standpoint of the media and the attention her death garnered. Reporting of her going missing and killing were not on the margins of the news as many other murder victims. From her disappearance to finding her body and the funeral, vigils and prayer services, to ultimately the trial, there was media coverage. In fact, at one point there was nearly daily coverage of what was transpiring.

Given the way Dr. Jenkins was murdered and the limbo of not

The Mediator

knowing her condition for about a week wreaked psychological havoc on her family and friends. Of course, they confronted the issue of whether she suffered and if so for how long. Well how are they now coping six years later?

Although some of the symbols of her murder have been altered, such as the demolition of the abandoned house where her body was found, and one of the defendants has died, the grief and pain is still evident.

The family still misses her, and her voice and radiant smile. One especially devastated group was the family grandchildren and her nieces and nephews, Rocky, Devin, Cris and Lisa. Although she did not have any children, she viewed them as hers, taking them to parks, plays, and the movies, and playfully harassing them. She loved them and they loved her back.

Unquestionably, the pain and grief continue. The immediate family members have spread some geographically. It stands to reason that the core family members and friends' responses are varied about the grieve they are encountering.

Darryl, a close friend of Karen and the family, related how he thought that his grief was subsiding. However, he is projected back into some level of pain if he meets someone named "Karen." It reminds him of the tragedy and he simply cannot address that person by name, and instead refers to them by other pronouns.

He further comments: "Karen was the sweetness woman I know. One could only marvel at her intelligence, drive and unfettered desire to make the world a more loving and equitable place. She often wanted these things without sufficiently considering her own safety. At times, she had to be reminded that not everyone shared her goals and dreams, and some people had inimical thoughts towards her drives. Nonetheless, how she put it all together escaped me. I will never figure it out. We shared a love of travel and the outdoors. Personally, I will miss her touch, hopeful glean and contagious smile. She accepted me for who I was, a man, for years, without a car; but a man with a huge and caring heart."

Kenneth and his girlfriend, Frienda, reconciled to the reality of Karen's death by trying to keep the family together. To do so, they hosted several family events.

Crying has been anesthetic for Lisa. She cried throughout the trial and still cries when Karen's name is mentioned. She has channeled much of her energy to helping other victims, becoming an advocate for victims of domestic violence.

Cynthia, tough and vibrant, has sought to console Lisa. But she allows that she may not have set a good example because she "now cries at the drop of a hat."

Now 20 years old, Devin has joined the military and his career projections are to be involved in law enforcement, and Cris has moved to another state with his wife and young children and appears to be adjusting well.

A native of the Republic of the Congo, Professor Chiwengo fights for the rights of women in the Congo who have been tortured, raped and killed. Karen's death made murder "real" for her and was a personal experience at feeling the effects of violence, beyond any other experience in her life of assisting others.

Wendy revealed how she and Karen would talk for hours about many issues. It was not unusual for a lunch or dinner between the two to last for 4 hours, filled with talking and laughing. "Her death was the hardest thing I had to go through", she explained. "I am no longer the same person and have not become close to anyone else since her death."

Reflectively, but not surprisingly, many of the survivors and friends are involved in humanitarian efforts or professions

The Mediator

dedicated to serving others, such as counseling, or combatting domestic violence and victimization of women. Others take care of ailing family members.

During family get-togethers, they still review the senselessness of the murder and its impact on their lives. One of the more telling discoveries and comments was from Devin, a great nephew and her sister Bobbie's grandson. He observed that the adults had sheltered them and not talked much in their presence about the murder. He felt left out, even though he did not believe it was malicious and instead was intended to protect him.

In his revelation, he brought out that kids at his high school had joked about his aunt being killed because she was really involved in dealing drugs. Even though he knew it was untrue, it hurt deeply. Neither Ken, Cynthia nor Wendy had ever heard that rumor and were all angered by it and sorry that it had affected Devin.

Wow! they thought. She had not been involved in dealing drugs; but in healing and dealing hugs!

Consistent with the studies and research on the issue of how survivors deal with murder, survivors often have thought about or reimagined the process of suffering. Tearfully, what was she thinking or feeling during the murder? The worst possible scenario happened for Karen's family.

And it reflected what Cynthia instructed her grandson one day after he expressed fear about the moon: "It's not the moon that will hurt you, it's people." She had no greater pain in life; and this one was not the result of an illness, or accident, or the moon. It was the work of other people.

Cynthia knew that monsters were not four-eyed and grizzly and snarled. They were two-eyed, walked upright, quiet, and were often within your company. Monsters were people.

The Mediator

The family knows that life must proceed, but how is the question?

Ken sums it up by suggesting they start with what to make of Karen's life, rather than her death. He said the family is trying to focus on the "quality of Karen's life, not the cruelty of her death."[70]

Symbolically, the house where her body was discovered has been bulldozed. Now the stain of her death has been removed and an open field stands in its place, metaphorically decluttering some of the emotional scarring.

For Cynthia, Karen's killing is still fresh because it appears that, in managing the bar, either Karen's killing or another murder in Omaha often becomes the topic of conversation with her and the bar's patrons or employees. Omaha appears to be transforming into a larger metropolis, foisting some of the dangers and prevalence of violence of larger cities. Of course, every other murder there leads her back to thoughts of Karen. Continuing to travel that psychological path, while the bar does not allow her to escape from the tragedy, it allows her to console other homicide survivors, who are dealing with the grief of their loved ones.

Karen's life epitomizes scripture which teaches that no one lives for himself/herself and no one dies for himself/herself, but we belong to God, both in life and death. Karen lived for others, and died for others, yet belongs to the Lord. Her message to her family would probably read like the lyrics from the band Higher- "Don't be scared, I am watching over you from the stars."

May she rest in peace - in a place where mediation is unnecessary!

CHAPTER 4

THEY KILLED THE BODY BUT THE SPIRIT DID NOT PERISH

On May 13, 1966, Head Deacon and church Treasurer, Hosey Davis, was walking along late near midnight, headed home from church, when he was confronted by three young men on Piety Street, in a neighborhood adjacent to the Desire Housing projects in New Orleans. As part of a robbery, they demanded his money and one of the assailants pulled out a knife and began stabbing Deacon Davis, in the right cheek, and into his chest. And then a third and fourth time in his chest and back. Deacon Davis died on the scene before police arrived. He was 75 years old.

He was known to his descendants and relatives as "Papa Hosey". Born into a highly religious family on October 27, 1890, in Lettsworth, Louisiana, his father, Reverend Edward Davis, had been a well-known Baptist preacher for more than a decade in Pointe Coupee Parish. Reverend Davis traveled throughout the parish for nearly five more decades, providing brimstone sermons and spreading the word of God. Described as fearless, many of his sermons were about the injustices in the Parish to blacks and local farmers. Reverend Davis had been born and lived his early life in New Orleans as a practicing Roman Catholic. But he had a calling and entered the ministry, converting to a Baptist. Heeding his calling and internal spirit, he and his wife, Virginia ("Jinnie"), moved to Pointe Coupee Parish, since Jinnie was originally from Batchelor.

Pointe Coupee is French for "a place cut off" and has been referred to as the "sugar bowl" of the state, because of the prominence of its sugar plantations and crops. It is located in the South-central

Deacon Hosey

part of the state at the bend in the river, or the "instep" part of the state, which is shaped like a shoe boot. Lying 300 miles from the mouth of the Mississippi River, then, as now, the parish had several other small towns scattered throughout the jurisdiction, such as McCrea, Lacour, Innis, and Torras, with New Roads being the parish seat. Lettsworth, where Deacon Davis was born, is in the northern end of the parish nearing adjoining Avoyelles parish, and across the Mississippi River from the infamous Louisiana State Penitentiary at Angola. It is best known as being the birth place of Blues musician Buddy Guy and the father of journalist Howard K. Smith.

Novelist Ernest Gaines, who is from Oscar near New Roads, uses the lives of sharecroppers and tenant farmers in Pointe Coupee as the settings for his novels. And the great gospel singer Mahalia Jackson's mother was also from the same area as the Davises in upper Pointe Coupee on the Atchafalaya River.

It is also known historically as the region where in 1795 slaves banded together with some white abolitionists to rebel against slavery. Their catalyst was previous slave revolts in the Caribbean. They had also read or been informed about the Declaration of the Rights of Man, which was an ideology, emanating from the belief that because France had abolished slavery a few years before, they were entitled to their freedom. The revolt was aborted and many slaves were hung.

Additionally, some Pointe Coupee's citizens were more fluent in a Creole dialect than they were in English or French. Even after the abolition of slavery, most of the slaves continued to live on the plantations and even in the prior slave quarters.

Of course, the Davis' were a farm family, since the parish was made up of predominantly farmers. With a population of about 20 thousand residents in the early 1900's, there were more than 3,000

Deacon Hosey

farms. The farms which they worked as tenant farmers or sharecroppers were usually located in the Northwest area of the parish.

It is not clear whether the Davis' worked as sharecroppers or tenant farmers, or both. But for decades they worked hard in the fields of the various farms, fighting mosquitoes and heat through the Great Depression. During the time, both whites and blacks worked as sharecroppers or tenant farmers, but the major landowners were white. Some described it as a crude extension of slavery, which endured for decades after emancipation.

More than 50 percent of the citizens in the parish existed below the poverty level, with a median income of less than $5,000. Many lacked complete plumbing facilities and there was an accompanying lack of economic opportunities.

It was not an easy life. "In sharecropping land owners provided sharecroppers with a house and a plot of land, as well as all the seed, fertilizer, and tools necessary to cultivate crops. Owners dictated what crops were to be raised and supervised laborers who worked in the fields. In exchange, the sharecroppers worked the fields from seed through harvest.

At harvest, the entire crop was given to the owner, who sold it. After deducting the cost of supplies for which the owner had paid, the owner shared the remaining profits with the sharecroppers. Sharecroppers usually received between one-third and one-half of the remaining profits."[71]

However, weather, poor prices, and other factors affected the profits, if any, which sharecroppers received, often placing them in debt. They would sometimes make enough to purchase their own farms or some would leave in the middle of the night under the threats of violence for the debts. Many were also cheated in the way the books were kept. Others became tenant farmers.

Tenant farmers were more independent since they rented the land.

Moreover, they decided what crops to grow and were responsible for obtaining all the tools and supplies. They also decided whether to sell or use the harvest or crops. In entering into rent deals

Typical plantation houses for African-Americans in Pointe Coupee Parish, courtesy of Library of Congress

Evicted sharecroppers [72]

plantation owners decided whether they would take rent in the form of a cash payment or a share of the crop.[73] Similarly, many tenant farmers were able to make enough money to eventually own their own land.

"Planters owned the houses black people lived in, the stores they shopped in, the land their churches and schools were built on. Landlords controlled the mail and telephones, enabling them to limit the amount of contact their employees had with the world outside the plantation. White people also bestowed money, gifts, and favors on African Americans who kept them informed of developments within the black community. The likelihood that

Deacon Hosey

planters would find out about any expression of dissatisfaction or any attempt to organize workers made challenging the plantation system extremely difficult."[74]

Some dubbed the system as "slavery by another name."[75] Recognizing the unfairness of the tenant and sharecropping systems, in the 1930s Congress passed laws to help farmers acquire their own land. However, big businesses later developed farming systems which compromised the legislation.

Rev. Welton Washington (left) and Deacon Hosey Davis (right) at a New Birth B.C. baptism.

Deacon Hosey Davis had grown up in the church and continued his life there. His father was a preacher, one of his son-in-laws was the same, and a son and a grandson eventually became Baptist preachers. Thus, the family was steeped in the "word" and biblical nourishment. But he and many of his family members also worked most of their lives as farmers, picking cotton or raising sugar cane in the Louisiana delta, right off the intersection of the Atchafalaya and Mississippi rivers. Indeed, the education system was set up that black children were groomed to be farmers, since their school year was only three months (so that they could work in the fields),

Deacon Hosey

while the white children attended school nine months of the year.

However, they were not merely farmers who were fervent about their religion. They were also civil rights activists and served in the military, with the son of Hosey's sister Lucinda, Fagan Thomas Jr., being a casualty in World War I. He served with the 369th Harlem Hellfighters, died on the battlefield in 1918 in Argonne, France, and is buried at Arlington Cemetery.

Early Life and Pointe Coupee

Mr. Davis had five brothers, Andrew, Albert, Augustus, Sumler (sometimes referred to as "Sumner") and Talmage, and five sisters, Beulah, Sarah, Lucinda, Alberta and Lara. They lived for some time in Ward 1, in the small towns of Batchelor, McCrea, and Torras, in homes surrounded by swamps and bayous. It was venued in an agricultural economy. It was also an area of the state where natives were fluent in and uttered the Creole language, and also rich in the tradition of story-telling or "porch talk".

Unmistakably and unsurprisingly, the Davis' were not at the apex of the overall conventional social order (the large landowners were), given the history of slavery and racism in the area, but they were hard working and industrious. They were highly respected in both the white and African-American communities.

Behind the charm of vistas, abundant lakes, moss, and oak trees, life was tough for tenant farmers in the area. African-Americans constituted 70 percent of the tenant farmers in the parish.[76] During this period there also was heavy civil rights activism in the rural parishes, including Pointe Coupee, to eradicate discrimination regarding loans to black farmers and other issues affecting farmers.[77] The long-standing farmers were considered part of an elite class and controlled the federal funding and administration of the government's programs. This led to discrimination against those doing much of the labor.[78]

Deacon Hosey

Some of the planters were earning nearly a million dollars annually, while many sharecroppers and tenants were in debt. With a crop-lien system and extension of credit for food and supplies, many were lucky to break even at harvest time.

The sharecroppers and tenants organized to discuss issues, align with the Louisiana Farmers Union (LFU), which was an interracial organization, and plan a convention. Their efforts were part of a broader effort by African Americans for economic, political and social justice during the New Deal and following the Great Depression.

It was a high risk and courageous effort by Deacon Hosey and others. A similar effort had been undertaken in Arkansas, and nicknamed the "Green Uprising". Many families who had joined the effort and became part of the union were harassed and retaliated against by the landowners and evicted from the premises.

Decades earlier, and thereafter, in other parishes in the state hundreds of black strikers had been massacred by white mobs, angry at the economic impact of the strikes. Hence, Papa Hosey and others were not merely risking their livelihoods, but their lives.

There were arrests of several organizers, for instance, for allegedly libeling a planter, by distributing a circular complaining about the unfair conditions. Hence, an organizer could be imprisoned for criticizing a landlord who had treated his sharecroppers or tenants unfairly, if not illegally.

The government initially appeared more focused upon the LFU and black farmers' activism to address discrimination than they were the underlying unfairness and discrimination, initiating an FBI investigation.[79] Subsequently, the government enacted some legislation to control wages and agreed to loan money to many black farmers who had been evicted, so that they could establish their own farms.[80]

Deacon Hosey

Family elders often informed descendants of notable family history events. Deacon Hosey's great grandson, Warren Jones, III, who had not been born at the time of his grandfather's killing (and was Amelia's grandson), proudly relates how he had been informed about how Hosey and his relatives were central to the farmers' union and farm activism. Indeed, some of the meetings of black farmers took place in Papa Hosey's home. The activism was so passionate that the levees were manned by men armed with shotguns, to prevent snitches or invasion. The years of activism had been part of, or led to, broader protests and actions, such as the sugar cane plantation strikes ("Caine Mutiny") in the early 1950s.

Hosey had married Maude Thomas, when he was 25 and she was 17 years old. They had several children: sons Fagan ("Billy") and Harrison, and daughters, Amelia (Toussant), Gussie May (Hunter), Bessie (Lafayette), and Neale (who died as a baby). His oldest daughter by a previous relationship was Beatrice (LaCour), who initially lived with her mother, Rachel (Rebecca) Davis, in Innis.

After his mother-in-law's passing, the couple and their children moved in with her father in Pointe Coupee parish. They lived in the small town of McCrea, whose population was less than a thousand residents. His father-in-law, Fagan Thomas, a special mail carrier, had lost his wife, Lucinda ("Cindy") Golden Thomas, at age 55, in January, 1920 to a heart attack, which the family believe was brought on by grief form the death of their son in World War I. For many years thereafter, Fagan lived with Hosey and Maude.

But it was not uncommon for African-American tenant farmers or sharecroppers, such as the Davis family, to move from one plantation to another or wherever farm work existed. One example was Hosey and his family living on a prominent plantation in the parish - Keller's' plantation in Ward 2 in the 1930's and early 40's. But tenant farming and sharecropping were on the decline after the advent of some technological advances and government programs

Deacon Hosey

which hurt the poor.

Crescent City Bound

Slowly, one by one, the Davis children moved from Pointe Coupee, "the country", to New Orleans, which was about 140 miles away, shouldering the Mississippi River. Beatrice moved first, at about age 5 or 6, to live with a maternal aunt and great grandmother in the city. The other children would visit her, liked the liberality of the city and the many things which there was to see and do. There was the French Market, a good transportation system, solid schools, music and Mardi Gras. So, they also decided to move to New Orleans.

In 1940, New Orleans was the largest city in the South, and by 1960 had more than 627 thousand residents, the majority of whom were white. After all, it was already one of the most unique and culturally vibrant cities in the country. Even then, it was use to hosting of sponsoring large crowds for conventions and other social events. Tourist-oriented, the many railroads which entered the city allowed for free layovers in the city. And where else could you find jazz music, oyster luggers, streetcars and ferries, all in the same locale?

It had been labeled, in some publications in the latter 1920's, "America's Most Interesting City".[81] And with good reason, to all ethnicities, but particularly to African Americans. As depicted in O.C. Taylor's *Pictorial,* there were black businesses, such as Unity Life on S. Rampart Street, undertakers, like Carr & Llopis, on St. Phillip Street, Flint-Goodridge Hospital, uptown, social clubs, such as the Bulls and the Autocrat, and colleges, such as Xavier, Dillard and Straight.

There was also a mysterious and "open lifestyle" far different than what existed in the "country." As some described it, there were always a place open to dance, gamble and drink. Many of the nightclubs were open until the "cock crowed in the morning".

More importantly, there were jobs in the city. And the job market was vastly different than that which existed in the "country". While the vast majority of the economy in Pointe Coupee was focused upon agriculture, less than 1 percent of the jobs in the city was tied to agriculture.

In the 40's the nation was at war and there was shipbuilding at the docks of the river. In the 50's there were an ample number of jobs, building the Lake Pontchartrain Causeway. Additionally, Delta Shipbuilding and the Higgins Industries had established strong business footholds in the city and there were plenty of jobs in that industry. Delta built 187 ships during the war, taking an average of 2 months to build each of these massive ships. According to the *Times-Picayune*, Higgins grew from less than 100 employees shortly before the war until 20,000 by the war's end. By the 1960's, Avondale was the largest industrial employer in the area. Hence, many of the family members took jobs helping build ships, or with the supporting businesses. A few joined the armed forces and went off to fight on behalf of their country.

At first, in the shipyards during WWII, blacks had been prohibited from employment, particularly supervisory jobs. But because there were so many men who were serving in the military, the shipyards opened employment to African-Americans. Some of the Davis family members eventually obtained supervisory roles.

A conventional migratory pattern emerged. Most would live temporarily with Beatrice and her family or another relative then find their own accommodations in the city. Many vowed never to return to live in Pointe Coupee. However, they would visit family and friends or for funerals, but not return to reside.

Papa Hosey and his wife ("Mama Sweeta") were the last to make

Deacon Hosey

the move from the country to the city. They had struggled with the concept of city living, having lived for more than 50 years on a farm in the country. But the number of farms was beginning to decline in the parish, yet the average farm size increased. Large plantation owners and companies had begun to control farming and many were insensitive to the needs of sharecroppers or tenant farmers.

And they were family people and desired to be around their children and grandchildren. Additionally, his father, Edward Davis, had died in Pointe Coupee at the end of 1947. Most critical to the decision, however, was that his wife Maude wanted to own a home; so, they made the move. Once in the city, Maude had decided to be a stay at home housekeeper, since she stated she wished to avoid the humiliation and degradation which accompanied work as a maid to a white family.

LC LC-USW3- 034429-D [P&P] LOT 765 John Vachon, Higgins Shipyard workers at lunch 1943

Ironically, in making such move to New Orleans, Hosey was

reversing the path of his father, who had moved to Pointe Coupee, thus completing a migratory circle.

A Close-knit Family

The female family members met their future husbands and started families. Beatrice was the first to marry in 1937 to Nathaniel Lacour. Then in 1943 Bessie married Leon Lafayette and Amelia married Tommie Bibbins, both marriages occurring in Pointe Coupee. Gussie Mae and Arthur Hunter married in 1957, and after a divorce, Amelia tied the knot with Ernest Toussant, in 1956.

The Davis' were a close-knit family, most living in close proximity in the same Desire neighborhood, communicating and visiting frequently, and helping one another. This was not uncommon during this era, wherein family and neighbors created indirect support systems, often sharing food, shelter and security. Transferring the skills and industry from the farm, they were savvy and industrious entrepreneurs. Hosey's son-in-law, Arthur Hunter, Sr., purchased one of the only supermarkets in the area, the Delta Supermarket on Desire Street, and several of the family worked there.

It was considered the largest black-owned supermarket in the city, being rivaled only by African American owned funeral homes, a few insurance companies, and others, as economic success stories; however, all located in other sections of the city.

The supermarket was significant because, despite its many residents, the area was bereft of a hospital, department stores, or bank branches. Located on the corner of Desire and Florida, it drew in the residents from not only the Desire and Florida housing projects, residents came from as far away as the 7th Ward and Ponchartrain Park to shop for groceries. It also catered to the black middle class and city's celebrities. Many of the city's preachers and ministers visited, if only to shake hands with Mr. Hunter. It had 5 trucks for delivering groceries throughout the city.

It was a well needed service for the area, particularly after the Desire housing projects were constructed in the mid 1950's. The Desire, which had been more of an industrial neighborhood, was poorly served by public transportation and lacked businesses such as supermarkets and shopping areas. Delta offered food products, fresh produce, meats, and had a pharmacy.

In New Orleans parlance, it was where residents came to "make groceries". It was more than a supermarket however; it was also a "gathering spot", where people met and had winding social conversations. It operated until the destructive forces of Hurricane Katrina.

The Neighborhood and church

The Desire was one of the largest public housing developments in the country with 248 buildings, 1,860 units and more than 13,000 residents. Final construction was completed in 1956 as part of the post war urban renewal programs, at a cost of $23 million. However, it had been built on low lying swamp land and a landfill and constructed with inferior materials. It was also bordered by a polluted canal and railroad tracks. "Desire planners created the biggest and most densely packed housing project in the South, and even at its inception was too big for police to patrol."[82] As a consequence, it began to present problems for its residents early on.

In fact, according to the Office of Policy and Planning, residential development in the Desire area was to be considered the "stepchild" of industrial development.[83] Nevertheless, although sparsely populated then, its construction had displaced many families.

It had the identifiable characteristics of most public housing projects: population density, minimal funds for security and maintenance, and poverty of its residents. These factors undoubtedly influenced the growth of crime in the area. In fact, by 1958 it had the highest population density in the city, with the vast majority of residents being less than 18 years of age.

Church members including some of the Davis family members

Those issues were exacerbated by Hurricane Betsy in 1965 which flooded the first floor of most of its buildings. And by the mid-nineteen sixties some of the buildings had already been shuttered because of their conditions. This was further aggravated by overcrowding, continuing its distinction as the most densely populated area in the city.

The Desire later began to take on the profile or characteristics of many urban housing projects – populated mostly by women, children and young men, bereft of economic opportunities and seemingly dependent upon government benefits. Nevertheless, many struggled to free themselves from this dependency through education, military service or, unfortunately, crime. Despite its misgivings it was populated by many citizens who were conscientious, righteous, and principled. Most of the families

Deacon Hosey

existed on less than $3,000 per year.

Prior to the building of the Desire some of the Davis' had purchased land in the area and had "Pittman homes" constructed on the sites. In contrast to other large cities which were lacking in space for new home building, New Orleans had begun to expand home sites by draining the swamps and wetlands. In addition, it would have been difficult to buy existing homes in certain sections of the city, since under the Jim Crow era many deeds contained language which explicitly forbade selling to black buyers. Thus, black home ownership was promoted in areas such as the Desire and Pontchartrain Park, the latter of which was intended for affluent and middle-class blacks. Between 1950 and 1960 more than 350 single homes were built in the Ninth Ward.

Desire Housing Projects, 1956, courtesy of New Orleans Public Library, City Archives

African American homeownership was promoted in the area where the Davis' were interested in building in the Desire neighborhood, and most lots were in the $3,000 to $4,000 range. "Pittman homes" were custom homes which sat high upon concrete slabs and were constructed by the Pittman Construction company. The company eventually became one of the construction contractors for the nearby Desire Housing project.

Even though the adjoining neighborhood was close to "the Desire projects," it was populated with neighbors who were close and overall unassuming. But its proximity to the Desire and overall topography presented challenges. Aside from the emerging crime, Hurricane Betsy had also flooded many of the houses in Papa Hosey's Desire neighborhood. This was after the city and Corp of Engineers decided to divert rising waters from the Mississippi River through the Industrial Canal to Lake Pontchartrain, rather than having the flood waters affect more wealthy parts of the city.

Growth in the Ninth ward was not unexpected since in 1960 it far exceeded the population of any other ward in the city, with more than 130,000 residents. Then, the majority of residents were white and there had been suggestions, politically, to divide it to create several wards. [84] Notably, it was in the Ninth ward which produced the plaintiffs for the major school desegregation lawsuits in the city.

Hosey Davis' home was a double located at 3022 Piety Street, the next street to the east of Louisa Street and about three blocks south from the church. Although it was dissimilar to the houses uptown, which had thousands of feet of square footage and cornstalk fences, or the large Victorian homes lining Esplanade Avenue, it was comfortable and new, and all that "Mama Sweeta" had desired. He lived in one side of the double shotgun home and other family members lived on the other side, including his daughter Gussie and her husband Arthur Hunter, and later his daughter Bessie and her family.

It was a neighborhood of people, who were close. Many church members and officials lived nearby. Pastor Washington and his wife Helen lived two blocks north on Piety Street and Brother

Deacon Hosey

Brown's home was one or two blocks south. Most of the deacons lived along Piety, Louisa, and the intersecting streets. In the same block with the Davis' were, for instance, the Church, Lee, Amos, and Lloyd families.

In 1951, they also helped organize and construct the church from whence Deacon Davis had departed on that fatal day - the New Birth Missionary Baptist Church, in the 3300 block of Louisa Street. Its website identifies its founders as Pastor and Sister Welton Washington and Reverend Fagan Davis, with Reverend W. B. Mitchell chosen as its first Pastor. The name "New Birth" was selected by the members.[85] Under the leadership of Rev. Washington it ordained many other ministers. It had been birthed in Pastor Davis' living room.

Fagan, or "Billy" to family members, was one of Deacon Davis' sons from Pointe Coupee parish, who had come to the city along with his other kids, before he arrived. He, his father, and others started planning the idea of the church shortly after Fagan arrived in New Orleans around 1943, even though he was not ordained until the 1980's.

What began as a small family church began to gain increasing membership. By 1966 it had blossomed into a popular Baptist church in the Ninth Ward with 300-400 members, rendering it one of the larger churches, in terms of membership, during that period. Most of the members were from the newly minted Desire Housing projects.

Spiritual worship at New Birth was active and highly participatory with members joining auditorily in prayers, testimony and song. It was certainly more colorful and aural than most of the surrounding Catholic churches. Its ministers often spoke of a societal vision free of racism and classism, and emergence of a melting pot. Thus, the church was more than a spiritual house of worship; it was wrapped

Deacon Hosey

into politics, civil rights and human assistance.

The church members lived as a family, particularly the deacon board and ministers. They considered one another "brothers" and acted accordingly. Deacon Hosey was the head deacon and the others respected his leadership. On weekends, they would visit the homes of the others and commiserate about spirituality, politics and "Nawlins type of stuff." Some of those topics was voter registration, protests by students in the business district to integrate lunch counters in the city's department stores in the early 60's, the passage of the civil rights laws in 1964, and the killing of Medgar Evers in Mississippi.

One critical element of the deacon brotherhood was looking out for one another and serving as each brother's protector. So, it was not ironic when he found himself cornered on the night of the murder, Deacon Hosey would call out to Brother Brown. He was being assaulted on the block where Brown lived.

Intersection of Piety and Miro Streets, 1961, courtesy Nutrias.org

While the Davis clan grew, personal tragedy from illness struck.

Deacon Hosey

Maude Davis had taken sick in 1959, became very frail and passed away in September 1960. Two weeks earlier, Maude's sister, Betsey ("Bessie"), who was living with them had also passed away. Thereafter, Hosey began living with his daughter, also named Bessie, as he grieved the death of his wife.

By the 1960's the city and neighborhood had been through a transition. A bridge had been constructed between the east and west banks of the city, construction of the interstate through the city was ongoing, and it boasted the second largest port in the country.

Moreover, it had become more Americanized with the influx of many immigrants, and had an old-world feel. Its inhabitants were more diverse than most cities and was blossoming with an intermixture of cultures, inclusive of jazz and unique food, and Mardi Gras.

Members of the Davis family (Papa Hosey, far right)

The sixties also reflected significant social changes in the city. The civil rights era was in full swing. Efforts were afoot to desegregate schools, restaurants, amusement parks (Lincoln Beach vs. Pontchartrain Beach), and theaters in the city. There had been protests in some of the major department stores downtown and the public schools. Critically, it was the churches which often served as the gateway for African-American leaders in the city as it was transforming socially.

1966 in particular was notable for the Vietnam War, Martin Luther King's campaign to expand his activities from the South to northern cities, rioting and protests in Watts, and there was serious discussion of a professional football team in the city – the Saints.

New Orleans' geographical references were still uptown, downtown, the lake, and the river. The East had developed as the swamps continued to be drained. The Desire, though, was still considered hidden away and isolated.

Horrific Stabbing

On the heels of the civil rights movement in the early 1960's the Desire community had begun to thrive in some ways. Businesses sprang up around the projects, despite its isolation from the rest of the city, as the population had grown. However, there were plans by the city to build even more public housing on scattered sites in the area.

Despair had also set in because of environmental concerns as well as crime. Violent crime had begun to surge into the area, with robberies of those receiving benefits and murders were on the rise, but still not as rampant as they would later become.

Although there had been a slight spike in violent crime in the mid-sixties, there were more significant spikes in, for example 1973 and later 1994. 1966 became a bellwether year for homicides, when there were 140 murders in the city, compared to 110 the previous year and 117 in the next year (1967), or 199 in 1974. Additionally, nearly 80 percent of the city's murders for that year were cleared by arrest or identification. Less than twenty years or so later, the Desire became one of the more violent sections of the city, with frequent robberies and murders.[86] In 1988 there were 19 murders in the Desire development alone,[87] and 13 in 1994.[88]

Thus, the stabbing of Hosey Davis then was a shock to many, because of who he was, as well as the relative civility and closeness of the neighborhood residents who surrounded the perilous project. The weekend of May 13 however was a forecast of what the Desire was to become – a killing field. That weekend four persons were killed in the Desire neighborhood.

There was media concern then that the city was becoming unbearably violent. In November of that year, the *Times Picayune* ran a story which declared that New Orleans was "fast becoming the murder capital of the South", with 17 murders being unsolved. Deacon Davis' slaying as well as the other killings in the Desire that weekend were mentioned among the unsolved killings.[89]

That deadly weekend in May seemed to set the Desire neighborhood in a downward spiral. Crime became so bad that by 1980 Arthur Hunter, Sr. was forced to sell the legendary Delta Supermarket after it had been robbed several times.

To this day, there are some clear facts about Deacon Hosey's death such as the motive – robbery - the number of assailants – three, and how he was killed – by stabbing. What transpired leading up to his murder is less clear, but there are varying theories among family members regarding whether he had been "set-up".

But why kill him? This is as elusive today as it was then. Did the killer just want to add to his "rep" as one of the "baddest" or toughest? Because certainly Papa Hosey could not have fought

Deacon Hosey

back and none of the evidence suggested so. Or was the assailant simply a cold-blooded murderer?

Unequivocally, it is agreed that he did not have enemies nor had he quarreled with anyone. It is rather clear that the motive was robbery, since the money he was carrying was not on his body. And it was not uncommon for robbery murder victims to be considerably older than the robbers.

The theory that most family members settled on was that he was not a random victim, there were multiple assailants, and he was possibly lured to the spot of the assault and tried to escape from his assailant when he was stabbed.

Deacon Davis, along with some other family members, had attended a memorial service for a deceased church member that Friday evening at the church. Several in attendance that night remember him praying, singing in the choir and drinking coffee. Notably, Deacon Hosey had delivered the ultimate prayer that night, something along the lines of: "Lord, I want Your will to be done. I will not be walking alone, by myself. I ask God to take me home!" Were his words a typical ultimate prayer or that of prophesy and prognostication?

Among the family members in attendance were his daughter, Gussie, and her husband Arthur Hunter, Sr. Hunter, who was also a deacon in the church, and his wife started to depart from New Birth about 11:45. He recalled that Deacon Hosey had left a few minutes before. He and others had offered Deacon Hosey a ride home but he had refused, saying that he would rather walk home.

Papa Hosey was returning home alone from the church and apparently started to take the same route, through the Edith Sampson playground, that he had taken hundreds of times previously. The playground was between Louisa Street, where the church was located, and Piety Street to the east, where Deacon

Deacon Hosey

Davis lived. As his granddaughter, Delores says, he had taken that route so often there was a worn path in the grass which depicted his footsteps.

According to police, as he was walking home Deacon Hosey approached a teenager, whom he knew, and suggested that, given the late hour, the teen go home to bed. The teenager, who lived in the Desire projects, did as Deacon Hosey suggested and headed home.

However, immediately on the heels of speaking to the teenager, three young men, ranging in age from 18 to 20, approached him. They demanded his wallet and money. He was not big in stature (about 5'7), and albeit not frail, he was 75 years old and therefore in no condition to fight. In sum, despite the many years on the farm and in the field, it was a no-win situation for him. At first, he refused their requests for money, saying he did not have a wallet and sought to escape by running. "Give up the wallet, give it up", they demanded.

He called out to Brother Brown to help him, "Help me, Brown", "Help Me! but Brown was apparently not in the vicinity. His assailants ran after him into the 3100 block of Piety, less than a block from his home, and attacked him, stabbing him and taking his money and wallet. Some witnesses thought that the strikes were punches but later learned that they were stabbing motions.

In what police described as a "brutal" murder, he was stabbed four times, with the most critical wounds puncturing his lung and heart. Three of the stab wounds were from a small blade knife and one was from an icepick. These wounds caused massive internal bleeding and the highly lethal condition of a stab wound to the heart.

The teenager whom he had counseled earlier, witnessing the attack, turned around and frantically headed back to help Deacon Hosey.

Deacon Hosey

He saw the assailants run towards the Desire projects, just a few blocks to the northwest. As he was approaching Deacon Hosey, he recruited two other teenagers in the block, who had also witnessed the attack, but they were too afraid to become involved. The commotion had attracted neighbors and onlookers. He then asked one of the neighbors, looking from her door, to call the police.

Nearing the same time, two female church choir members were headed home when they vaguely saw a man lying on his right side on the sidewalk bleeding, with a teenager trying to assist him. The body was on the sidewalk, somewhat off the path Deacon Hosey usually traveled, in the 3100 block of Piety Street. But he was still only about a block from his home. The choir members had left the church just moments after Hosey and had taken the same path he normally took, through the playground, as they made their way to their homes in the Desire project.

When they observed a body along the street on a more dimly lit area of the sidewalk, they used a match to illuminate the area as they stood above him with the teenager. It was indeed Deacon Hosey! He was still barely alive. His breathing was shallow, as if at a whisper-level and he was groaning. Shocked and in disbelief because they had just saw him at the church, they ran screaming back to the church in search of Pastor Washington.

Breathing hard and visibly trembling, they alerted the few members still at the church about Brother Hosey, and police were summoned a few minutes past midnight. Fortunately, as they ran up, Gussie and Arthur were headed to their car to depart for the evening. The shaken choir members and other church members simultaneously ran to the homes of other Davis family members in the area to notify them of the tragedy.

Arthur anxiously hopped in his car and raced to the block where Deacon Hosey's body lay strewn on the sidewalk in the gutter aside

Deacon Hosey

a red 4-door Chevy car. His famed white straw hat and brown rimmed glasses were next to him, as his body was somewhat tangled on the sidewalk. Dressed in a blue suit, with white starched shirt, his head faced the river and his feet faced lakeward, closer to the intersection of Benefit Street than Treasure Street. Next to his blood-soaked body was a somewhat shiny object. It was at least one of the murder weapons - a 4-inch fishing knife. When Arthur arrived, he knelt close to him and heard Deacon Hosey take his last shallow breath, "umm", and everything turned silent for a moment. The sigh was irrevocable, and signaled death.

Arthur, Sr. stood up and looked toward the family home, a block away. Gussie's heart was pounding. Others would soon be on the scene also. Arthur then had the heartbreaking task of identifying his father-in-law's body for the police, as they arrived.

Word of Deacon Hosey's death reverberated quickly in the community. It seems that within minutes of his body's discovery, people came from everywhere filling Sampson playground, as an unofficial way of honoring this beloved man. It was before the advent of the Internet and cellphones, and word usually spread by someone banging on neighbors' doors and sporadic phone calls to those who had landlines. Some came driven by curiosity, but most came due to their love and feelings for him.

They hovered in the area for hours. There were whispered exchanges between neighbors, as well as boisterous comments. Some were angry and wanted revenge. Others held their mouths in disbelief. Still in shock and mourning, some stayed until daybreak. "A moment I will never forget," says Arthur Hunter, Sr.

When the sun rose the following morning, a few mourners still littered the playground. "I can't believe it," a man in a skull cap said.

Hosey's granddaughter Delores, who was 16 at the time, vividly remembers many of the details surrounding that night. She remembers someone knocking on their door, summoning for her father, Fagan Davis. When he asked, what they wanted or why they were there, they responded alarmingly that "Brother Hosey has been killed!" She let out an expectant gasp, as though she had been hit by a car.

They were about to go to bed for the night but immediately got dressed, summoned other family members, and ran to the area where his body was on the sidewalk. Shortly before the knock, they had heard the sound of the sirens sifting through the trees and front door, since the scene of the murder was so close. But that was not enough to alert them to anything askew because sirens were not alien to the neighborhood.

Although the ambulance had arrived and the police were on the scene when they got there, Hosey Davis was already dead. The stab wounds were deep and had caused him to bleed to death. Screaming and crying replaced the sounds of the sirens which now had faded. Later, they sank into prayer, even amidst befuddlement about why such a horrible thing had happened to such a beloved man.

The autopsy confirmed that Deacon Hosey had died from massive hemothorax and hemopericardium. Hemothorax means that blood had built up in his lungs, causing difficulty in his breathing. As a result, the lungs collapse. Similarly, hemopericardium meant that blood had also built up in his heart causing his heart not to be able to fill and consequently to stop.

The search for the suspects

Yet, who would want to kill such an elderly man? He obviously had not done anything to them, aside from possibly resisting their robbery and assault, and been a potential witness to the crime. Did they know that he was a church deacon and was on his way home from church?

It is reasonably believed by many that the robbers were aware beforehand that Deacon Davis had cashed his Social Security check a few days earlier or may have been bringing the church's offerings home for later deposit into the bank during the week. They probably laid in wait for him to bend the corner or come along his normal path home to rob him. The robbers also must have contemplated harm, since one was armed with a knife and another had an ice pick.

It was customary then for Social Security recipients, such as Deacon Davis, as well as workers, to cash their benefits checks or paychecks at the local supermarkets and carry the cash on them. Many simply did not use or trust the banks. It was close to that time of month when Social Security checks were delivered in the mail.

Not only were some residents' recipients of Social Security benefits but many had also received funds from the government, as payments in consideration of damages from Hurricane Betsy, which had hit the area in September 1965.

Ironically, his daughter Bessie had warned him a few days prior to his murder about carrying so much money on him. Arthur Hunter estimated that on that Friday Deacon Davis had $300-400 on him. His pockets were empty when police checked him, strongly suggesting a robbery.

According to Delores, the location of his body was suspicious, since it was somewhat off the path which he had taken so many times before. It was as though he had been summoned by someone or had been lured to the faintly lit area near the sidewalk. She conjectured that someone must have known that he had cashed his check just a few days before and had planned to rob him.

There was also conjecture to the contrary; that it was a random robbery and killing since the weekend before there had been some robberies at or near Sampson playground. According to news accounts there also was a similar robbery and stabbing by two brothers, who were later captured, in the area (3500 block of Louisa) a few months later.

More critically and incredibly, there were four murders and one attempt murder in that same neighborhood that weekend. All five incidents were within a mile of Papa Hosey's killing, and most a few blocks away. Moreover, the slayings, all in the Desire area, were murders by stabbing, with three occurring within one hour. The *Times Picayune* reported on Monday morning that "Assailants in Stabbing Deaths Are Being Sought."

It was described by the *Louisiana Weekly* as the "hour of death": at 12:50 a.m. a 36-year-old man was stabbed to death in the 2600 block of Desire; at the same time, a 38-year-old man was stabbed to death in the 3100 block of Florida (at the intersection where the Delta Supermarket was located); and a 32-year-old man was stabbed to death in the 3400 block of Pleasure Street, at about 1:55 a.m. These killings all followed on the heels of Papa Hosey's stabbing.

Although each murder was traumatic in an individual sense, if the murders were linked it would create even greater concern for police and the community because it would be an indication that there were assailants who were possibly indiscriminately killing citizens. These would be considered "stranger" murders, since the assailants were not associated with the victims. And those murders tended to be more difficult to solve than others, where there was a relationship between perpetrator and victim.

Sergeant Robert Mutz (who had been involved in the investigation of Clay Shaw for the assassination of President Kennedy) and

Deacon Hosey

Detective James Alphonse, led the homicide investigation of Papa Hosey, simultaneously with their investigations of two of the other stabbings. The detectives knew from experience and the escalation of violence in the area that an area of focus for finding the suspects was the projects. Thus, police interviewed residents of the neighborhood and the projects, gathered crime scene evidence, took photos of the body and crime scene, gathered forensic material such as blood and clothing, and traced the projected routes of the assailants. They found his wallet, empty, in the housing projects about two blocks away. They continued their efforts by following leads for months, interviewing various suspects.

Critically, the killers were careless and had left one of the murder weapons at the scene. One of the assumptions which the police operated upon was that the victim left traces on the perpetrator and he/she may have taken away traces of the victim or scene.

There were forensics limitations then, however, which are now well accepted, such as DNA analysis, which was not used in criminal investigations until about 1985. Of course, there also were lingering questions for the police about whether Hosey's murder was linked in any way to the other murders and robberies in the area. At least two of the weekend murders had similar modus operandi, i.e., stabbing in the course of a robbery by several young assailants.

Hence, there were various reasons for NOPD to solve Pastor Hosey's killing. One, he was a prominent, and well respected, figure in the community. Second, his killing may have been linked to others in the area. And, finally, there was pressure from the community to curb the emerging violence in the area. However, both homicide detectives were involved in many other investigations, since there had been an uptick in murders and violence in the city; and in 1968 Detective Alphonse was killed in an automobile accident.

From the police's perspective the murder would be solved through crime scene reconstruction, bloodstain analysis, the recovery of trace and microscopic evidence, and, most importantly, working to obtain information from people with more direct knowledge of the murderers.

Police knew that it was important to be flexible, looking for both consistencies between the murders and prepared to go where their instincts and evidence led them. They also knew that in this instance their duty to the family was profound.

The Hosey family was aware of the racial divide which even then existed between the NOPD and the community but commended their investigative efforts in Papa Hosey's murder. It was clear that the detectives were cognizant and respectful of his impact on the community.

There was a cacophony of suspicions and innuendos about the murderers, and even some leads. The detectives followed these leads. However, none of the leads ever panned out in arrests.

The neighborhood was riveted with fear for a while, due to the senselessness and randomness of the killing. There had been murders before in the neighborhood, but it usually did not involve strangers in such a compacted time period.

Nevertheless, it was also a senseless, heartless crime because there were no precipitating factors. It was not surprising for the police to draw some immediate conclusions: the killers had to have had a high capacity for rage to commit such a killing and there was a strong likelihood they lived in the area. They realized what many others already surmised.

Regardless of which theory one espouses or accepts, or if suspects were identified, Papa Hosey was brutally murdered!

Deacon Hosey

Reacting to His Killing

As Hosey's grandson, Nat LaCour, discusses, he and his mother Beatrice were at his grandfather's home on Piety that day, having traveled from uptown earlier during the day. They were sitting around talking to their relatives, waiting for him to come home. He cannot recall whom or how they were informed of his grandfather's stabbing but all of a sudden all of the people ran from the home to where his body lay strewn on the sidewalk, partially in the gutter, a block or so down the street.

What he recalls is the intensity of the moment; all of the women were screaming, wailing, and crying uncontrollably. Some fell to the ground; others punched the muggy air. Not only the shrill in their voices, but their bulging eyes revealed the horror of the predicament they were literally facing.

Police were called and it seemed to him like a long time before they arrived, though it probably was not. It was clear that he was dead and not an ounce of life remained in his body. His body lay on the sidewalk for quite some time though, while they investigated.

Another grandson, Reverend Fagan Davis, Jr., following in the family tradition of men in the ministry, related his memory of the dreadful day. He says on that afternoon the church was awash with Davis family members; nieces and nephews and cousins and aunts and uncles. Although he was only 8 years old at the time, he remembers a spiritual reverence surrounding the church and his grandfather.

Similar to his older cousin, Nat, he recalls the female family members wailing and crying upon learning about the stabbing. Along with other minors, he was not allowed to attend the funeral services. He comprehended it as a way of protecting them from such horror and the psychic pain associated therewith.

Although nearly all murders are brutal it was difficult to comprehend a knife and icepick stabbing in this scenario. A stabbing is normally considered a more personal homicide than guns or other weapons. The assailant has to be close to his/her victim and it is often utilized in crimes of passion.

Deacon Hosey's murder is reflective of the murder weapons of the time. In the 60's stabbings were more common than the 90's, with nationwide knives being used in 22 percent of the murders.[90] In particular, ice picks as weapons of murder, dissolved many decades ago. In the 1960's, however, an ice pick assault was not uncommon and it was still considered a weapon of terror, in part, because they were easy to obtain and inexpensive to purchase.

To date, no one has ever been identified or charged with his murder. His case, however, did not fall off the NOPD's radar. They conducted a rather thorough and diligent investigation, and kept the case open, regularly inquiring of family members about potential leads. They had canvassed the blocks where the murder occurred as well as the housing project. That night was very busy in the 5th District as officers and detectives rushed from one murder to another in a short time span.

It was reasonably assumed that as popular as the Delta Supermarket and Arthur Hunter, Sr. were that communal word or rumor would spread about the killers and wind up in the ears of those operating the store. Moreover, they wanted to know, were the killers involved in other murders that weekend or similar crimes that occurred later during the year in the neighborhood? They would inquire whether the family had heard anything. Arthur, who rubbed shoulders with and served all in the neighborhood at the market, including drug dealers and killers, had not heard anything.

There was more to know and understand. But those questions were never fully answered. After a while, however, the murder languished into another unsolved homicide in the city. This is despite the murder clearance or solved rate for the city during this era being much better than it is now, with the rate hovering in the 75 to 85% range.

A few days later when his son Harrison arrived from Los Angeles California, he and his son, Hayward, and Hosey's grandson, Henry Lafayette, walked the neighborhood searching for his elusive killers. They were armed and angry, impatient, and intent on seeking some form of justice, since the police had not yet apprehended anyone. Thus, Harrison got his gun and went to every bar in the Ninth Ward searching for the assailants. The next day he even hid among trees near the park hoping that the killers would appear to rob someone else, so that he could capture or retaliate against them.

A retired military man, his look was menacing, and questions of bar patrons, made it clear that just because Deacon Hosey was a religious soul, the violence against his father was intolerable. There were no killers to be found that night, however, or the ensuing days when he searched.

There were, of course, questions or considerations of whether better police-community relations or people with information coming forward would have helped solve the murder.

It was rumored in the neighborhood that one of the persons who had committed the stabbing had later been imprisoned for another crime, but there was no confirmation for such by police and it was mere conjecture. Another rumor, years later, was that one of the killers, had himself been murdered in the Ninth ward. Thus, the killers were never caught but have been left to account to God.

Communal Pain

Deacon Hosey's death came as a shock to most because he was so well-liked and had a generous and giving spirit. It is believed that the nearby high school, G.W. Carver High, held a momentary tribute to him, even though he had never attended the school as a student. Of course, Nat was a school teacher there and several other family members attended the school.

There was some news coverage regarding his death, with a few print articles and a typical flash report on the televised news the next morning, identifying those who were murdered the previous evening. Commenting on news media coverage, family members recall later reading in the *Times Picayune,* the leading print media for the city, a sparse segment in the Crime section, no more than a couple of brief paragraphs about the murder, highlighting only its sensationalism. Reverend Fagan Davis Jr. says frustratingly, "in light of his achievements and what he added to the lives of others, any article should have been at least 1 page, if not 2 pages."

The Baton Rouge paper, *The Advocate,* which was more attuned to Pointe Coupee parish, however, published an article which discussed more fully the achievements of Deacon Davis. And the one African-American published newspaper in the city, *The Louisiana Weekly,* devoted more detail regarding Mr. Davis' murder, discussing his death, both in a communal article addressing several murders in the same neighborhood and a single article related to his stabbing.[91] The latter article mentioned his life as a shipyard worker and identified his burial services and his instant survivors.

Even that could never account for the everlasting devastation of such a tragedy, since even presently its ramifications are still heart felt among his survivors.

Each day leading to the funeral brought new rumors and conjecture about what had happened, why it had occurred and who possibly had killed him. It was like a nightmare which kept repeating itself, but without any substantive resolution. The wake and funeral were upon them before they knew it.

Funeral services were held for Papa Hosey on May 18 at New Birth Missionary Baptist Church, with one of the church founders, Rev. Welton Washington, officiating and throngs of mourners from the neighborhood, Desire projects, religious community and all walks of life, lamenting his loss. It was probably one of the larger funerals, in terms of attendance, in the city that year.

Emotions again were raw at the funeral with many family members crying and, reportedly, Harrison screaming out at the casket about why someone would kill his father. He was verbalizing with strong emotions what many others in attendance were thinking - "why"? They also were not going to allow his life to be minimalized based upon his ripe age of 75, with sentiments about how full a life he had lived. He was still entitled to a full life, they reasoned; not one cut short by a dagger.

Nat Lacour - courtesy American Federation of Teachers (AFT)

Some were still so shocked they were numb. Their sense of security had been fractured, but not their faith. In a ceremonial closing, Papa Hosey was buried in Providence Memorial Park cemetery.

One of the more scarring memories for Delores was listening to the news on the television the following morning and hearing her grandfather's name identified as being among 5 people killed in the city the previous day.

"Ooh that was devastating" Delores exclaims, as she discusses what it was like "seeing her father grieve like that". "It was a bad feeling". She wanted to scream. For her, after 50 years, the grieving has subsided but she remembers "piece by piece" the night's events. And even if they wanted his money, she pondered "why kill him? Was it a means of punishment because he had resisted, so as to not leave a witness to the robbery, or simply bounded in hate?

In the aftermath, although the adults did everything reasonably possible to protect the children from emotional harm, there was only so much they could do. Delores could not enjoy her graduation from high school, a few weeks later, because the murder kept "reappearing in her brain."

Reverberations

The Davis family had migrated from the "country" in Pointe Coupee, where murders were uncommon, even in the neighboring largest city, Baton Rouge, where in the 50's there were an average of 8 to 9 murders annually. Suddenly, the blessings of the Big Easy exposed the dread of living in the city.

He had obviously faced grave danger when he stood up to the oppression of the farmers and sharecroppers in Pointe Coupee Parish, but was unexpectedly killed in a community which he loved and cultivated.

As Reverend Fagan Davis Jr. relates, his father (Fagan, Sr.)

admired that his son's grandfather was so well known and respected in the Desire community. Hosey's life was an inspiration to his son and grandson, who later also turned to the ministry. Despite decades of hard work and community commitment, he never let his family believe they were any better or entitled to anything more than their neighbors in the projects.

Hosey Davis' WWII draft registration card

Deacon Hosey

And Arthur Hunter, Jr., one of the younger grandchildren, believes his grandfather shaped his life, albeit indirectly or subtly. He recalls how he would sit with his grandfather and watch all of the "cop" and "justice" television shows, e.g., *Perry Mason*, *The Untouchables, The Fugitive,* and *Highway Patrol*, and sometimes discuss life or moral lessons to be gleaned from the screen. In real life, as a child, the city did not have a representative number of black police officers or detectives.

Hosey's grandson, New Orleans Criminal Court judge, Arthur Hunter, Jr.   **Another grandson, Rev. Fagan Davis, Jr.**

As a career path, he first worked as a police officer, possibly subconsciously as a result of his grandfather's killing, patrolling the same neighborhood where he was raised, inclusive of the Desire project and Sampson city playground. One of the first things he did when he was assigned to a one-man unit, was to drive

Deacon Hosey

to the park and block on Piety Street, get out of his car and walk to the spot where his grandfather was killed. Miraculously, there would still be something there that an evidence technician would have missed, he thought. Or maybe, more practically, he could perceive the scene now with a background of training as a police officer.

He remarks emotively: "It made me sad, but reinforced one of my reasons for becoming a police officer, which was to make a difference." He then practiced law and is currently a criminal court judge in the city.

Now, after more than 50 years, the locale of the murder was destroyed by Hurricane Katrina. Although the pain has subsided substantially for loved ones it has not gone away. Many elderly family members found it too hurtful to talk about the murder. For some, the emotions which they feel are measured and deliberately spoken, yet it is a texture of feelings which many have not discussed or spoken about outside of the immediate family. There is also a level of consciousness about his life, such that they recently found ways to honor his memory by dedicating a family reunion with a brief discussion of his life.

Fagan Davis, Jr. who organized the first family reunion, moved from New Orleans, to rural Greensburg, Louisiana, which happens to be only 90 miles from where his father and grandfather were born in nearby Point Coupee Parish. Six months after the reunion he was installed as Pastor of a church in Batchelor, in Pointe Coupee which his great-grandfather Rev. Edward Davis founded nearly 100 years ago. Rev. Fagan Davis, Jr. also established the "Hosey Davis Memorial Christian Leadership and Service" Recognition Award. The award recognizes men, women, and children who exemplify Christian Leadership and Service in the Church or Community as Bro. Hosey

Deacon Hosey

Davis had. Established in 2012, Rev. Fagan Davis Jr. (pictured above) and the Sons of New Birth Founders has recognized five individuals, 3 in New Orleans including Hosey Davis' only living child, Bessie Davis Lafayette, and 2 in Pointe Coupee Parish which include the oldest living civil rights worker, Herbert Carter, who lived to be 104 years of age.

In this way, he honored the legacy of generations - his great grandfather, grandfather and father, by continuing the work of the Lord which they had begun. If there could not be any earthly bonds there would be everlasting spiritual bonds!

For Reverend Fagan Davis, Jr., biblical section John 11:25, 26, encapsulates his spiritual and eulogic feelings, popular to many death sermons:

Jesus said, "I am the resurrection and the life; he who believes in me, though he die, yet shall he live, and whoever lives and believes in me shall never die."

Hosey's reverence and gentle manners are what granddaughter Delores remembers. He was also quiet. Even when he disciplined the grandkids orally, it would be at the same amplification of his normal talking voice.

His knowledge and people skills far exceeded his formal education. Still, to her, he was "country" and brought his old-world ways with him to the city. She recalls how he was not accustomed to using a telephone and would neither say "hi" nor "bye" on the phone and would speak as though he was in the other person's presence. It was not intended to be rude, but instead was rudimentary.

For others, his quietness and gentleness were puzzling, as though he was always in deep thought. His appearance was both methodical and reverent. However, his face did not tell the story of his life. Some had no idea of his past as a tenant farmer and

Deacon Hosey

sharecropper, and more importantly, a civil rights farm activist. His mind and heart were apparently heavy.

"One of the finest men you could ever be around", remarked Arthur Hunter, Sr., the oldest living family member. He had been around Deacon Davis for years before marrying Gussie, and they had lived with him several years after marriage. He often drove Deacon Davis to work and was keenly aware of his interactions with people. He was "a piece of gold" and a "light in the community", he said.

The lives and achievements of his descendants are testament to the resiliency of a family overcoming tragedy. Even if his life was only tangentially influencing for their successes, the results are significant in the area of professions which assist and uplift the community. The family spawned, for instance, several ministers, deaconess', a judge, the head of a national teacher's union, several teachers, entrepreneurs, and nurses. Had his civil rights efforts, such as those with the Louisiana farmers, emboldened his descendants to similarly fight for others?

Whether consciously or subconsciously, they have some of his DNA in applying his life principles to their careers. For instance, Nat Lacour is credited with pushing a tough liberal agenda as Executive Vice President of the American Federation of Teachers (AFT), and advancing education reform and greater assistance to poor students.

In connection with his retirement, the AFT passed a resolution which stated, in part: *WHEREAS, although Nat LaCour's leadership roles in the labor and civil rights movements are so extensive that no resolution can fully encompass the scope of his accomplishments, they include establishing the United Teachers of New Orleans as the first fully integrated teachers union in the Deep South and obtaining the first collective bargaining agreement ever won by an education union in a Southern-right-to-work state.*[92]

Similarly, Arthur Hunter Sr. was part of an era of establishing black businesses in poor neighborhoods in the city. And his son, Judge Hunter, Jr., has been identified as a "legal rebel," in his efforts to ensure application of the Constitution to the criminal trials over which he presides, and founding a court-reentry program to address recidivism. In doing so, he was upsetting the status quo,[93] tackling some of the most challenging legal issues, such as unanimous verdicts in criminal trials and government funding of criminal defense for indigents.

As noted, Reverend Fagan Davis, Jr. has adopted the spirit of his grandfather and the migratory route of his great grandfather as a minister. He insists on carrying his grandfather's messages of hope and spirit to others.

Undeniably, Deacon Hosey was a man of great faith and had treasured family. Church was at the center of the Davis' lives and he was the epicenter of the church. He is still remembered. More importantly, his spirit lives on. Indeed, the church's website bears an adage which seemingly reflects the family's inner feelings:

We now know our past. We know where we presently stand. We do not know, however, what our future holds but as believers in Christ Jesus, we know who holds the future.

CHAPTER 5
BRITTANY RAY

In July 2000, along with Baltimore Police Department (BPD) Homicide detectives, the United States Marshals Service was seeking Charles Donnell Johnson in Baltimore for first degree murder. Well, Charles was on the run, literally.

The Marshals Service are crime fighters on the hunt in the ultimate cat and mouse game – finding and arresting people who are on the run from the law. They are not usually crime solvers in determining "who done it" but they "solve crimes" by capturing the bad guys. Those they seek have often eluded local law enforcement and are in a desperate game of avoidance. So, when they execute an arrest warrant it is usually with several marshals as a show of force, as a means to prevent violence, escape by the elusive fugitives, and overall physical safety of officers. U.S. marshals are usually the lead on task forces to locate fugitives.

When the marshals from the Fugitive Task force in Maryland sought to execute an arrest warrant on Johnson on July 21, in the 1200 block of West Lombard in Baltimore, he ran, scaled a roof and jumped, seeking to avoid capture. He catapulted nearly 18 feet to the sidewalk below and was captured, with fractures to his legs and injuries to his back; and then transported to University Hospital. He was arrested and charged with first degree murder in the death of Brittany Ray.[94]

Brittany was a mere innocent, angelic baby. Three days earlier, on July 18, 2000, she had been murdered at her home in the 1200 block of Glyndon Avenue, in Baltimore's Mount Clare neighborhood. Brittany was 10 months old when she was killed; an infant who had just begun to walk, with assistance. Police and an ambulance had been called to the scene for a baby being injured and not breathing, but Brittany was dead on arrival at the scene.

Discussing murders or killings of infants usually is not a comfortable or easy topic. The resulting court cases are also usually difficult and highly emotional.

Even in cities and localities marred with violence, the killing of children is jarring. The toll of suffering and outrage seems to be elevated for victims who are toddlers. The headlines or story lines with respect to child murders are usually dressed in horror:

- *Little Mason Hunt died Feb. 3, 2015 after District Attorney Jack Whelan says the boy was "terrorized" and beaten the last two days he lived.*[95]

- *The 18-month-old boy found dead at a home in Dell Rapids on Thursday had been hit on the head six times until his skull fractured.... Minnehaha County State's Attorney Aaaron McGowan also says that the autopsy showed bite marks on the little boy's body.*[96]

- *Her ribs, arm, leg, and skull — all fractured. The baby suffered "severe brain injuries," according to a Miami-Dade police report. Her left arm had been pulled clean from its elbow socket, an autopsy revealed.*[97]

- *She placed duct tape across the body and mouth of her four-day-old son, placed him in a black plastic trash bag, and left his body in a trash dumpster, resulting in his death.*[98]

- *A teen mother killed her newborn baby girl — who was only minutes old — by throwing her from an eighth-floor window because she feared her family's reaction, officials said.*[99]

> - *The petition says she wrapped a belt around his neck, choking him, and even lifted him off the ground by holding onto the belt.*
>
> *Other abuse includes Blair standing him in the tub naked, and throwing hot water on him which caused his skin to peel off, according to the petition. She also forced him to drink window cleaner and put plastic bags over his head, the petition said. When he tore through the bags to breathe, she used "Force Flex" bags to suffocate him until he passed out, according to the report.*[100]

The reasons persons kill infants or toddlers are much different than why adults are killed. Attached to the killings are other collateral consequences, such as mothers losing parental rights to other children or any remaining children being removed into foster care, or killers, if convicted, being placed at risk in the general population of prison as "marked" men, targeted for assault.

From the perspective of the greater public, possibly no murder draws as much public anger or outrage as the killing of an infant or toddler. This may be attributable, in part, to their innocence, helplessness and vulnerability, and often they are gruesome killings. At least an adult or even an adolescent can make an effort to protect themselves and, at a minimum, can speak out for themselves. Additionally, an infant is too young to have harmed or mistreated anyone, providing no cause or basis for retaliation or reprisal. Thus, they are considered "pure innocents".

More graphically, in contrast to most adult murder victims, child murders are often the result of torture since they are abused over the course of days or do not die immediately, because they are usually beaten.

As a consequence of these types of factors, most states have passed legislation enhancing the penalties or sentences for those who kill children and, with greater medical technology and training, identifying more infant deaths as murder.

Pure Innocence

Brittany was a beautiful infant with a dark brown complexion and big, bright eyes. She was nicknamed "Des Des". She was puny with long, slender fingers. At one time, Brittany smiled on contact, but a couple of weeks before her death she had started to whine and cry out more often.

In her killing, Brittany's name was thrust into the media when she would have probably otherwise lived a normal life, barely beyond the radar of anonymity. There was some print and local media coverage of her killing in the local newspapers and one spot on local television news coverage. Otherwise, her death was another statistic, listed among the FBI's uniform crime reports (UCR) and BPD's annual police report.

A warrant was issued for Johnson's arrest on July 20. With a "never quit" culture, the marshals put their investigative techniques in place, tracking Johnson the next day to the 1200 block of West Lombard Street, about a mile from where the infant was beaten to death. He saw them, ran, resisted, and was captured, and then had to face the consequences of a charge of murder.

The home which Brittany's mother was renting on Glyndon Avenue, was a typical two-story row home, in an impoverished neighborhood, situated on a skinny street, not far from the downtown section of the city. Within its approximately 1,100 square feet was a small kitchen, living room and half bathroom on the first floor, and two small bedrooms and a bathroom on the second floor.

Brittany lived there for her brief life, along with her mother, 22 years of age, maternal grandmother, two older brothers, and her mother's boyfriend, Charles Johnson, 21. Johnson had recently moved into the home about 7 or 8 weeks before the murder.

Brittany's mother had met Charles through a mutual friend at a party and they began dating. From initial indications he was okay with the children and appeared to have some bond with them. He had a child from a prior relationship and did not have a recorded history of child abuse. However, he used and smoked weed, but not in excess. But the family had already lived on Glyndon Avenue for about a year, without incident, when Charles arrived.

Most of the homes along the block were brick or stone-faced, with some boarded up and others needing significant repairs. Nearly all of the homes had been constructed in the late 1890's or early 1900's and were known as "two story and attic" row homes, for which many still existed in the city, more than 100 years after their construction. Commonly referred to by residents as "Pigtown", the overall crime risk for this area was very high. Drugs, violence, assaults and burglaries saturated the neighborhood.

But the grandmother said that despite its impoverished condition, the neighbors were close knit. They all adored Brittany and spoke about her angelic ways and swarthy complexion.

Baby's Killing

On the morning of the incident, Brittany's mother headed to work leaving her mother, three children and live-in-boyfriend, Charles Johnson, at home. It was on a Tuesday about 6:30 a.m. when she alighted the few steps on the row house and boarded a bus to her job as a Nurse Assistant at a local hospital, where she helped take care of AIDs patients.

The mother arrived at work about 7:15 and began her rounds. She had talked with her mother briefly about the grandmother running some errands and leaving the children in Charles' care. Otherwise, there was nothing unusual about her day. Until, about noon or so when she received a call from a neighbor who said Brittany had been taken to the hospital. She immediately rushed from John Hopkins to University hospital, which was about 2 1/2 miles away.

The mother later told police that when she left for work early in the morning, Brittany was "sleeping peacefully." The baby was breathing, and did not have any marks, bruises or injuries. The baby had slept in the room with her and Johnson the night before.

Brittany's maternal grandmother, telephoned her about 8:30 or 9 a.m., and said that she needed to go to run some errands and asked whether it was okay to leave Brittany with Charles "for a minute" while she went to pay bills. The grandmother told her daughter that she would be gone until about 12:30 midday. Brittany's mother responded that it was "okay", even though Johnson, 21, had only been part of the family unit for a few months and had lived in the house since June. But Johnson had baby-sat the children on several occasions before that tragic Tuesday.

The day before the grandmother had asked Johnson several times whether he was going to be okay watching the kids and he assured her he would.

A family friend from across the street on Glyndon Street had come to the house shortly before 11 and Johnson informed her that the "baby was asleep." Because the family often kept the front door unlocked, the neighbor often came unannounced. She came back about a half an hour later to see if Brittany was awoke. The neighbor was checking to see if Johnson needed any assistance with the kids. Again, Johnson noted that Brittany was sleeping. The neighbor noted that Johnson was agitated, pacing and fidgety. About an hour later, about noon, he was screaming for the older sibling and went around the corner searching for him, as the child rode his bike. When he found him, Johnson told him to go and get

Brittany Ray

the neighbor who had visited earlier because Brittany had fell and was not breathing. "She's not breathing", Johnson exclaimed.

Johnson ran further out onto the middle of the street, screaming for someone to dial 911. The family did not have a house phone. "Call an ambulance, call an ambulance," he repeated frantically. According to the neighbor, who called the police, Johnson said that the baby had got out of the bed, got a bobby pin stuck in her throat, and then also fell down the stairs.

When EMS arrived, Johnson told them that he had been watching a movie when the baby fell. They noticed, however, that the stairs where she was alleged to have fallen, were heavily carpeted and there was no evidence of trauma on the carpet. When EMS tested the baby, she flat lined. Brittany was already dead.

Johnson repeated that story to detectives about the falls when they arrived on the scene. He said he had put the two youngest children (which included Brittany) back to bed but allowed the oldest child to ride his bike outside. He said he fell asleep while watching a movie. He alleged he awoke when he heard the baby crying. But he later would modify his account of what occurred.

When the grandmother arrived, the police officers would not allow her to enter the home and provided her with scant information. The children were isolated in a separate room in the home, evidently to protect them from the trauma of the circumstances and ensure the integrity of the investigation. When she called the hospital, they connected her to her daughter, who had arrived from her job at Johns Hopkins. Through heavy tears, she told her mother, "Brittany did not make it; she is dead". Upon hearing the news, the grandmother fell to her knees and sought counsel from the Lord. And she needed it.

Later, when reunited with her grandchildren, the youngest one asked where was Brittany. The grandmother gulped hard, looked toward heaven, and said, "Brittany's gone; she won't be back anymore." She had never imagined she would have had to have a conversation with a grandchild so young (barely a year older than Brittany) about death. She was not sure he understood.

The grandmother had just played with Brittany the previous day. The grandmother had taken her to lunch. Mysteriously, at about 11 a.m., while at the offices of the gas company she felt strange and said to one of the workers there that she needed to rush back home. But they assured her that it would not be much longer, but it was.

The grandmother described this mysterious feeling as "a very strong spiritual thing". Analogously, she said it was similar to what behaviorist describe as the feelings of twins- they can feel what the other is feeling. She loved Brittany so much, it was though the grandmother was feeling the pain or fear of her grandchild.

She also regrets that she did not bring the kids with her when she ran errands that day. But she said, "it was so hot, that day", they would have been miserable. It took some time for her to recognize that she was not responsible and had done nothing wrong.

Doctors pronounced Brittany dead about 1:30 p.m. that Tuesday at University Hospital, where EMT had taken her. The following day, the state medical examiner's office in Baltimore ruled her death a homicide by blunt-force trauma. Not only did they believe the evidence supported such a finding, it would be left to the prosecutor's office, with support from the police, to make a legal determination of charges.

When an infant or child dies suddenly, from the outset law enforcement are taught to proceed under the assumption that there has been foul play and maltreatment. Standard protocol in these cases require, among other things, that police officers interview witnesses and interrogate suspects, particularly the last caretaker, investigate and document the scene and evidence. They are also taught to review and analyze old and new injuries brought out in the autopsy and post mortem reports, and review the child's medical history and events of the day of the incident.

Since the vast majority of these cases occur in the home, the focus is usually on the person whose care the baby was in at the time of the injuries, and all others in the home. In this instance, the caretaker was undeniably Johnson, and at the time the three young children were the only ones in the home, except for a neighbor who checked in on them. The older of the children was in and out of the house riding his bicycle.

The investigation fell to Baltimore Detectives Lynette Nevins, Chris Dyson, and Blane Vucci. At the time Detective Nevins, was the senior among the three, and had been an officer for about 17 years. Vucci, who was a member of the Criminal Investigation Division (CID) had been with the department about 9 years, and with the homicide unit about 18 months. Dyson, Officer No. A99262, had also been on the police force for at least 9 years and had investigated numerous crimes involving violence and drugs. All three had seen their share of murders, with a few involving infants.

Homicide work is gratifying by solving the most serious crimes, but is also depressing and unsettling to family relationships, because of the long unpredictable hours. But, according to them, the murders of infants, tend to linger longer in their mind than some others because of the vulnerability of young children. Moreover, the crime scenes are usually the homes of the children and infants, replete with cribs and diapers and bottles.

After their investigation at the crime scene on Glyndon, the detectives began a more detailed and formal interview with Johnson at police headquarters. They did not know what to expect but did not anticipate that he would tell them the truth.

Brittany Ray

He told them several conflicting accounts of what had occurred, with distinctions, among them, regarding where Brittany and the two other children were at the time, whether he was upstairs or downstairs, the time sequence regarding what he had done with respect to the infant, what he was doing at the time, sleeping or watching a movie, how she accessed a bobby-pin, what the grandmother had revealed to him or the children, and the efforts at CPR.

Tellingly, with respect to the children, he also informed detectives that 'they all got different fathers". "I am not any of them father," he noted, without solicitation, and distancing himself from them emotionally and genetically. When questioned about blood on the sheets where the baby slept with him and her mother, he said the mother was "on her period".

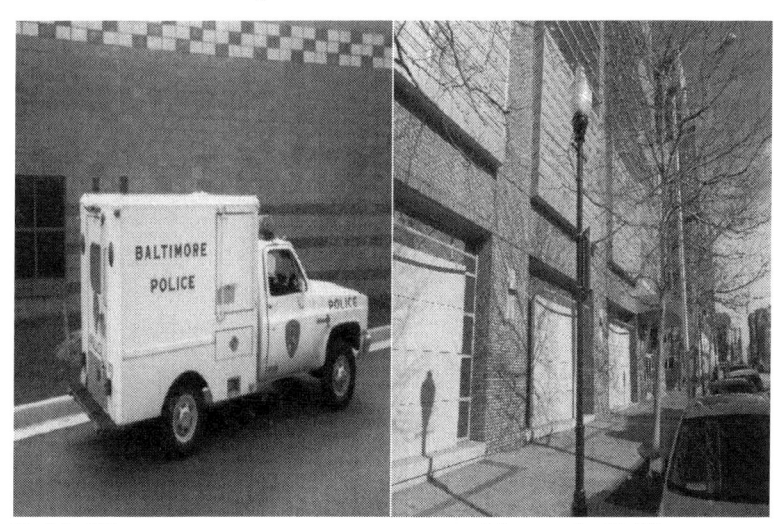

Paddy Wagon   **Morgue in Baltimore**

The detectives doubted Johnson's story, but needed more to obtain an arrest warrant. That something more would come with the Medical Examiner's post-mortem findings. They received that a couple of days later. The ultimate finding - her death was the result of murder.

The specific findings were that Brittany was beset with numerous injuries, some fresh and others healing, to the majority of her torso, extremities and internal organs, including a lacerated liver and hemorrhaging of the right lung. There were fresh and healing rib fractures and others to her thigh, flank, chest, hip and wrist. The Medical Examiner's office (ME) in its autopsy found a constellation of injuries which were diametrically inconsistent with Johnson's account of how she fell. The ME's opinion, in its post mortem report, is set forth below.

Detective Nevins swore out an affidavit to be presented for a judge to sign. The witness statements, along with Johnson's cloudy and inconsistent depictions, and the medical findings, were adequate for a judge to issue an arrest warrant for Charles. Judge Mitchell did so on July 20, finding probable cause that Johnson had committed murder. This set the police and marshal's office on their hunt, leading to his run and ultimately to his arrest.

When the grandmother learned that Charles had killed Brittany, she was hurt because she had trusted him and he had betrayed that trust in a monumental way. Of course, she looked back and saw several reasons why she should not have trusted Johnson.

On the day of incident, when the grandmother returned home, Charles came over to her and gave her a hug and said, "I'm sorry". It put a chill through her and she knew then that something other than an accident had occurred. She thought back about other occasions when he had appeared edgy and nervous and had disregarded it.

On one occasion, a pediatrician had questioned the mother and grandmother about some of Brittany's bruising on her cheeks. But she and her daughter foolishly thought it was the result of her teething, and because her complexion was so dark, the bruises were

Brittany Ray

not easily recognized. Additionally, when the grandmother would bathe Brittany, she recalled that Johnson would usually appear and try to distract her. But at the time it was occurring she did not put it all together. And though the grandmother did not know whether it had anything to do with his abuse of Brittany she recalled that he often washed his hands and clothes in heavy bleach.

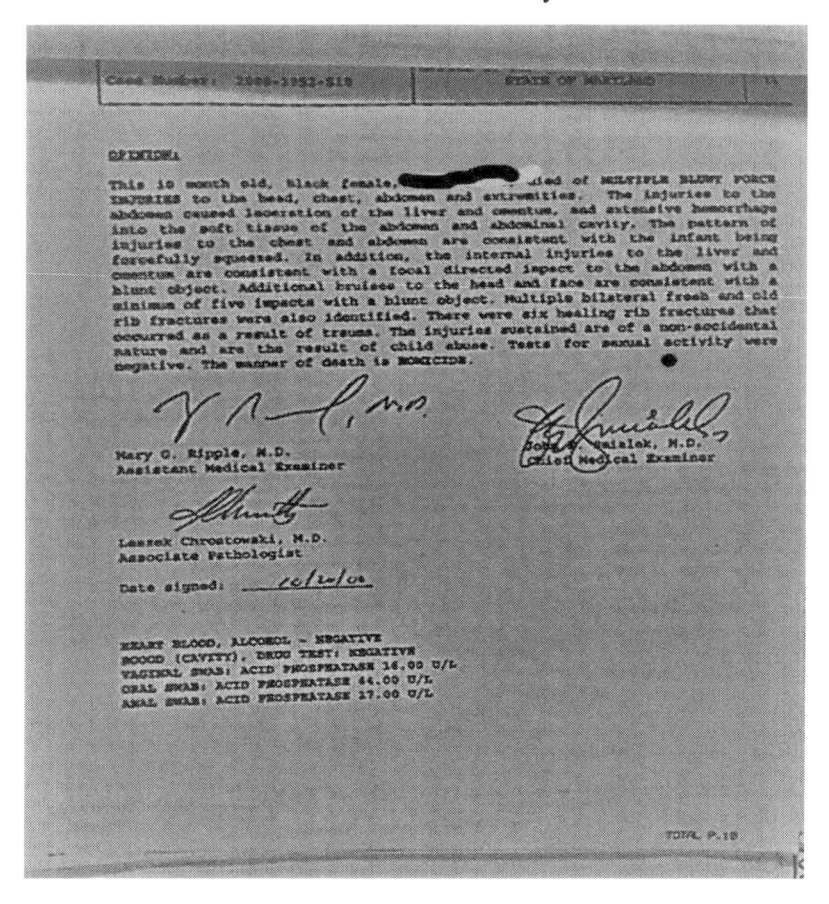

Brittany's Post-Mortem report

The next step was an indictment by a grand jury and then a trial before a jury to determine whether Johnson was guilty or innocent.

The indictment was issued in August 2000, commencing the criminal litigation process.

Trial and Court Proceedings

Brittany's case was considered a high-profile case, as is most murders of children, particularly intentional murders such as hers. In April, 2001, a jury trial began in Baltimore Circuit court before Judge Thomas Waxter, commencing April 6.

The predominating question for the trial: Was it intentional murder, or an accident as a result of the infant falling down the stairs, or the application of CPR by Johnson or a neighbor?

The prosecution asserted strongly that it was murder. As the prosecutor exclaimed in her opening argument, Brittany had lived only 314 days before she was killed. She further argued that Brittany had been entrusted to Johnson's care and he had fabricated his account of what occurred. According to her, Johnson's account did not, in any manner, line up with the medical evidence which the State's witnesses would present.

On the other hand, Johnson argued that it was either not his fault or an accident. He attacked the legitimacy of the medical and scientific findings, claiming their findings were flawed.

There is no rational reason why anybody would torture and kill a little baby.

Arguing to the jury in her opening statement, Julie Drake, the Assistant DA, and a long-term prosecutor who prosecuted many of the child murder cases, sought to answer the question which, obviously, may have been on the minds on most jurors. Drake uttered the above, posturing that she did not have a clear answer but whatever the reason it defied reason.

One of the first witnesses for the State was Brittany's maternal grandmother, who told the jury that she left to run some errands;

pay the electric bill and get some food for the house. Before leaving, she testified she peeked in on Brittany and saw that she was sleeping in the bed with Johnson and doing fine. She acknowledged that Brittany had recently begun to cry more often and required frequent diaper changes.

The grandmother further testified that Johnson began to stay with the family in the house in about June, a month or so before the murder. She said that he had babysat Brittany about 5 times. She had noticed bruises before this instance, after Johnson had babysat her, but had not taken it as serious as she possibly should have. She had informed Johnson the night before of her plans for the next day and asked that he watch the children.

A neighbor, who lived across the street on Glyndon Avenue, testified that she had come over earlier that morning after the grandmother had left, but defendant was too agitated to hold a conversation. He said the baby was asleep. Thus, the neighbor left and went back across the street to her home. She came back again about a half hour later and spoke briefly to Johnson but left again. The neighbor revealed to the jury that shortly thereafter, Johnson ran across the street to the neighbor's screaming that the baby had fell down the stairs and was not breathing.

When the neighbor ran over, she testified Brittany was on the living room couch. Brittany was cold, her tongue was purple, her eyes were open, and she was just staring; a grim stare devoid of life. She could not feel a pulse, and the baby was not breathing. Defendant said to the neighbor that he did not know what had happened to her. He claimed he had been smoking some weed. Another neighbor who had some medical training, was summoned and she attempted to resuscitate the baby, without success.

One critical piece of testimony came from an EMT technician who testified that Johnson rode with him in the ambulance transporting

Brittany to the hospital. During that ride, he stated that defendant exclaimed, voluntarily and incriminatingly to him: "Oh my God, what did I do? Stupid! Stupid!".

As in most similar infant death cases, the core of the case was whittling down to a battle of medical experts – doctors Walker and Ripple for the prosecution and Dr. Piatt on behalf of Mr. Johnson. The defense withdrew Dr. Piatt as a witness on the first day of trial.

Consequently, the trial testimony was dominated by medical personnel who had examined the baby's body or forensic documents. Dr. Ripple, an Assistant Medical Examiner who had supervised the autopsy, testified, consistent with the autopsy report, about the injuries which Brittany had suffered. Having been involved in many other child murders, Ripple knew the subtleties of infant homicides and had developed an expertise in this slice of pathology and forensics. Critically, Ripple was of the opinion that there was no way that the pattern of injuries could have occurred as a result of a fall down stairs, as Johnson had asserted. Additionally, she testified that if the child fell down the stairs her injuries would include a bump on the head and bruises to the extremities, because of how her weight was distributed.

Ripple testified there were multiple blunt force injuries to the head, chest, abdomen and extremities. Important to the prosecution, there were no injuries to the brain or a skull fracture, which may have been indicative of a fall down the stairs, as Johnson had claimed. There were at least 5 impact blows with a blunt object and, in her view, the injuries could not have been caused by inexpertly performed CPR. The rib fractures occurred up to ½ hour before her death and the healing rib fractures had occurred a few weeks before Brittany's death.

In sum, the Medical Examiner testified that Brittany:

- Had 18 fresh fractures to her ribs
- Had been squeezed with significant force
- Suffered facial injuries with imprints on her face and head
- Suffered a torn frenulum- which is the tissue between the lip and tongue, and is a classic indicia of child abuse
- Had suffered a tremendous blow to the abdomen which completely lacerated her liver

The other prosecution medical expert from Johns Hopkins University, Dr. Allen Walker, is a nationally renowned child abuse expert, who has appeared as a prosecution witness in numerous child murder cases. His testimony was similar to Dr. Ripple's. He also thought it took a significant amount of concentrated force to break the flexible ribs of the child. On cross-examination, he conceded that incorrectly performed CPR could have produced some, but not all, of the injuries.

Johnson attempted to lay the blame on others. He says that the grandmother left the children in the care of the two older children, 7 and 2 years of age. He had fixed the children some Oodles and Noodles that morning and Brittany had first got a hold of a Bobbie pin and then fell down the stairs, since there was no child gate on the stairs. Defendant argued that the broken ribs and other injuries likely came from the fall or they were the result of the attempts at CPR which he and the neighbors had attempted.[101] None of that was his fault, he contended.

His lawyer also sought to explain his incriminating statement to EMS personnel as reflecting his concern that a child in his care is no longer alive, not that he had committed an intentional murder. She also asserted that he had two other children for whom there had never been any allegations of abuse. Hence, why would he want to hurt Brittany?

In sum, his defense was typical. It went something like this: He was not responsible. The child's mother or someone else in the house must have committed abuse against the child that resulted in a delayed death. His only possible involvement in the injuries, according to him, was the result of him trying to save the child's life after Brittany fell and stopped breathing. In fact, the child had not even been entrusted to his care but the grandmother had left her to be cared by her two older brothers, not him.

The medical examiner and prosecution expert rejected his claim about how the injuries occurred, testifying that it is rare that a child suffers a broken rib during CPR and that a child's fall down stairs usually results in head and extremity injuries not broken ribs. The ME confirmed that given the flexibility of baby's bones it takes a large degree of force to fracture 19 ribs. In this instance, that degree of force also caused a contusion of the lungs.

She opined that the injuries were the result of continuous squeezing of the child. She further determined that about a third of the child's blood volume had hemorrhaged inside the baby. Because your organs need blood, including your heart and brain needing sufficient amounts of blood, with this amount of loss, they stop functioning and a person dies. This is what happened to baby Brittany!

The culmination of the trial reflected an apparent weird mixture of emotions, spewing from the various Brittany Ray family members and friends. For instance, not surprisingly, there were those who were angry and wanted some level of revenge against the defendant. It was so evident to the defendant's counsel that she asked for relief from the judge because of what counsel complained of as "aggressive looks" towards defendant and how he had to traverse a phalanx of people who were staring at him.

Brittany Ray

On the other hand, Brittany's grandmother provided the following victim impact statement to the court following Johnson's conviction: *Your Honor. I just want to say this. That was my only granddaughter. I may not have another granddaughter. I loved Brittany with all my heart. I'm sorry. I don't Charles. I'm sorry. I don't know what happened to you that day. I'm sorry Charles. I'm sorry. I hope that God gives you grace, be gracious to you and forgives you and blesses your soul. My heart goes out to you. I can't point my finger at you and blame you because it wasn't only you. It was circumstance, it was society, it was what had to be done that day. The responsibility for having three children may have been too much for you. If you had thought and said I need some help. If you went to a neighbor or a friend and asked for some help, I'm sorry I was delayed. I tried to get home as fast as I could. I thought about you. Thought about you Charles. I was thinking about you when you were doing the act. I don't know, I don't know why, all I know is dear God in heaven is coming back here one day. When he comes will you and I be there? Will I be able to look you in the face and hold your hand and say it's alright? Something went wrong that day, something. Something terrible. Brittany bless her little heart, paid the penalty. She was sacrificed. There is so much evil in the world. It's always out there. I don't know what happened, but I'm sorry that it did. My granddaughter is gone, she's gone. I'm sorry it happened. I don't know why. God help us all in the world today. Thank you.*

The grandmother unquestionably struggled with misplaced guilt and a sense of failure. She blamed herself a lot. Psychologically, there was a failure to protect her grandchild, as well as a failure to provide a better life for her daughter, and relatedly for her grandchildren.

But the grandmother recently explained that her statement in court was intended to explain that she had given the issue to God to resolve and was coming to peace with herself and Johnson. She expressed that she wanted God to have mercy on his soul, but it was not her he had to deal with. It was God-only God could show or provide the mercy which he needed. "I had to make myself forgive him", she says.

Carrying all of that anger would destroy her, she thought.

In contrast, Brittany's natural father requested of the judge that defendant be given the maximum sentence, and for Johnson to "man up" to face the consequences of his actions.

In this case, it is clear the jury did not accept Defendant's depiction and instead accepted that of the government. After an emotional trial, the jury found Johnson guilty on all counts: second degree murder, child abuse, and manslaughter. The judge sentenced him to 30 years in prison. This sentence may have taken into account the possibility of an accident.

Under the Maryland sentencing scheme, with good time, Johnson was, practically, facing 21 years in prison.

However, Johnson appealed his conviction and sentence to a higher state court. The appeals court agreed that the prosecutor had made an improper closing argument to the jury at his criminal trial. In an unreported decision, in May 2002, the Maryland Court of Special Appeals overturned the trial court's decision and jury verdict. It found that he had been prejudiced by the government's closing arguments and the trial court's acceptance of inconsistent verdicts related to murder and manslaughter by the jury.

Rather than retry Johnson a year later, the Baltimore prosecutor's office worked out a plea deal with him in May 2003. He pled guilty to second degree murder and was sentenced to 15 years in prison. With the new sentence, Johnson could expect to serve about 10 1/2 years in prison, with the application of education and other good time credits.

Some family and friends believed the 15-year sentence was wholly inadequate and insulting to Brittany's life and the pain of her loved ones. Others had factored in the collateral consequences they felt Johnson would face in prison for being the murderer of an infant. It had been fairly well-established that child murderers, pedophiles, and rapists fall to the bottom of the social stratum in prison society and often despised or considered "marked men" by other inmates. And he fell into that category.

Children, Infants and Toddlers as Murder Victims

Notedly, murders of infants and other children have occurred since the advent of mankind and is thus not a recent phenomenon. The recent cases have been memorable. In Houston in 2001, Andrea Yates drowned her five children, who ranged in age from six months to seven years. China Arnold of Dayton, Ohio was sentenced to life in prison in 2008 for placing her 3-week-old baby in a microwave oven, literally frying her to death. In 2008, in Florida, Caylee Anthony went missing from her home, and her mother was found not guilty for her murder. These types of deaths fueled greater public concern about child abuse and the safety of children.

Nationally, in 2000, 349 infants (under age 1) were murdered-129 by neglect, 29 by strangulation or suffocation, 12 by firearm, and 182 by beatings and other means.[102] The death rate per 100,000 persons was 9.2, which was 1½ times that for the rest of the population (6.1).[103] And, coincidentally, the 9.2 rate was the highest rate for infants during the period 1970 to 2013.[104] In fact, there were nearly as many homicides of infants (349), as there were for the next age group (1-4 year olds), for which there were 356 children murdered.[105] Thus, the youngest children were at the greatest risk.

According to the Statistical Assessment Service, the United States has the highest infant murder rate in the civilized world, prompting a comment, that "America is witnessing something barbaric happening to its young children."[106]

There has been abundant research concerning infant and child murder.[107] Overall, child homicide rates have tripled since 1950,

whether the increase in numbers is the result of better diagnosis or more murders. During the period 1996 through 2011, homicide was the leading cause of infant deaths due to injury, accounting for 28 to 31 percent of such deaths.

Aside from Brittany, there were 66 other infant black females killed in 2000, at a rate of 22.16, which was about 4 times that of white female infants. None of the deaths involved a firearm and constituted 26 percent of all deaths from injury.

Placing these types of figures in context, these statistics are incredible. For instance, the CDC determined that in 2011, 256 infants were killed. Yet, in that same year no infants died as a result of a range of diseases and conditions with which the medical community has placed great emphasis: among other possible causes, measles, chicken pox, mumps, polio, tetanus, diphtheria, gonococcal infection, or disorders related to long gestation and high birth weight.

Moreover, nearly seventy-five percent of the infant killings were committed in the home, indicative that they were usually killed by a relative or someone they knew. And the majority of times the perpetrator was alone during the commission of the crime.

There are also research findings which support a theory that both homicides and fatal cases of child abuse are undercounted. There are a number of factors which bear on an undercount: for example, some births may have been kept secret and the resulting murder may not be known; some deaths were mistakenly labeled as an unintentional injury or from other causes, including the sudden infant death syndrome.

Child Deaths and Murders in Maryland and Baltimore

The infant mortality rate for infants for Maryland for 2000 was 789.7, a whopping 28 times greater than for the next age grouping of 1 through 4-year olds. There were 550 infants who died that year in the State, with 11 being the result of homicide.[108]

There has been notable overall concern about infant deaths in the city. In 2000, its infant mortality rate per 100,000 residents was incongruous with the country's rate and that of Maryland, with the applicable rates 7.0 and 7.5, respectively; Baltimore's comparative rate was about 12.0. As one commenter noted, "A community's infant mortality rate is considered to be the most sensitive sign of the overall health of the community. In Baltimore City, there are typically more than 200 total fetal deaths (also referred to as stillbirths) and infant deaths every year. Baltimore's infant mortality rate has traditionally been one of the highest in the country and is a serious public health problem."[109]

Concentrating on child murders in Baltimore, there were 8 infants less than 1 year's old who were killed in Baltimore in 2000. For the later period 2001 through 2015, 63 children, from new births to age 4, were murdered in Baltimore. The vast majority of them (51 or 80%), were infants or toddlers, aged from birth through age 2.

Nicknamed "Charm city", it was known for its row houses, crabs from the Chesapeake, Preakness, and emerging sports teams. Baltimore was once considered a blue-collar city, comprised of many neighborhoods. It had been transformed into a city reliant upon the tech sector and service industry, with the latter resulting in lower wages for many of its residents. However, it is also a city of many memorials, balloons, and stuffed teddies, however, because of its many murders, not necessarily its charming aspects for other reasons.

Baltimore has generally fit the nationwide profile for murders of children in urban areas. Still, most of the murderers of infants less than 4 years old were their parents. However, the numbers of murders by boyfriends, which is pertinent in Brittany's case, is disproportionate to the national profile. Of the 71 murders of young children (from new births to age 4) noted above, for the period 2000 to 2015, at least 14 were committed by boyfriends.

Who are Their Perpetrators?

When an infant or young child is murdered, the most frequent perpetrator is a victim's parent. Beyond that, research and studies vary regarding the prevalence of other perpetrators. One study, focused upon the period between 1976 and 2004, concluded that 30 percent of all children murdered under the age of five were killed by their mothers and 31 percent were killed by their fathers. Another study in 2004, found that 63 percent of children under the age of five were murdered by their parents in the United States.[110]

A similar study in 2014, found that parents, acting alone or with another parent, were responsible for 79.3 percent of child abuse or neglect fatalities. More than one-quarter (28.0 percent) were perpetrated by the mother acting alone, 15.0 percent were perpetrated by the father acting alone, and 21.8 percent were perpetrated by the mother and father acting together. Nonparents (including kin and child care providers, among others) were responsible for 15.7 percent of child fatalities, and child fatalities with unknown perpetrator relationship data accounted for 5.0 percent of the total.[111]

One fact that has remained consistent is the murderer of children within the first 24 hours of life. Almost all are committed by mothers; fathers are rarely responsible. The mothers are usually teenagers, who have live births at home and act impulsively.

Generally, the perpetrator changes with the age of the child. The older the child gets the more likely the chances are for the perpetrator to be a person unrelated to the child. In the first week of life, mothers are the perpetrators in the vast majority of cases.[112] In fact, experts conclude that there is a clear distinction regarding the motives between children murdered within 24 hours of birth and murders which occur thereafter.

One positive statistic for law enforcement is that when there is a determination that the death was the result of homicide, the closure and conviction rates meaningfully exceed the rates for the general public.

Interestingly, this area of homicide has spawned a unique range of terminology to describe the killing circumstances: Filicide identifies those circumstances when a parent(s) kills their child. Paternal and maternal filicide, respectively refer to when the perpetrator is the father or the mother, respectively. The term *neonaticide* describes murder of an infant within the first 24 hours of life. Infanticide, which occurred in Brittany's homicide, refers to the murder of a child before he/she reaches age 1.

Answering the Why

It is only natural to ask: Why did Charles Johnson kill Brittany? Let's start with the broader question of why anyone would want to kill a child, an infant, or toddler?

The various studies have shown that the reasons people kill children are vastly different than the reasons why adults are slain. More granularly, the reasons perpetrators kill and the means used are different for infants and toddlers less than1 years old than the more comprehensive grouping of children 5 years of age or below.

The reasons for killing of a child ranges from an undesired pregnancy to the perpetrator having mental health or psychological issues, such as postpartum depression. In many instances, the triggering event was less complicated and resulted from the child crying, bedwetting, or feeding problems. In other circumstances, the killing resulted from the killer's frustration, or hatred for the child.[113]

There are also the truly bizarre experiences, – e.g., the 3-year old child who died after his father forced him to box with him to toughen him up and prevent him from being gay. Or consider allegations in the China Arnold killing, that she confessed to her cellmate that she put the baby in the microwave because she was afraid that her boyfriend would leave her if he found out that he was not the baby's biological father. And in Baltimore in 2009, a 16-month old was starved to death after a cult leader forbade her followers from feeding him - because he didn't say Amen before meals.

There has been significant research regarding why adults kill children.[114] For this discussion, we are not here dealing with the deaths of children from negligent parenting or neglect (although such can be intentional), such as malnutrition, crib deaths or accidental suffocations, leaving a child in a hot car, but rather intentional killings.

One of the more often cited pieces of research is that of Dr. Phillip Resnick, professor of Psychiatry at Case Western Reserve University, who has studied parents' murder of one's own child, for more than 50 years and testified in several high-profile cases involving child murderers. Broadly summarizing, he has identified five general circumstances where parents kill their children.

The first reason, termed "altruistic filicide", the parent thinks that it would be better for the child if he/she was dead and in their best interest, so that the child can escape the suffering that they suffer in society. They may illogically believe they are helping the child.

A second reason is psychosis - a mental illness or condition where they believe they are being told to kill the child. Psychosis seems to be common in men who commit filicide. Two studies, for instance, found the rate of psychosis for men who killed children was 40 percent.[115]

Another reason for such murders is mothers who hide a pregnancy and birth of a newborn, because the child is perceived as a hindrance or will cause the other spouse to leave.

A fourth scenario is abuse; although often considered accidental because not intending to kill the child, parents are sometimes prosecuted for murder because the intent may be to abuse or beat him/her leading to death. As a result, many states have adopted "homicide by abuse" statutes, which penalize abuse cases where the results lead to murder.

The last reason is revenge against the other spouse or partner; also, termed revenge filicides. In killing the child, they are getting back at the other parent for what they perceive as having been wronged or mistreated, typically after infidelity.

Dangerous Boyfriends in the Home

Brittany's killing involves another phenomenon, related to infant murders, which may incorporate some or parts of Resnick's categories - boyfriend killings.

Boyfriends living in the home create a high risk of death by killing for children.[116] The phenomenon of boyfriends killing the children of their girlfriends are now well documented.[117] It has been described as the "boyfriend issue", or "dangerous men in the home" concern.

One study, conducted in 2001 in Missouri, found that children residing in households with adults unrelated to them were 8 times more likely to die of maltreatment than children in households with 2 biological parents.[118] In another study, based upon children from birth to 8 years old, researchers found that children who had a father surrogate living in the home were twice as likely to be reported for maltreatment after his entry into the home than those with either a biological father or no father figure in the home.[119]

Another study in 2005, regarding fatal child abuse in Missouri, found that children living with their mother's boyfriends were more than 45 times more likely to be killed than were children living with their married mother and father.[120]

Young children who reside in house-holds with unrelated adults are at an exceptionally high risk for inflicted-injury death. Most perpetrators are male, and most are residents of the decedent child's house-hold at the time of injury.[121] All told, children living in households with an adult unrelated to them were almost 50 times as likely to die of an inflicted injury than children living in households with 2 biological parents.[122]

Strangely, Johnson's defense was common to those charged with murdering a child. In other cases, defendants have similarly argued that the injuries occurred in administering first aid or was an accident. Indeed, Dr. Walker, the expert on child abuse in the Johnson case, had heard similar legal defense gymnastics about 6 months before, in connection with the killing of 5-month-old Ta'mar Hamilton in the same East Baltimore neighborhood.

Ta'mar's killer, Walter Pinkney, 25, was convicted of first-degree murder in connection with the November 1999 murder of the infant. Pinckney was the boyfriend of the infant's grandmother, who was raising Tamar in a Lombard Street rowhouse, not far from Brittany's killing.

In probably no other murder circumstances is the testimony of a medical expert as critical to the success of prosecution as it is in a child murder situation, such as Brittany's and Ta'mar's killing.

As the court described the critical facts in the Pinkney case:

At approximately 10 a.m., Ms. Pinkney went to the store for diapers, leaving the children in appellant's care. She checked and saw that Ta'mar was asleep before she left. According to appellant, while Ms. Pinkney was away, Ta'mar awoke and began crying, so he went into the room where Ta'mar was and picked him up to try to calm him. He tried to feed Ta'mar from a bottle, but Ta'mar only drank a small amount, approximately 3 and a half ounces. Appellant testified that he was changing Ta'mar's diaper following a suspected bowel movement when Ta'mar gasped for breath and stopped breathing. Immediately, he called 911 and began giving Ta'mar CPR. He was still trying to resuscitate Ta'mar when Ms. Pinkney returned home. An ambulance then arrived and transported Ta'mar to The Johns Hopkins Hospital ("Hopkins").

Ta'mar was admitted to the Pediatric Emergency Department. Dr. Allen Walker, Director of that Department, was contacted to evaluate Ta'mar. Dr. Walker diagnosed Ta'mar as having sustained a severe brain injury. Dr. Walker interviewed Ms. Pinkney and appellant, trying to ascertain what had happened before Ta'mar was brought into the hospital. During the interview, appellant described Ta'mar's constant crankiness, refusal to eat, how Ta'mar had stopped breathing while he was changing his diaper, how he had immediately contacted 911, and his attempts at CPR. Thereafter, Dr. Walker spoke with the police.

The autopsy revealed that the cause of Ta'mar's death was blunt force trauma as a result of four injuries to his head. After receiving the autopsy results, Detective Peckoo asked Ms. Pinkney and appellant to come to the police station for a second interview. They did so voluntarily on December 3, 1999, and he took recorded statements from them both. During this second interview, appellant indicated that he might have hit Ta'mar's head on the bed rail while trying to get him to respond after he stopped breathing. He also admitted that he had shaken Ta'mar a few times.[123]

Brittany's grandmother's cautions that women should be careful whom they date and even more careful about who they trust around their children.

The Challenges of Determining that a Murder was Committed

Infant and child murders often present challenges in proof. Invariably, there are questions, along a sliding scale, about whether it was the result of an intentional act, maltreatment or an accident. Was it negligence, a horrible accident, irresponsible conduct or intentional, and if so, was it child abuse, manslaughter or second-degree murder? These are the typical questions facing prosecutors.

Retrospective studies appear to confirm that the vast majority of infant deaths are the result of sudden infant death syndrome (SIDs) or accidents and not murders. Murders have been found to have occurred in only 5 to 7 percent of the deaths.[124] As discussed herein, nonetheless, far too many infants are being murdered.

In infant murders, the child's body is generally considered the most critical piece of evidence. They usually involve dueling experts regarding the cause of death, with one medical examiner arguing an accidental death or the result of an illness or deformity and the other contending it was the result of an intentional act. Moreover, these cases almost never involve the traditional weapons used in the murder of adults - guns and knives.

Brittany Ray

Each year there are about 1,500 child deaths which are labeled as resulting from maltreatment. This is all in the context that there are limitations of what medical experts can prove legally and conclusively. Often cases are identified as, a diagnosis of exclusion. These difficulties have often led to charges of child abuse or manslaughter rather than murder being brought or pursued.

The investigation of infant homicides also may differ significantly from that of adults. Investigations are designed to determine cause, manner, and circumstances of an infant's death. This will include emphasis on factors, such as the infant's prior medical history, post mortem changes in body, mental health and social histories for the caregivers, prior siblings' deaths or abuse, and doll reenactments.[125]

As a leading expert on child abuse investigation, notes:

Everyone involved in the investigation of a child fatality must understand that these cases differ from typical homicides in many ways, including the causes of death, the offender's motivations and legal culpability for the crime, the methods used to inflict the fatal injuries, the types of injuries that the victim sustained, the forensic and physical evidence involved, and the investigative techniques used.[126]

Generally, there is tremendous stigma associated with families of infants who have died. Thus, the forensic analysis differentiating SIDS from infanticide is crucial.[127] Innocent parents or caretakers often feel responsible for the death because they feel they contributed or should have been able to prevent the death.

Some of these cases simply defy logic. For instance, there is the example of a case in Tennessee where a father is accused of leaving his 10-month-old in a tub of water. Alone in his care, when he returned and found the child lying face down in the water not breathing, he did nothing for 5 minutes. He then wrapped the child in a blanket. He then drove around the city with the child in the car making several stops over the course of several hours before he took him to the hospital.

One common and notable factor is the absence of witnesses; a crime rarely committed in public; there are rarely weapons used; and DNA evidence is usually less useful, because the child has a connection to the perpetrator.

The other mystifying aspect of murders of infants and toddlers is the high clearance rate of arresting perpetrators. Given the high clearance rate, why would most perpetrators murder an infant? This higher clearance rate may be attributable to the fact that because perpetrators are usually caregivers, whether they are parents, relatives, boyfriends or other persons, they are easier to identify and focus upon than in other crimes. The clearance rate may be deceptive however, because there appears to be significant research which indicates that child homicides are underreported and perpetrators are often not charged criminally. This is so in part in light of the difficulties of putting some cases together for prosecution or the caregiver may be only charged with child abuse in domestic court.

Injuries to Infants

What are those injuries like which led to the child's death? "Postmortem findings in cases of fatal child abuse most often reveal cranial injuries, abdominal trauma (e.g., liver laceration, hollow viscous perforation, or intramural hematoma), burns, drowning, or exposure as the cause of death."[128]

It is difficult to fathom such suffering to an infant or small child. The following descriptions of the injuries from a few cases, paints a morbid depiction of infant murders:

Brittany Ray

A court in Minnesota described the injuries as follows:

Medical personnel from both hospitals testified extensively about their observations, care, and diagnosis of A.C. Ultimately, doctors discovered that A.C. had a skull fracture that took up the entire surface of the top of her skull. The fracture could only have been caused by direct impact to her head with the amount of force that would occur in a car accident at 29 to 45 mph, a fall from a three-story building, or being hit by a baseball bat. Her brain was severely injured. There was also evidence of healing bilateral rib fractures of the type that are only seen in child-abuse cases.

The hospital notified law enforcement of possible child abuse. A.C. was placed on life support. After five days, the doctors told Shane that A.C. was not likely to survive and that if she did survive, she would be "neurologically devastated" and would be in a vegetative state.

State v. Shane, A06-1581, 2008 WL 660543, at *1–3 (Minn. App. Mar. 11, 2008)

Another court in Maryland described the injuries just as shockingly:

Dr. Walker testified in great detail about the extent and cause of Ta'mar's fatal injuries, explaining that (1) severe brain injury was his initial diagnosis, (2) Ta'mar's chance for survival was almost non-existent, (3) the injuries were almost everywhere, i.e., the brain and skull had been virtually destroyed, (4) violent force, similar to the force when someone is thrown through the windshield in a car crash or falls from a third floor window, was required to inflict the type of injuries that Ta'mar had sustained to his head, and (5) such violent blows would have rendered Ta'mar immediately unconscious so as to make him incapable of crying or drinking formula. Dr. Walker also described the rest of Ta'mar's stay at Hopkins, explaining that for a couple of days he was maintained on a number of medications and a ventilator because he could not breathe for himself, and that, during that time, his brain died.

Pinkney v. State, 827 A. 2d 124 (Md: Court of Special Appeals 2003).

An Alaska court opinion, describing the injuries, is similarly painful:

According to the testimony presented at the trial in this case, Takak starved Christina to the point where the infant had essentially no fat left in her body, and her muscles had atrophied. One witness testified that Christina looked like a famine victim at the time of her death. The jury found, however, that the immediate cause of Christina's death was Takak's act of intentionally dropping Christina on the floor head-first, causing trauma to her skull and brain. This physical assault (which preceded Christina's death by one to three days) caused Christina's brain to hemorrhage and swell inside her skull, leading to her death.

Johnson v. State, 175 P. 3d 674 (Alas. Ct. Appeals 2008).

The Immense Pain of a Mother

The death of a child, particularly from murder, is unquestionably one of the most painful experiences a human can suffer. Studies reflect that of all homicides, it may be accompanied by the greatest and most lasting stress, for survivors, particularly parents. In addition, it is complicated because the stress and pain of the infant's siblings usually mirrors that of the parents.

The details were sketchy for Brittany's mother. When she got to the hospital on the day of the murder, Brittany's mother was confused. At first, she wanted to believe Johnson's version of the facts. But Brittany's mother could not focus, could only respond in a faint voice, and would tear up on the slightest thoughts of her baby girl. Brittany's mother internally questioned whether she should be feeling sadness or anger.

For Brittany's grandmother there were no definitive or pressing indicators that Johnson was dangerous in this manner. She was aware that he had some prior arrests for drugs and violence, but nothing related to children. But it is obvious Johnson was having some internal dialogue and troubles, since the forensic evidence showed that the baby was being abused over a period of time. Many of her injuries had not been sustained on the day of her death, but prior thereto.

The motivation for Brittany's murder is cloudy still, more than 17 years later. It is theorized by some that Johnson was trying to retaliate against Brittany's mother because the mother maintained a cordial friendship with Brittany's father. Second, Brittany's mother, who had two sons and one daughter, was unable to conceive again after Brittany was born. Hence, taking away Brittany would be extremely hurtful to the mother because she would lose her only daughter and would be unable to conceive or have another female. This would be much more abusive and damaging than anything else.

Brittany's mother knew then her life would never be the same. For her, it was not a murder but an atrocity. She was not the same since the murder and the road through life took her into a lot of dark curves.

She felt as though she had failed in her most basic duty and responsibility as a mother: she had not protected her infant daughter. Her precious baby! Brittany's mother had learned from her mother and the rest of her family that you always protect your children; don't put them in unsafe situations. A significant error in emotional or romantic judgment, nonetheless, would change her life. From there it was an emotional and psychological rollercoaster.

On that day in 2000, all life as her mother knew it was shattered. Her precious little body later lay in a small casket at the New Light Church of St. Luke in Baltimore. In attendance were many of the neighbors, fellow nursing students of the mother, and family from different parts of the country. Bishop Benedict Dorsey performed the services and Warren, an uncle on her father's side, delivered the eulogy.

With somewhat of an edge, Bishop Dorsey reminded those in attendance that Brittany's murder was not an act of God, but rather was that of the devil. This was "pure evil", he extolled. "Who takes a baby's life"?

She and her mother had sought to protect the two remaining children from further emotional trauma and did not bring them to the funeral. Brittany's mother simply could not take it, was overcome with grief, and passed out.

She was pained because her two other children were either in the home when the murder occurred, or nearby, and had seen Brittany as a dead infant. How could she now shield them from the loss? Of course, she thought about how she could have missed this dark side of a man who would kill her daughter. She wondered aloud: Is there life after death and is my daughter happy?

Brittany's mother embarked on a somewhat predictable emotional journey after the loss of a child. Conversations which had begun with "going to be" about the baby were now reduced to silence and not answering. The previous stares and comments of neighbors and passers-by about such a "cute baby" were converted to looks that she deemed incriminating or suspicious, even when neighbors were still supportive. The only way to escape this pressure was to leave the area of the murder.

Brittany Ray

Family Devastation

The devastation from Brittany's killing was also deep, wide and lasting. The most immediate family members' lives spiraled out of control. They moved away from Baltimore to get a restart on life.[129] Brittany's mother suffered a nervous breakdown and eventually was arrested for several crimes of violence, which her relatives attribute to her breakdown. Her grandmother suffered PTSD and became seriously ill. Her oldest brother was charged with, and convicted of, robbery and was incarcerated. And her natural father was in a serious automobile accident.

What about the kids? Poor kids, they could not unsee what they had seen - their baby sister's lifeless little body, not breathing, with EMT hovering over her. They had been exposed to a lot. They became fearful and anxious. The oldest son in particular became worried about his mother and younger brother – he thought who would be next?

The real challenge in the aftermath of such events is how to explain the tragedy to the other children - especially family members and playmates of the deceased.

The myth that younger children are not affected by violence has been debunked by behavioral specialists. Children who are exposed to homicides in a neighborhood are subjected to cognitive impairments and are subject to fear, hopelessness, and horror.[130] Most experts believe that children who are raised in abusive homes learn that violence is an effective way to resolve conflicts and problems. They may replicate the violence they witnessed as children in their teen and adult relationships and parenting experiences. Additionally, living with domestic violence significantly alters a child's DNA, aging them prematurely 7-10 years. Brittany's brothers represent the real children behind the statistics and varied studies.

Brittany Ray

Surely, there were many days when the following anonymous quote from a grieving mother followed her.

Please don't treat me like
I'm sick or crazy
Sometimes, I just miss my baby.
　　　　-Grieving Mother

Both siblings were significantly affected. It was tough for them. They exhibited the classic effects customary to children who are survivors of violence.

Before the killing, the oldest son thought he would be safe. Afterwards, he had many thoughts about his safety and those around him.

Research has established that children witnessing violence, particularly intra-family, learn violence as the "norm" and often become abusers later in life. Moreover, witnessing violence is the single highest predictor of juvenile delinquency and adult criminality. This, unfortunately, affected the oldest son.

As the oldest child grew older his emotions bubbled from frustration and anger to violence. He was arrested at age 19 for armed robbery and sent off to prison. During the robbery one of his co-defendants was killed. Even after being released on parole, it was hard for him to adjust and his parole was revoked, and he was placed back in prison.

His younger brother also had classic effects of grief, and experienced difficulty in school, often "acting out" and being suspended. His level of pain and suffering was unmistakable. In one instance, while in a counseling session, he literally tore some hair from his scalp.

It was evident, nonetheless, that the younger child was intelligent and talented. One of his counselors identified him as his favorite student, being so creative and intelligent that he created a game which the other students played and simulated. Yet, at age 19 he had not yet obtained his GED and was still fighting psychological anguishes which were more than likely brought on by his sister's murder.

One of Brittany's great aunts described the pain and aftermath from the murder. She said that after the murder, the two remaining kids were placed in foster care temporarily for their presumptive protection. Along with Brittany's killing, she remarked how this resulted in the mother suffering a nervous breakdown, and the grandmother seeking counseling. The cognitive load was simply unbearable!

The great aunt also adds that these actions affected her personally since she felt guilty about not helping better the family's living conditions, even though she lived more than 500 miles away. She had met her great niece briefly on a visit. Although the aunt had not seen anything that evidenced abuse of Brittany, she was concerned about the family's level of poverty and living conditions. Two weeks later Brittany, whom she had held and kissed on the cheeks, was murdered.

Upon learning of her murder, the great aunt's mind could not escape the thoughts of failing to assist her family, even though she did not perceive any danger, and it likely would not have altered the bases or reasons which existed in Johnson's psyche for killing the infant.

Brittany was now gone, long before she could "have even dreamed" or an opportunity at life. "Evil has to be lurking in your bones to brutally murder a baby," contends the great aunt, tearful, with eyes watering.

Brittany Ray

Nearly seventeen years later, the emotional scars of Brittany's death remained palpable. Her mother could no longer even discuss the murder, still at time finding herself crying uncontrollably, and was still receiving counseling. Reflecting the depths of her pain, in the summer of 2017 she attempted to commit suicide, suffering numerous permanent, life-threatening injuries and paralysis, including loss of a kidney, after she jumped from a bridge.

Was she punishing herself for Johnson's crime and her baby's resultant death? She often found herself alone and crying. Because she also could not have any other children, consequently she suffered deep emotional conflict. Clearly, the burden of the murder was so heavy that it was not difficult for some to envision that if the grief did not kill her if not treated, she could possibly resort to suicide, which researchers have found to be common among survivors. As a result, her relatives often tried to ensure for years that she was not alone.

Nor was she alone in suffering deep pain. The grandmother reveals how she sees young women, about 17 years old, in the community and wonder what Brittany would be doing at the same age, and how she would look. The grandmother's refrain sounds familiar: "I will never see her graduate. I won't see her married or have kids."

Although at first hesitant and in evident pain about discussing Brittany's murder, the grandmother agreed to talk about the topic because she hopes some of what she says will help other families and children who may be in danger. Her message is that when it comes to the safety of your children or grandchildren, parents must "double-check" those whom they allow to be in contact with, or care for them. "They cannot fend for or speak for themselves and depend upon loved ones to protect them." It was a tough lesson learned, for her, under the most tragic of circumstances.

In the summer of 2017, Brittany's grandmother says she had been looking for a sign that things will get better – but it had not come. Fighting back tears, in her final comment, she says, "It was terrible what happened"; Brittany is never far from my thoughts." Then, she refocused, turning her attention to questioning whether Brittany's murder would result in the premature loss of her daughter and grandsons.

Well, the pain of her daughter (Brittany's mother) ended in 2018. After her suicide attempt, Brittany's mother endured an even greater existence of physical and psychological pain, being transported into and out of numerous hospitals and rehabilitative facilities. After being admitted to her ninth hospital in the year, in mid-March, she passed away on March 23, 2018. She was only 40 years old.

From the outset family members knew that Brittany's murder was simply too much for her mother, and the ultimate price would be greater. There was the murder, then the overwhelming sense of guilt and failure, followed by a feeling of injustice regarding Johnson's sentencing. Sadly, in practical terms, Brittany's mother had given up on life and, unfortunately, her obituary was written on the date of Brittany's murder.

Upon her passing, her aunt commented regarding Brittany mother's premature death: "God has a way of healing, and that was his way. I hope she is now with her baby."

CHAPTER 6
THE OTHER JACKSON FAMILY

Life seemed to be on the upswing for the Jacksons in New Orleans. There was renewed energy in the Jackson family, as they sought to escape or turn around certain setbacks. Four family members, the parents and two infant daughters, were on their way back home after meeting with builders to start construction of a home on a vacant lot which they had purchased in Pearl River, Louisiana, an area across Lake Pontchartrain from the city. The Jacksons had agreed to an architectural design and construction had just begun on the home.

They were moving from renting to land and home ownership. This was a significant accomplishment in the backdrop of where their lives had been and what they had endured. More importantly, they wished to escape from the rough and tumble of the inner city to the quiet of the suburbs. There were not many families from their neighborhood who were financially able, and others not willing, to move from the beloved Treme or Seventh Ward neighborhoods. Most of the lots which were being sold in the area were at least several acres, and relatively economical for purchase. Although it was located in the city's defined metropolitan area, many of the youngsters in Treme had never heard of it, normally burrowing close to the neighborhood.

It was also a bold move, since it was the mid 1970's, before integration was fully implemented in the school system, and they were moving to an area of St. Tammany Parish which was more than 90 percent white.

It didn't happen. On this tragic day of July 16, 1975, three of them were killed, and one survived.

Jacksons

As the father, Freddie Jackson, steered his car along a dark, curving, newly constructed highway in Pearl River, he misjudged the road and the car hit an embankment and flipped into the air, causing severe damage and instant carnage. Freddie was hurled through the car's windshield, 2-year old Darrilyn was ejected through the window, and his wife Evola and daughter Dana, 10 months old, were disgorged from the car onto the grassy knoll adjoining the highway. Freddie, Darrilyn, and Evola were killed instantly on the winding Louisiana roadway. The other younger daughter in the car, Dana, then 10 months old, was knocked unconscious but was still alive. Her mother's dead body covered her on the ground, apparently shielding her from greater harm.

Less than 9 months later, on April 8, 1976, another Jackson family member was dead, this time as a result of gunfire. Aaron, then 21, was shot and killed – by his older brother Arnold, 22. About a month later, Arnold pled guilty to manslaughter and was sentenced to 10 years hard labor, with 9 years suspended, and with 5 years of active probation. He served a little more than a year in prison.

These four deaths were the preview of tragedy and devastation which affected the Jackson family. The psychological impact was instant but also continuing.

The Tragic Preview to Everlasting Grief

As they had on other occasions, on the night of July 16, Deborah joined her brothers across the street at the family home for some good ol home "stoop talk." It was jovial with music and dancing on the sidewalk as they talked about the "good old days", the challenges which they had overcome, and those which lay ahead. The younger brothers, Alvin and Ronald, were generally the family entertainers, with new and acrobatic dance moves and, imaginary mike in hand, cracking jokes. But all joined in. Little did they realize that during their festivities there was family tragedy

Jacksons

occurring at the same time less than 40 miles away.

Deborah and her husband, Arthur Meyers, nicknamed "Tegu", who had married young, were also waiting for her parents to return home from meeting with the builders. They lived across the street from her parents and other siblings. Both 22 years old, they had planned a trip to Texas for a festival and were waiting for her parents who had vowed to rent a car for their trip. Seven o'clock crept to 9 or 10 at night and she began to worry and become agitated. It was certainly unusual for her mother to stand them up or even be late.

Tragically, her concerns materialized into fear and then downright horror. When she answered the phone at about 10 p.m. that night it was a police officer from Pearl River. Speaking with a Cajun-like or backwoods accent, he asked her rather calmly, "Do you know Freddie Jackson? She responded "yes, that is my father". His tone was a mixture of sensitivity and matter-of-factness. There was then something of a pause in the conversation. Alarmed, she asked: "Is this about my mom and dad?" Apparently sensing her anxiety and incapability of handling the impending news, the officer asked to speak to her husband. She handed the phone to Tegu. He listened for a while, then grabbed his head and, with his lips quivering, began screaming. Mind racing and stomach wrenching, she then knew something bad had happened, but Tegu was in shock and could not speak.

Tegu was tough and a former star high school athlete in track. She had, however, never seen him in that level of stress. His facial expression was of utter tenseness. What could have been said that would make him react in that manner?

When he could muster enough strength to speak, he said shockingly still, "your mother and father are dead." Concerned about her sisters, she worriedly asked: "what about Darrilyn and

Dana?" He then exclaimed that "one of your sisters is dead", but Pearl River authorities could not identify which of the two sisters had survived. She immediately broke down, emotionally and physically.

However, she still had to move quickly because one of her younger sisters was alone and without family in the hospital near Pearl River. She gathered two of her brothers, Alvin and Arnold, and Tegu, and her grandfather, and headed towards Pearl River, about 35-40 miles north of New Orleans, near the Mississippi border. Ironically, she told her brothers, apologetically, that she "really did love her father." They knew what she meant because there had previously been discussions between her and Aaron about how she and her father were not meshing with one another. They simply were not getting along and she felt distant from him, even though they lived only across the street from one another. In fact, that topic had temporarily fractured the festive moments that very night, before the telephone call.

The telephone call from Pearl River authorities had set the stage for the ensuing trip. In what she describes as the longest car ride of her life, the car traveled along the long, dark, winding road in a rural stretch of highway, encrusted with fog from when the coolness of the night had merged with the muggy heat of the afternoon. She immediately sensed the danger her family must have faced traveling this dark, curvy, narrow road which was bereft of sufficient lights or traffic signs. It seemed as though the swamp, cricket sounds, and moss was their only companions along the shadowy road.

The brothers, also sensing the tragedy and that the curtain had fallen on their lives, were nervous but tried to withhold their feelings. They knew the ride along the dark, moss tree lined highway would be locked in their brains forever. More disturbing was that their parents were on the way home to celebrate a joyous and momentous occasion – construction of a new home.

To an outside observer, it would have appeared that Deborah was more anxious and nerve-wracked than her brothers. But they would later acknowledge to others that their hearts were in the pits of their stomach. They could hear themselves breathing. No amount of machismo or testosterone could block the awful feelings they had.

When they arrived in Pearl River, Deborah was so emotional authorities would not allow her to the morgue-area of the hospital to identify the bodies. They knew that the viewing would be traumatizing for her, or indeed, for any immediate family member. Thus, Arnold and her grandfather went into the back room of the hospital where the temporary morgue was located and, themselves shaken, with lumps in their throat, identified the three Jackson family members. They spent the night with Dana in the hospital in Pearl River before returning to New Orleans, with Deborah now bearing the title and responsibilities as "mother", and Arnold as "big brother", like never before.

Alvin, who was often chided by his siblings as a "mama's boy," because of their closeness, felt numbed by knowing that his mother was dead in another room in the building where he was standing. He was motherless. He questioned himself about whether anyone in the future would understand his feelings the way his mother had? And there were simply so many unanswered questions about what would happen with the rest of his life.

Their uncle, Irving Williams, who was Evola's brother, was likewise devastated, when he learned of the car accident. He had joined the Job Corps and had returned to training in Texas after a brief visit home, a week before, where he had laughed and joked with his sister, Evola, and brother-in-law, Freddie.

He was sitting on his bunk clowning around with some other

student-residents of the Jobs Corp in the dormitory when a dorm monitor approached him and said, "the counselor wants to speak to you". He immediately thought he was in trouble. So, when he walked in the counselor's office, he presented a defensive approach, seeking to ward off any punishment. "What I done now?", he exclaimed; "if this is about the fight in the cafeteria ..." The counselor cut him off and said, "sit back and relax". "Your sister and brother-in-law were in a car accident, and we need to send you home", he added. Irving looked at him in disbelief. He dropped his head in his hands and struggled to avoid crying. Even then, he simply could not let his fellow students see him cry.

Leaving the office, he ambled to his bunk and only informed his bunk mate about what had occurred, who in turn informed the other dorm students to "give Irving his room and let him be." Irving departed the next day for the trip back to New Orleans.

It was a Wednesday night during a summer month, which was not a day of the week when single car accidents were likely. They usually occurred on a weekend night between 6 p.m. and 6 a.m., and often involved the driver having been drinking, which affected the safe operation of the vehicle. Those were not the precipitating factors here.

When Evola's mother, "Miss Odette", learned of her daughter's death she did not cry; she wailed. Bereavement was paralyzing for her. She had three children and now essentially two were gone. Her daughter was killed in the accident and her son, Herbert, had previously been sentenced to life in prison without the benefit of probation or parole for a double homicide. This meant that absent a pardon he would die in prison. Under tremendous strain, she had to help plan for the funeral services for her daughter.

Olivia Odette Williams, affectionately referred to as "Miss Odette", had been the neighborhood beautician for decades. She

Jacksons

had a shop and also "did hair" from her home on St. Phillip Street, which was next door to her daughter Evola and her family, before they moved to Rousselin street. One of her side jobs was styling the hair of the dead bodies for services at the funeral home across the street, Charbonnet-Labat Funeral Home, a family business which had been in existence since 1883. As a result, she had seen the evidence of death many times as a funeral home beautician, seeking to hide or modify the vestiges of death, through make-up and hairstyling.

The deceased Jackson family members' funeral was scheduled to be held at Carr-Llopis' funeral home, however, another funeral home around the corner. Now, could she bear to style her daughter's or granddaughter's hair for their funeral, which was going to occur at Carr-Llopis'? She could not bear to do so, and eventually fell into a state of deep depression, closing her beauty salon and instead taking a job at Charity Hospital in the city.

At the funeral, on July 21, distressingly, there were three caskets, containing Jackson family members, at a time and a place when none were expected because they all were dead long before it was expected. A small casket for a young child will usually cause sadness for even the most experienced funeral directors. Deborah says, "I could not believe it. I was burying my parents and a young sister". "I remember crying out to God to help me and my family," Deborah says.

Crying among the families of Freddie and Evola was so widespread that it was both comforting and assaultive. Freddie had been the patriarch of his larger family in Hahnville, Louisiana, where he had been born and raised for a time, but now he was gone. Their deaths were beyond shocking for many.

Reverend George Alexander Beacham of Greater Old Zion Baptist Church, in the neighboring Fifth ward, held the religious services for the Jackson family members. The drive to the cemetery was unusual in several respects- there were three bodies rather than one and more hearses than attendant cars for family members. All three bodies were interred at Mount Olivet Cemetery in the Gentilly section of the city, near Dillard University.

Although children lose parents during their youth, when both parents are lost unexpectedly at the same time, such as the Jackson's parents, the loss is seismic. Support groups seemed non-existent at the time. The children were suffering from a combination of sensations: isolation, helplessness, and a gross lack of information regarding what to do next. They also had to go through a process of "role reorganization", i.e., determining who would play which roles to replace their parents, even if the process was informal, at best. They were sure that Evola's parents would be in their lives, but they were not sure of what that meant. And they simply could not mask the pain.

Some of their emotions were typical or predictable, then as well as later in life: could they continue to love others; would they have a future; problems with alcohol or drugs; and irritability and anger directed at others, including family. Furthermore, they recognized that despite their role reorganization, the roles and obligations were fractured and imperfect, and their parents would not be replaced - ever.

One comforting element was that they had one another to lean upon. They also were close to their grandparents, who lived close, and therefore had some support in decision making. Freddie's' mother had died years before and most of his relatives were more than 50 miles away in Hahnville; but they offered support through phone calls and cards.

What the siblings did not recognize was that they were vulnerable. Though they had acquired some lifelong skills and were physically

Jacksons

tough, they were vulnerable to the vices of immaturity; there were those prone to lure them into drugs, crime and immorality.

While each of them handled the loss differently as they fought through the stress, they recognized that indeed they were not alone. As unfortunate as it was, they also had suffered previous tragedies which had strengthened them to endure loss and pain: their father and uncle had been incarcerated and they had lost an older brother unexpectedly, when he was a baby.

The Jackson children were both scarred and scared. Although they had to engage in a monumental process of healing, just as critical, they also had to move forward and reconstruct their lives. Because the children were now responsible for their own welfare, they could not put off their lives or escape new found obligations and responsibilities which were thrust upon them, emotionally, financially, and judgement-wise.

Nevertheless, the goals which their parents had instilled in them remained intact: get an education and remain a family.

Not Yet Beyond the Grief

When April 8 arrived, only 9 months had passed since the accident, and the family was still grieving. They still had not settled in or answered the fundamental questions about how and where they would live. Although wise for their ages, they were still young adults or adolescents, and had not had leadership roles before. Hardly any family member could say they were beyond the shock of the accident. Life was extremely hard and distressing. And now another heartbreaking loss was lurking around the bend.

This is when the tragedy between Aaron and Arnold befell the family. The tension between the brothers began soon after their parents' death. They were only about 1 year apart in age and then without sufficient male supervision or presence at the time. After their parents' death, the four sibling brothers lived together in the family home on Rousselin Drive. Arnold tried to be the big brother and surrogate father to Ronald, the sibling who was considered most reckless, immature and in need of supervision. Their grandfather had stepped in a few times to offer guidance on how to deal with their emotions and one another.

Their older sister, Deborah, only a few years their senior, had become head of the family by default, and lived across the street. She had recently graduated from Southern University in New Orleans (SUNO) and married, and her husband was her age. Several of her brothers had been in her wedding.

Thus, the only realistic male supervision for the boys was their grandfather on her mother's side, and even he was somewhat out of touch with their youth stresses and the grief that they were struggling with as a result of their parents' death. Additionally, he was in a state of grief as a result of his stepdaughter, Evola's, death.

As Deborah acknowledges pertaining to her brothers, "they could not handle the grief and lashed out at one another. Their parents, who had always provided discipline and advice, were no longer there."

Although she looked in on them and provided all the emotional support she could it was tough, given that she was only a few years older and not prepared for parenting, enduring a new marriage and at the beginning of her employment career, all concurrently. The stress of it all eventually led to the failure of her marriage about a year later.

One of the vestiges of grief for children who lose their parents is whether they will lose another loved one. They often ask of themselves, about their other siblings and close relatives: "will I lose you too"? For the Jacksons' this became more than a grieving factor or element. It unveiled as part of their reality.

Jacksons

On the fatal Thursday morning in April at about 10 a.m., Aaron and Arnold had begun to argue and tempers flared in the home. The home, in the 1700 block of Rousselin Drive, was a double shotgun duplex which was a narrow one-story residence, with each shotgun being about 12 feet wide with a front door and back door. It was raised on brick piers, with a narrow concrete porch to the front which was covered by a roof apron. It consisted of a living room, three bedrooms, kitchen and small bathroom. Being a shotgun home, it was possible that persons in other rooms could see into the room where the brothers were and undoubtedly could hear their entanglement.

They were yelling and cursing at one another. And neither brother would back down. Others were in the house, with some milling in and out of the area where they were arguing. None of the witnesses at first suspected that it would become physical and certainly not with gunplay. They assumed that it was an argument that would blow over and be "squashed".

The previous day Aaron and Deborah had clashed, which was not typical. It was not atypical, however, for Aaron and Arnold's interactions to become heated and full of sibling testosterone. Arnold was viewed by most as the pacifier and peaceful of the bunch while Aaron was deemed to be more stubborn and feisty. Some would term him "humbuggish", ready for a fight and not willing to turn the other cheek.

The Jackson children had recovered a small amount of money from their parents' modest estate, but the argument was not related to money. What they were arguing about is unclear but was more than likely trivial or insignificant in light of their other personal struggles. Their uncle, Irving, close in age, had tried to mediate and bring calm to the dispute. However, it became physical, and Arnold and Aaron began to grapple with one another and punches were thrown.

Jacksons

At some point during the confrontation, Arnold pulled out a .22 caliber pistol from his trousers and they struggled for the weapon. During the struggle, the weapon accidentally discharged and the bullet struck Aaron in the stomach. The early morning bang of the pistol shook the small house and alarmed some of the neighbors. An undeniable panic then set in.

Arnold hurriedly, but nervously and panicky, ran across the street and asked Deborah to borrow the keys to her Volkswagen Beetle. Cursing himself, and tearing up, his eyes had the haunted look of a troubled man. He did not have time to explain to her and Tegu what had happened in any level of detail. The other brothers and uncle had seen the skirmish, but never thought it would result in one of them dead and the other facing prosecution.

Arnold then loaded Aaron into the car and rushed Aaron to the hospital. During the hectic, yet speedy, drive they cried together and talked, apologizing to one another for the fight. Through gasps and groans and bleeding in the car, they seemed to have resolved what had caused the argument.

As usual and customary, Charity Hospital was abuzz with activity, possibly even other gunshot victims. There were doctors, nurses and interns, seemingly everywhere. They took vitals, force air into his lungs and rushed him into a trauma room. Despite the legends of medical miracles at the hospital, Aaron did not make it, however, and was pronounced dead upon arrival at about 10:25 a.m., at the same hospital where they were born.

It was easy to speculate why Aaron died so quickly, with delayed intervention from medical staff? A number of factors could have influenced this fatal conclusion. One, is how long it took to arrive at the hospital before he received medical assistance, even though there was no doubt that Arnold had sped to the hospital. Additionally, a misconception among some of the public is that a

Jacksons

low caliber gunshot from a .22 caliber handgun does not cause damage equivalent to that of higher caliber automatic weapons. That is true only in part. Wounds from .22 caliber bullets often cause more damage because it may not enter in a straight line, and instead tends to advance at an angle, bouncing off bones and causing damage and bleeding along the way. Horribly, Aaron was dead.

Immediately, there were at best, two victims - Aaron and Arnold.

Arnold cried uncontrollably and was in shock that his brother was dead. He wondered aloud about how his siblings would view him. More than likely, he also contemplated how his parents would have perceived him had they been alive. In any event, despite significant evidence of the shooting being accidental, prosecutors in New Orleans charged Arnold with murder.

The look on Deborah's face was grave when she learned of Aaron's demise. This simply could not be happening to them again! The drive to the hospital by Arnold with Aaron in tow had to be as dreadful, if not more so, than the long ride by the family to Pearl River nine months earlier. But this time her car bore some of the bloodstains of her brother's last gasps at life.

The next day, the local newspaper reported that Aaron Jackson 21, was "slain at his residence", having been shot by a .22 caliber pistol. His death was chronicled beneath a headline which was titled, *Three Murdered in N.O. Shootings*.[131]

There was not much of a criminal proceeding, with appeals, or botched evidence, with Arnold admitting the shooting, and pleading guilty, yet explaining that he had never intended to shoot his brother.

Of course, the killing did not make sense and was hard to comprehend. Arnold was not sociopathic or mentally disturbed or suffering any of the other mental health phenomena associated with most killings within a family. He did not hate his brother. In fact, he loved him, deeply and protectively. Nevertheless, it did require some soul-searching.

Both brothers were strong willed, with Aaron usually being more assertive about his position, though Arnold was the elder male sibling and described as heavily family-focused. It all seemed to have calmed, however, when about a month before the fight Aaron and Arnold had entered into sort of a truce, vowing not to fight anymore. To avoid some of the conflict, Aaron began hanging out more with younger brother, Alvin. Similarly, Arnold sought refuge in more quality time with his sister Deborah.

What is undisputed among family is that the shooting would not have occurred had their mother been alive. She was the family interventionist and had settled differences between her sons on several occasions. Thus, the deaths on the Pearl River winding road had indirectly cascaded into another devastating family event.

Deborah and Alvin now had to bury another family member. Feeling immense stress, she thought to herself, "isn't there someone else who can do this." There was not. She was the senior Jackson member and the "anyone else" that she hoped for were also still grieving to the point of breakdown. Alvin had matured greatly in the nine-month period and was able to help with the planning.

Like a bad hand in a game of poker, Miss Odette also considered herself a triple loser. She had effectively lost her son to prison, then her daughter, son-in-law and a granddaughter in a car accident, and now a grandson to gunfire.

It is clear that at the time of Aaron's death, the family was still grieving the loss of their family from the car accident. In August of 1976, Ms. Odette and the remaining family members honored Evola's death and birthday with a memorial in the newspaper:

Jacksons

"Another year has sadly passed since you were called away, but fondest memories still remain and hopes to meet in heaven someday." A month later, the court finalized the succession papers on Freddie and Evola's estate.

A Close-Knit family

The family members were close and had an inseparable bond.

Married in 1952, Freddie and Evola had instilled in their children values of hard work and loyalty to family. They played together, prayed together, often lived within close proximity to Evola's parents, and stayed in contact with Freddie's relatives in Hahnville, across the river from New Orleans.

Similar to the famous singing Michael Jackson family from Gary, Indiana, the Jacksons in New Orleans were a large brew of 10, consisting of the parents and 5 sons (Arnold, Aaron, Alvin, Ronald and Reginald) and three daughters (Deborah, Darrilyn and Dana). The oldest child was Deborah and the youngest was Dana. They lived much of the time in Treme or the 6th Ward section of the city until they moved to Rousellin Drive in the 7th Ward.

They lived in an era and neighborhoods where their neighbors usually bonded and were close. On St. Phillip Street, for instance, they could rely upon "Ms. Clothile" or "Ms. Laverne" disciplining them if they caught them doing something wrong. At a minimum, the ladies in the neighborhood would telephone their mother or bring them home and "tell all" about what they had observed them do wrong. They lived as part of a village, meaning that others helped raise or mentor them. And there was plenty of discipline meted out or trips by the collar to their home, with one of them in tow by a neighborhood elder, most particularly Ronald.

In the same vein, neighbors shared food or household items when there was a need or funds were short. "Go over to "so-and-so's" house and get a cup of sugar" was a common refrain. "Can you run me to the store?" was similarly a common inquiry when a family did not have a car or it was in disrepair. Some residents watched television at the homes of neighbors when their utilities were cut off. This was part of communal living in the hood.

The neighborhood was beset by a few diffcrent architectural styles – mostly shotgun doubles, a few bungalows, a gallery four-plex, a wooden, narrow but long church, and a reconstructed brick funeral home. It was as though the 1600 block of St. Phillip where they lived was never "closed". There was "comings and goings", and "where ya at's" well past midnight, most nights. The stories told on the stoops were a mixture of educational and life insights, as well as a labyrinth of truths mixed with fiction about personal exploits.

Photo of Aaron Jackson

Overall, their lives were marked with indelible tragedy, grief and pain. There had once been 10 family members, and now there were only 3. Inclusively, 7 of the 10 family members succumbed to untimely and tragic deaths, as a result of accidents, homicide or illness – Reginald 20 days old (crib death), (April 1960), Freddie 45, (auto accident) (July 1975), Evola Mae (Marshall) 42, (auto accident) (July 1975), Darrilyn, 2 years old, (auto accident) (July 1975), Aaron 21, (homicide) (April 1976), Dana 32, (cancer) (June 2007), and Arnold 53, (auto accident) (October, 2007).

Labat-Charbonnet Funeral Home

Freddie was educated and athletic. He was only one year short of graduating from college and had played semi-pro basketball and baseball. Several opined that his skills were refined enough that he could have played either sport at the NBA or MLB levels. Even though he did not get such opportunity others still sought him out for his athletic acumen. In fact, college and high school coaches would consult him about strategies for their sports teams. He had also served a stint in the military.

Despite these talents, it was difficult to find reasonable paying jobs in the city and he had given serious thought about moving his family to California for employment purposes and a better life.

Freddie had always been concerned about and talked with his children, particularly his sons, about violence and the "streets" and looking out for one another. He had ample reasoning for worry and concern since he had himself once been on the other side of the streets and hooked within the criminal justice system. In 1967, Freddie had pled guilty to being an accessory to a double homicide which had occurred in the city. He was charged with being one of three men who had been involved in a botched robbery of two businessmen, leading to their murder. In pleading guilty as an accessory, he was sentenced to 4 years in prison. The other two men, one of whom was his brother-in-law, Herbert Williams, were convicted of second-degree murder and sentenced to life in prison, without the benefit of probation or parole.

So, Freddie Jackson knew the dangers of the streets, the perils of weapons and handguns, and importance of resolving conflict. Even while incarcerated he had been the directional and emotional rudder for his family. He had returned from prison, recognizing that he had been incarcerated during some of the critical formative periods in his children's lives. He realized the mistakes he had made and sought to transform his life.

As a mother, Evola was passionate, calm, and protective of her family. Others would say "she is so sweet". The neighborhood children would often turn to her for advice and comfort. Similar to how she handled her kids, she was calm and her tone was encouraging.

In her life, she had not escaped the tragedies of violence, which was so endemic to the Big Easy. Her father, Paul Marshall, had been murdered by his mistress with an icepick in an alley on Claiborne Street in 1937, jealous over his marriage and treatment of her. He was 24, and Evola was only about 2 years old at the time of his death.

Initially, Freddie had returned to the double shotgun house next to his mother-in-law on St. Phillip Street, where his family had lived while he served his prison stint. His family had struggled emotionally and financially while he was imprisoned. They moved often and Evola had to work several jobs to meet their financial obligations. Eventually they had to obtain welfare and Deborah had to go to school and work, simultaneously. When paid, she would provide her entire paycheck to her mother to help with the family's bills. Arnold, who was in the military, also sent part of his military pay home to help defray expenses.

After his incarceration, Freddie and Evola both had jobs and were saving funds. They were committed to providing their children with a better life. They had created the economic means and found the path to sustainability. Freddie had rehabbed himself during and after prison, learning a trade, and became an electrician. Despite his imprisonment, the children were well mannered and had career goals.

Along with church and discipline, one of the values which their parents had instilled in them was the importance of education and training. Each parent had been incubated in households where education was stressed. Consequently, both attended the premier boarding high schools in the city for African Americans, with Evola graduating from the prestigious Caudet school and Freddie graduating from Gilbert Academy, a private Black educational institution in the city. Evola and Freddie then attended college during the early civil rights era, with Evola a student at Clark College in Atlanta, Georgia, then Dillard University in New Orleans. Freddie also attended Clark College, for three years, entering the last year of Dr. Martin Luther King's attendance at Morehouse, across the street from Clark. This is where he and Evola developed their life-together plans.

These were significant achievements for Evola and Freddie, given the struggles which their families faced, the climate of segregated education in the city, and the long odds of obtaining a college education for African-Americans in the South during this period.[132] However, both had solid ancestral settings, who pushed education and achievement. That discipline and drive was transferred to their children.

Dana followed in the footsteps of her mother and attended Dillard where she graduated with a degree in Mass Communications; Deborah obtained a degree in Sociology from SUNO and a Doctorate in Divinity from Howard University; Arnold became a licensed Master Electrician; and Alvin attended divinity school.

Although their father was talented and had some rough times, they considered their mother as the ultimate pillar. She had to carry the family financially and emotionally while Freddie was imprisoned and some corresponding fragility in the marriage had set in. Nevertheless, she had to ensure the requisite level of compassion and intervention in keeping all of the personalities in the home in harmony.

All told, before their parents' unexpected deaths, to most observers, there were little manifestations of the troubles they had faced. This was, in part, because their trouble or struggles were similar to most residents in the neighborhood; financial difficulties; some members being "in trouble with the law"; utilities being temporarily shut off; and parents figuring out how to best navigate the raising of their children, amidst drug dealing and other crime in the neighborhood. In this sense, their struggles were unexceptional.

However, the car accident and shooting placed the Jackson's in an advanced category of struggles, and in their reliance upon God. Their faith would carry them through.

Jacksons

Aaron's Dead!

Aaron's killing was shocking to many in the neighborhood because the brothers were close and often hung together, including the youngest, Ronald, tagging along. The word was spread throughout the neighborhood as friends and neighbors inquired "what could have happened?"

The brothers were protective of one another, at times having to fight on behalf of another sibling. And they played together on neighborhood athletic teams, even if it were informal pickup teams.

Sometimes the family living room resembled a sports arena with tackling and wrestling and brothers cracking jokes, or "ribbing" one another. For many families, this is typical sibling interaction and many believe a good training ground for dealing with interpersonal conflict in life.

One of the family's closest friends, Cheryl Grisson, who had known the family since she and Deborah attended grade school together, discussed how the Jackson boys would gang up on her and other females who visited Deborah. All in fun and good-natured, she jokes, "we would have to fight them off." Negative and physical reactions were reserved for those who threatened or fought any of the brothers. Fighting one of them meant possibly fighting all four of them.

They were all gifted athletically, playing the various playground or high school sports, particularly basketball and tackle football. Alvin, (AKA "Dog") who grew to be tallest, excelled in basketball and was known throughout the neighborhood for his athleticism and smooth skills. Ronald, (AKA "Cheaky"), the youngest, was very fast and shined in the sprints and at running back. Arnold ("Jack") was big and strong and good in football and aspired to be a track coach. Aaron probably had the most diverse athletic skills because he had a blend of all of the aforementioned skills; strong, deceptively fast, somewhat shifty, and a leaper. Alvin notes that he would have been an excellent wide receiver because of his hand strength and ability to catch the ball.

Deborah described Aaron as "funny and he was a natural." He was intelligent and would debate most things by questioning "why"." It was not surprising that he aspired to be a lawyer; not just any lawyer but a powerful one who would fight for his clients. He was cagey and savvy enough that his nickname was "Slick." He lived as if he had a promising contract with life.

On the other hand, Arnold was considered a gentle protective soul, who always put family first. After graduating high school, because it was difficult to find jobs, Arnold went off to serve in the military, part of it in Vietnam. Because he was closest in age to Deborah, they tended to have a close relationship. And Alvin and Aaron bonded because of their proximity in age and interests. But the entire family was close.

However, their parents' and little sister's death was nuclear for them. They were then thrust into the world alone, without the direction and mediation which Freddie and Evola had always provided.

Although those in the neighborhood were not surprised that the brothers argued or feuded, they were shocked by the killing. However, knowing what they did about the family and Aaron and Arnold, no one can remember others commenting that it was anything but an accidental shooting. "Arnold simply would not kill his brother like that," some neighbors commented.

Handling their Parents' Loss

All of the remaining siblings dealt with the tragedy differently. Not only were their parents' dead, but two siblings (Reginald and Darrilyn) had now died before reaching two years old. As Alvin

Jacksons

remarks, their parents were the "pillars"; without the pillars the family began to disintegrate.

The devastation and grief were palpable. Aaron once was seen crying and bellowing that even though they had a small amount of money from the succession, "it did not mean much because they would never see their mother again." Alvin and the others comforted him, even though they were hardly in a position to help themselves emotionally.

Jack withdrew and suppressed his feelings because he felt he had to be the "big brother" to the younger siblings. His emotional struggles were also compounded by some of the same hurdles his father had faced. Despite being a veteran of the Vietnam war, his efforts at achieving a profession and employment were still blocked by a brief prison record and the other travails and stereotypes facing an inner-city young black man.

Even absent the criminal record, many Vietnam veterans were facing problems in employment, obtaining benefits and drug and alcohol abuse. Several found themselves locked into the throes of the criminal justice system. In 1978, nearly 1 in 4 prisoners were veterans.

Deborah was very close to her mother, almost as though they were sisters, and sought her guidance on most matters. As noted, Evola was the pillar to which most of the children sought guidance and comfort. They were so dependent on her that Alvin was kidded about being a "mama's boy".

Deborah turned to her composition of school and neighborhood friends for consolation and advice. She had left the family home to work on her marriage but she was left with the unforeseen task of caring for Dana. And she always lived in close proximity to her brothers.

Jacksons

What was ironic about her becoming a mother to Dana was that her father's mother had also been raised by her older sister due to unforeseen tragedy in their family.

Alvin turned to basketball and tried to sharpen his skills in the mold of his father. He was talented and would saunter from one neighborhood basketball court to another, oftentimes playing for hours on end. Although it was not enough to fully recover from the tragedy, it did relieve some of the stress and emotional turmoil.

The youngest brother, Cheaky, had not learned to cope, and turned to "the streets." He was in and out of trouble - at school, with police, and friends. He was living true to his nickname – "Cheaky." However, he possibly never recovered from this and the ensuing tragedies.

Their uncle, Irving, who had been guided by his older sister Evola, now turned to Deborah and Arnold for guidance. He knew he would recover, since he had faced tremendous tragedy in the imprisonment of his older brother, but he did not know how to best answer the questions which class mates and friends would ask.

Similar to many families, even though they were close, there were already some frictions in place as tragedy struck on July 16. One of the more noticeable discords was Deborah had an ongoing disagreement with her father. Thus, one of her first comments to her brothers, as she sought their help going to Pearl River, was to exclaim love for her father. The penultimate question going forward was whether the deaths would separate or unify the family.

The Grief Never Ends

After Arnold ("Jack") returned from serving in the military there seemed to be familial progress. Gerald Ford was president and the country was transforming from the war in Vietnam, where Arnold had been part of the military during a tough war time period. Jack and Aaron were enrolled as students at SUNO, and Alvin was preparing to attend Delgado Community College in New Orleans, where he was also going to play basketball for the school's team. Hence, there was remarkable progress, given what had wretchedly beset the family.

But the grieving and pain, which had not gone away because of the automobile accident, now intensified after the accidental killing. Less than a year had passed since the auto accident and they had to deal with Aaron's death. Their brother, they reasoned, had barely made it past the age of majority, and was just entering into manhood. Now he was also gone, vanishing into the list of the many other victims who had been killed in New Orleans.

On April 12, Aaron's funeral and wake was handled by Charbonnet's funeral home in their old neighborhood on St. Phillip Street, across from their former home. His church services were likewise officiated by Reverend Beacham, at the same church as the services held about 8 months earlier. Reverend Beecham reminded those in attendance about sticking together as a family and turning to God to "help lead your life."

He was buried in the same section of Mount Olivet Cemetery, as his parents, sister, and infant brother.

For most survivors to a tragedy or murder, the stress attributable to the murder itself is often compounded by a number of other stressors. Some common noted stressors are shock, confusion, impact of other life changes, role changes, economic pressure, and the reactions of the criminal justice system.

The surviving Jacksons were afflicted by a variety of these classic stressors. One of the biggest surprises for the children was that it shattered their new-found assumptions of the world. They never fathomed that they would lose another family member so unexpectedly, and so soon. And then it did not seem there were any social or government programs to assist citizens who were survivors to murder or accident victims.

Although in many ways they handled the loss miraculously, it was difficult to overcome. Imagine that Deborah had to nearly concurrently: handle a brother going to jail; Ronald becoming out of control with the loss of his parents and two brothers; having to seek guardianship of her 10-month old sister, and raising a child she did not anticipate having to rear; handling the estates of her parents and Aaron; and trying to endure a marriage through all of these stressors.

Ronald reacted as he had in the past; by turning to the streets. He felt the core of family had been destroyed and looked for refuge in a wild lifestyle. Even though physically tough, and maybe even liking to fight, he had seen this script before and felt its psychological pain, and the only solution was escape. The result was foreseen and he became hooked into the debilitating criminal justice system, being charged with crimes such as burglary, theft and battery.

After Ronald got into trouble again and was sent to prison, Alvin struggled emotionally because he was now all alone in the house and had to mature really fast. He was responsible now for the rent and bills. He says, "I was messed up."

For Alvin, he recounts that forgiveness for Arnold came easily "because of the love I had for my brother". The automobile accident was not easy to bear but it was easier than the killing of Aaron. Their parents' death was an accident, without any indicia of ill will.

Aaron's death, on the other hand, was never supposed to happen, even though it could also be considered an accident, and he considered it such. But it was avoidable and there was a gun and unnecessary violence involved. He thought about what he could have done to prevent the conflict from building to such a tumultuous ending.

Alvin recounts how one of the police officers at the scene pulled him to the side, in an effort to comfort him, since he observed right away that this was not the typical murder in the city. The officer said sadly, "brothers fight all of the time, but in this instance a gun was involved." Yes, the gun that was in the house to protect them against others, was used in a fight among family members.

Deborah recounts that she had to plan a funeral for one brother while at the same time seeking legal help for another one. This is a classic dilemma when victim and perpetrator are siblings or related.

Deborah again found some comfort in her friends, but she was so overwhelmed now with added responsibilities that she did not have time or space to be depressed or anxious. She attended the court proceedings related to Arnold's prosecution to lend family support. She would also visit him frequently while he was in jail and provide funds for his commissary and other necessities.

According to her, Arnold was more concerned with how what he had done hurt his brothers and sisters than any prison sentence he would have to serve. It got to the point where he began every jail visit with an apology about the incident, and query about how his other brothers and sisters were coping. His facial expressions revealed the pain that he was suffering.

Although an accident, Arnold knew that his judgment could have been much better. His last good-bye to Aaron had been as he was struggling with the immense pain one suffers from a gunshot to the stomach. Why did he need to even have the gun, he thought?

On the other hand, Alvin refused to go to the court proceedings when Arnold was charged, because he did not agree with the decision to prosecute his brother. He still had love for both, his brother slain and his brother standing before the court. He did not consider it a difficult choice, nor socially awkward, since he forgave Arnold and believed that Aaron's killing should not be compounded with further damage to his family, with his other brother being incarcerated.

On the date of Arnold's sentencing, several family members attended the proceeding. They waited in the courtroom for him to appear. Similar to all of the other jailed prisoners appearing in court that day, he was held in a holding cell behind the courtroom until his case was called by the bailiff. When he appeared before Criminal Court Judge Becker, he appeared strong and resilient. After the judge addressed the family and asked Arnold whether he accepted the guilty plea, he replied "Yes," in a soft voice. The result was that although his sentence was 10 years, because 9 years was suspended, he would serve about a year in the Parish Prison jail, with 5 years of active probation.

Overall, the family never abandoned Arnold. Every Sunday either his grandfather or grandmother would go visit him at the Orleans Parish prison, and place money in his commissary account. When he was released, Miss Odette came up to him, greeted him by his nickname "Papa Jack", and gave him the strongest hug she had ever given him, and said "I love you".

While jailed, Arnold wrote to Alvin, asking his forgiveness. He was not only grieving Aaron's death, he felt he had embarrassed his family. According to Alvin, Arnold commiserated in the letter about how sad he was about what had transpired. Alvin's parents had taught their children to hang together no matter how difficult the circumstances. Thus, in his responding letter Alvin forgave him and encouraged Jack to improve his life. He said "Brother, come and make a life for yourself". And he did. When he was released, he came to live with Alvin. Although he had spent about a year in jail, he had been a "long way down."

Jacksons

Jack's release and coming to live with him was as therapeutic for Alvin as it was for Arnold. With Aaron dead, Arnold in jail, and Cheaky also locked up at the time, Alvin felt he was alone on an island. He now considers that year or so to have been the loneliest of his life.

Tegu sought to control his feelings in order to be strong for his wife. They had been together since their freshman year in high school, and as a result had dealt with some juvenile-related and maturity issues. But the stress may have been too much for someone who was thrust by marriage into another family facing such unforgiving tragedy. It was eventually too much for him to deal with, leading to disintegration of the marriage.

One of the first family members Arnold consulted with upon his release from jail was his uncle Herbert, who had been incarcerated at the time for more than a decade. He traveled to Angola, up the river from the city, where he and Herbert met for a face-to-face, heart-to-heart, man-to-man discussion. Arnold was Hebert's godson and they were close. He had always counseled Arnold about doing the right thing. It was clear to Arnold when they embraced in the visiting room at the prison farm that they were still close and his godfather had not abandoned him.

Herbert dropped his head as they talked and said, "I know you did not mean to do this". "You did 1 year in jail and I am in for life," he said. "Take it in stride and better yourself", he counseled Arnold.

In a subsequent phone call to his mother, Herbert said "support Arnold, regardless of what he did". He had been in a similar position. His mother was already on that bandwagon and merely shook her head approvingly. Irving, his younger brother, overheard the conversation and commented later, "that is family love". "That is true family love, man!"

The Pain Remains - and Continues

When asked "How did you overcome it?", Alvin responded that "you never overcome it". "But," he says, "God awakened me, and began to guide my life."

Many years later Deborah, Ronald, and Alvin acknowledge that the pain still lingers from those tragedies. With time, experience, and some professional training, they reflected on their past, and established links between their grief and pain and some negative behavior or emotional challenges.

Now an ordained minister, Alvin recognizes that the deaths had been affecting his behavior earlier in life but did not know that during the times it was happening. He became more of a loner and sometimes turned to the streets. He states, "I still had issues. I no longer trusted anyone and as a consequence there was no one who I could turn to." He contrasted his adaption to that of his sister Deborah; "she had an inclusive set of lifelong friends, I didn't."

Psychologically, it did not occur to Alvin immediately why he felt alone and without a mass of close friends. It clicked later that he was suffering from the loss in a hard manner because his blood brothers were his closest friends. He then confronted a psychological transformation because his parents and "friends" were missing.

Presently, also an ordained minister as well as a licensed social worker, Deborah took a shot at analysis. She opined that the tragedies had both immediate and long-term consequences.

For the rest of the world listening or reading, the question which was posed to the remaining survivors was "how you get through it?" The pain cuts deeper, Deborah says, because the assailant was a brother who you also love - a good brother at that! But for each of them the thought that maybe they could help someone else deal with tragedy was more compelling than pitying in their losses.

Are there life lessons from the Aaron homicide? There are many lessons learned; and just as many tough questions raised. Life is hard enough without confrontations, and violence, and murder. The emotions related to the killing are compounded, however, when the assailant is a sibling, parent or family member. Can you support both sides or do you have to choose sides in such sibling killings? Should you testify against your blood brother under those circumstances? Even if you think you understand, you don't.

Of course, Arnold struggled to seek forgiveness from his siblings as well as from himself. He suppressed a lot of his feelings because he did not feel equipped or prepared to deal with the pain of having taken his brother's life.

According to Irving, forgiveness was the strongest card in the family's deck. Reflecting upon the life of Jesus Christ, he remarked that "forgiveness means forgives all wounds." "That is what Jesus Christ's life teaches us," he remarked.

The family was fractured geographically for a time period. Deborah and Dana had relocated to the D.C. metropolitan area, Ronald to California, and Arnold and Alvin remained in New Orleans. But again, with calamity the family melded together, with all of the brothers relocating to Maryland to join Deborah and Dana, after Hurricane Katrina. The shadow of family tragedy lingered.

Adding to the heartbreak, Dana passed away from cancer at age 33 in 2007, after living in Maryland for the last twelve years, and only a couple of years after the reunification of the family. Arnold, who like his father, became a Master Electrician, was then killed in a single vehicle automobile accident, about 4 months later, at the age of 53, in Washington, D.C., after he had relocated to the Maryland

Jacksons

area. His car struck a tree as he was on his way to work. It need not bear reminding that their deaths, only a few months apart, were reminiscent of their parents and Darrilyn's, and then Aaron's, deaths, also months apart.

Arnold was buried in Mount Olivet Cemetery in New Orleans, joining Aaron and the rest of the Jackson family. Sadly, at the moment his body was interred, there were then 7 immediate family members interred at the same cemetery. All of their deaths were premature and none were natural.

After Dana's death, Deborah's mind was racing again, but she sprang into action, now as if by impulse or training, and arranged for grief counseling for Dana's minor children. She again took on the role of mother, this time for Dana's three young children. It has not been easy. Taking on such a responsibility has taxed her financially, spiritually, and emotionally.

Above: Ronald "Cheaky" Jackson; below: Arnold "Jack" Jackson, a year before his fatal accident

Her grief or sorrow is ongoing because to look at Dana's kids is to remember Dana; and to remember Dana is to remember her parents.

Alvin, now the "big brother", became mentor and surrogate parental advisor to Arnold's son. This was a responsibility he accepted willingly and with some enthusiasm, knowing that Arnold would have wanted his guidance and spiritual assistance with his son. Moreover, given the family's tragic history, it had become ingrained in them, despite some familial conflicts, to convert from uncle or aunt to surrogate parent.

The remaining Jackson siblings were inspired to tell their story and their missing family's legacy, with the hopes that it would help others suffering through family tragedy or fratricide, the killing of one's brother.

Searching for Why?

As set forth in the *General Eulogy* chapter, an overriding consideration in most murders is answering the demand about why did it occur? It is even more poignantly posed when the murder is intra-familial. A clear answer is just as elusive here.

Undoubtedly, other families have suffered multiple tragedies or murder victims. Yet, on the other hand, nothing about the Jackson's lives was "normal".

History is abounded with stories or accounts of sibling rivalries and fratricide, including the Bible, Cain and Abel, and Shakespeare's *Hamlet*. Some have described Cain's killing of Abel as humankind's first murder, and as the basis for the verse, "Am I my brother's keeper", in the Bible. Thus, one brother killing another frames the discussion and is the starting point of the topic of homicide.

Psychologists will tell you that it is not uncommon for issues over space and control among brothers leading to deadly results. Often, it occurs in the course of a heated argument, and termed impulsive fratricide; in contrast to psychotic fratricide, which is intentional and premeditated. Aaron's death fell into this further refined category. Moreover, the Aaron-Arnold conflict was consistent with the usual pattern of sibling homicides, with one brother killing another in 3 out of 4 sibling killings.

In the limited body of research concerning fratricide (killing of a brother) or siblicide (killing of a sibling) there are no clear answers. Their occurrence is rare. Siblicides constitute a small minority of homicides (less than 2%), most of the victims and perpetrators are close in age, and in a reversal of the common homicide trends, the perpetrators are usually older than the victims, with male-on-male being the most common occurrence. One notable factor was the loss or decrease of parental or guardian involvement.[133]

Weaving in the thoughts of Shakespeare, one commenter notes: "Like the legends from Rome and the Bible, Shakespeare focuses on the idea that jealousy and power are the corrupting forces that lead a sacred and pure relationship between brothers to become fraught with danger and death."[134] As discussed above, there may have been a sibling power struggle which emerged, but in light of the dynamics of the situation it is difficult to conclude this was the prevailing factor in Aaron's death.

Many of the cases of fratricide have also involved contributing factors of alcohol and substance abuse. None of these latter factors, however, appear to have been at play here, and thus it was unfathomable that any Jackson brother would kill another.

Thus, I posed this complex question to Deborah, considering that she has since obtained a doctorate of Divinity and is a licensed Social Worker. Her response was somewhat detailed, yet poignant, and helped place the killing in a sociological, if not psychological, context.

Jacksons

She says: "My brothers and I went through a lot when my father was briefly incarcerated. This was a very big void because my brothers did not get into any trouble until my father was incarcerated. The coaches and teachers usually denied them opportunities to play sports, which they all loved. Instead, she opined that some in the neighborhood saw them as delinquents and as a result they could not get jobs in the neighborhood." She further asserts, "we were basically written off and labeled by the school system. Instead of understanding that these children had been traumatized by the incarceration of their father, they advanced their trauma."

More simply, she described that Arnold and Aaron were inseparable and exemplified a great, loving relationship between brothers which had gone wrong during an argument.

It would also appear that their parents' deaths contributed to the atmosphere that led to Arnold taking Aaron's life. As one writer opined: *While some adult siblings' bond more closely after the death of their parents, others find that the loss brings unresolved tensions and old rivalries to the surface. Moving past the pain and anger requires a conscious effort on the part of everyone involved; the goodwill of one sibling may not be enough if others persist in clinging to old resentments.*[135]

Cheryl empathizes with the family she has known for more than 55 years: "Deborah and her brothers and sisters have gone through a lot. Although there was constant trauma and drama in Treme, the Jackson's basket was overloaded. I am not sure how they have been able to survive it. Without their strong resolve and faith, the remaining family members would possibly have cracked and been in perpetual counseling."

Another former neighbor of the Jackson's, Cynthia Doucet, whose son's murder is portrayed in Chapter 2 above, echoed a similar sentiment. "I don't know how they survived all of that tragedy", she said.

Going Forward

How do you move forward when tragedy is so central and common in your life? Rather than having extreme difficulty in dealing with others, as has been classically described by other grieving survivors, the Jacksons have been propelled into greater responsibility in dealing with and serving others.

Alvin remarks that if he didn't know what his life's calling was before, he certainly knew what it was after so many family tragedies and losses. It was to minister and help others.

Their experiences with death equipped them to better deal with those suffering physical and psychological maladies, such as terminally ill cancer patients and families who had lost members to violence. It also provided them with a perspective on hope, against long odds, which they could share with others, such as those imprisoned or institutionalized.

Jacksons

There was also something about their losses which help seal their relationships with their supreme beings. Alvin and Deborah embraced religion and education as mechanisms for sustaining their lives and helping others.

Dr. Deborah Jackson-Meyers

Alvin has sought to incorporate into his ministry the lessons learned from these tragedies. He has counseled others, including youth and those at risk of drugs or entering the criminal justice system. One of his recent trips as a minister brought him to Angola, the infamous prison in Louisiana where his father was once imprisoned.

After serving as a Social Worker and substance abuse counselor at Lorton prison, Dr. Jackson-Meyers sought to move beyond the emotional trauma of her father's and uncle's incarceration and the effects on other family members, by forming the Breaking the Chain Foundation. The foundation's mission is to break the cycle of family members who follow their parents or other adult family members into the criminal justice system and eventually into

Jacksons

prison. She was committed to not having the school system, neighbors and others treat other children the way she and her brothers had been treated because of the incarceration of a family member.

Death has been both painful and unforgiving for the Jackson family. Alvin, Deborah, and Ronald have endured the deaths of their parents, three brothers and two sisters; all tragically and all at uncharacteristic, unexpected times. None died what we would consider an ordinary or natural death.

Nevertheless, Reverend Alvin Jackson, smiled and said recently, "this year I celebrated my 60th birthday. In light of everything which has happened in the family, its' hard to believe, but my overall faith in Jesus Christ has brought me through".

A smiling Dana Jackson-Edwards, a few months before her death

In the same vein, Dr. Meyers offers this prayer to the public:

We are in desperate need of reconciliation in the community. Turn to your God for help. Ask God to make things different for all of us. The best way to do that is to maintain a personal relationship to your God and community.

At first, after the loss of my parents, sister Darrilyn, and my brother Aaron, I did not think anyone else had suffered the degree of loss which I had. But as I began to experience life and went through my career, I have seen significant loss and suffering among families.

I then lost my sister Dana and brother Arnold and was again questioning why, but for not a second did I lose faith. I am testament that having faith can bring you through struggles which are immeasurable. So, I say to you, Lord, bless the families and lift them up through their troubles. Show us the way to mutual love and respect, so that we may lead more honorable lives. Strengthen our families and the bonds that bind us and lead us to the door of salvation.

God, please watch over us - all of us regardless of race, creed or sex. May God's will be done, through us, to enlighten us with truth and love, to overcome adversity.

One close Jackson family friend commented that even the strongest of persons "would have bowed or fell apart" after all of their tragedies. But they did not.

One thing is for sure with respect to the Jacksons – they had seen and felt more than their fair share of unexpected death and loss. But they have endured through the unimaginable and not given up. When people hear their stories, they are both shocked and intrigued about how they recovered from their multiple tragic losses. When asked about their emotional and psychological courage, in their view they did not have any other choice but to be strong.

CHAPTER 7
BLOODY RED

Introduction

It started routinely. Biloxi, Mississippi police arrest a man for public drunkenness and lock him in the city's jail. Five hours later, 27 jailed inmates are dead after the arrestee allegedly intentionally set the jail ablaze. Another inmate died within a few days, and an additional 60 plus inmates, first responders, or correctional officers were injured. A 29th inmate died about a week or so year later, and a 30th inmate died after about 5 years, where he had been in a coma as a result of his injuries from the fire during that time. He was 34 years old at the time of his death. The victims ranged in age from 16 to 52. One of those murdered was 40-year old Clayton Reginald Austin, who went by the nickname "Bloody Red", and at the time was the second oldest victim in the city jail facility.

Local prosecutors considered it a mass murder, one of the most riveting murderous occasions in the state's history, with the largest number of victims from any killing in the state.[136] It became international news, and was the catalyst for jail and prison reforms throughout the country. Most critically, however, it left in its wake numerous survivors and loved ones of the victims.

Clayton's family's collective heart notched up a level when they learned of his murder. It came without warning. In a nutshell it was so tragic, so unpredictable, so untimely, and premature. At the time, he was being held on a burglary conviction, had already served time in state prison, and was about a few months from final release.

Growing Up as Bubba

Living rootlessly, Clayton moved from one part of the country to

Bloody Red

another. He lived his shortened life in places such as New Orleans, Biloxi, Seattle, Japan, Milwaukee and Florida.

He was born to Reginald Austin and Vera Edwards Austin in Biloxi, Mississippi. His name was a combination of his grandfather (Clayton) and father (Reginald). But his father died at age 44 from heart disease and organ failure.

Both of his parents were from well-established, respected families in the Biloxi area. He was the oldest of the brew but the only boy, with five sisters. There was Jane, Ceya, Eudith, Angela and Libby. His reality was not that of his siblings, however. They were mostly college-educated, held professional jobs, and married with families. Thus, while they were mainstream, he lived more on the edge.

As noted, as the only male child in the family, with 5 younger sisters, he was surrounded by females, whom he believed needed his protection as a "big brother". Clayton was nicknamed "Bloody Red", by his friends, based upon his complexion and hair. He was a light-skinned African American, with green eyes and reddish-brown hair. Sometimes friends and extended family would shorten his nickname simply to "Bloody". Hey "Bloody", they would yell.

To his siblings and family, however, he was known more simply as "Bubba"; certainly, more down-home and less foreboding than "Bloody". His face was at one time chubby as a youth, but usually adorned with a broad smile, and he was also a committed jokester. He had an engaging personality and could converse with nearly anyone - old, young, educated, uneducated. As he matured, he had a life partner, Theola Hall-Austin, who had several children, which Bloody helped care for.

Clayton's early existence was splintered between Biloxi and New Orleans. It started in Biloxi, however, where his immediate family lived with his grandmother, Corinne Edwards ("Mama Corinne")

Bloody Red

on Reynoir Street. His father's mother lived around the corner on Fayard Street, but passed away when he was 13 years old.

The neighborhood in Keesler (named for the Air Force base), was diverse, but still clannish and neighbors were close. His grandmother's home was modest with a porch and small rooms. However, it had a spacious yard, where she raised chickens and goats and also had an abundant garden of tomatoes, greens and fruit. She canned preserves from peaches and watermelon rinds and cooked shrimp.

There were various other kinfolk in the neighborhood. Clayton's uncle on his grandmother's side lived to the west about 3 blocks on Fayard Street. And just behind them, through the gate of the chicken coop was Clayton's grandmother on his father's side. Other relatives lived a few blocks over on Nixon street. Although small, Mama Corinne's home was often the meeting place for the extended family.

When it came to her grandchildren, it is said Mama Corinne liked the "bad boys." Another way of viewing it is that it was all a misunderstanding since she did not love her other grandchildren less; she simply believed the "bad boys" needed greater protection and were being mistreated by the criminal justice system. She was tough and brawny, with an edge to her, and even the police accorded her a greater level of respect than they did her neighbors. Nearing age 60, she had been accidentally shot in the leg by a shotgun while walking the neighborhood.

Biloxi was a port city of about 50 thousand and known as a resort area and military town. The family lived not far from the main streets, Division, Howard, and Caillavet, about a half mile from the Gulf of Mexico. The beach was lined with white sand and beautiful mansions.

Masked by the white sands and stately houses along the gulf, Biloxi

Bloody Red

was then awash with illegal gambling and petty corruption, and later an infamous political murder. Several years after the fire, in 1987, a Biloxi Circuit Court judge and his wife, a City Councilwoman, were murdered. Members of the Dixie Mafia, were convicted of the contract murder of the judge and his wife. Later, the city's mayor, Pete Halat, was also convicted of being part of the murder conspiracy. So, "sleepy town" could not be ascribed to Biloxi.

As he entered elementary school, the city was still segregated and divided along racial lines; thus, he attended the Our Mother of Sorrows Catholic school for black students.

Clayton was an adventurous sort, even as a youth. He would ride his bike in the neighborhood, once, at age 6, being hit by a car on Reynoir Street, and suffering a head injury. He sometimes joked about how it had made him "screwy" and bad in the head. But it was truly a joke because he was gifted and intelligent.

Otherwise, he did what most kids did back then, ride his bike, try to buy candy and sweets, later flirts with girls, and plays sports.

When his father passed away in December, 1953 (when Clayton was 11), the family had moved to New Orleans, 80 miles to the west. They moved into the rough and tumble Desire Housing projects in New Orleans, but he attended a prestigious parochial high school in the city, St. Augustine High School. The school had an entrance examination, which required a high level of intelligence, and he was smart and witty enough to be admitted - and excel.

He enrolled in the Air Force after graduating from high school. When he went off to the military after high school, he could not use the 26-mile stretch of beach along the Gulf of Mexico. It was restricted to whites. The schools which he attended in the city were also segregated.

Bloody Red

Upon entering the Air Force, he was stationed in Japan. At that time, integration had begun only about 10 years before in the military, and he was then entering into an integrated world. As a blue-suiter, he wore his uniform proudly and looked good in it. He emerged, speaking fluent Japanese.

Clayton's gravesite, with the permission of Stephen Ranum

However, the service may have been his turning point, because it was there that he was introduced to heroin. Thence, there were "ups and downs" in his life. He had been around the world but was still troubled by something. What troubled him most is subject to debate among family and friends.

After returning from the military, Bloody was bold and care-free. He turned to drugs, as had so many other servicemen. Whatever his troubles were, drugs eventually won out. He became hooked on heroin. At the time, there were few treatment centers for those addicted to this very potent drug. He moved around, first between

Bloody Red

New Orleans and Biloxi, and then between Seattle and Milwaukee, then "yo-yoed" back to Biloxi.

In this sense, his life was not much different than numerous veterans returning from abroad. Drugs were used to stave off memories of seeing death and misery. Yet, there were few who were willing to recognize or help heal the tragic wounds of war. In 1971, after visiting soldiers in Vietnam, two Congressmen - Robert Steele and Morgan Murphy - issued a public report and testified about drug use among U.S. soldiers who were serving or had served in Vietnam. They concluded that between 10 to 15 percent of the servicemen were addicted to heroin and that even larger numbers were potentially using heroin occasionally.

It was as though the military service also made him more of a risk taker and courageous. It was more likely the result of drugs which had erased some fears than it was maturity. He had a ruggedness that escaped some because of his green eyes and smooth complexion. As one of his cousins, about 6 years younger, philosophized that he admired Clayton because he walked around with an air of invincibility. He would visit the housing projects where he grew up (the Desire) and his younger cousins would feel safe with him, because even though he had moved from the area many years before, many of the neighbors still remembered him. He had that type of swagger which attracted followers and made those around him feel safe. It was as though he had no fears. He was, after all, Bloody!

He was truly a jambalaya of personalities and cultures - creolized and project-wise but also sophisticated and wise to East Asian cultural spheres. "A very likable dude" is how some described Clayton. He was every bit a salesman and philosopher about life. But he also was known for bad behavior.

Clayton viewed the world with hope and optimism. But with drugs in his life, for instance, sometimes he forgot whether or not he had

Bloody Red

slept, or where he had laid his head. Yet, he felt on top of the world and in control. Nevertheless, he was a giver, doing warm and sweet things for others. In fact, he would try to save others who also struggled with drugs.

Similar to most people who have drug addictions, of course, there were buried secrets. He was sometimes in a haze. It was unclear at times to Thelma and others where he received money and how the funds were being spent. On the other hand, on many occasions, he promised those close to him to stop using drugs and would give them the shirt off his back.

The Wrong Side of The Road

He downward spiraled, committing property crimes to support a nasty heroin habit. Thousands of soldiers had returned home in a similar predicament; addicted to drugs, with the magnitude of the problem being somewhat hidden or obfuscated by the Pentagon and Veteran's Administration.

Mirroring the life of many veterans, promise turned to tribulation, as he started to get in trouble with the law. There were several arrests, imprisonment, and arrest and imprisonment again. He had been arrested for several burglaries, including breaking in a church.

In the church break-in, he was found sleeping in the pews, glassy-eyed and high from "horse", a nickname for heroin. At the time, his world was somewhere between drug-induced poise and calamity. It was following the same pattern as a heroin high, on a pendulum between a rush and ensuing peacefulness. A judge had recognized that his use of drugs was at the center of his criminal actions, and as a result, required that he obtain drug treatment.

According to one of his first cousins, it was as though trouble found him, once drugs entered his life. The story line was a familiar one: get hooked on drugs, turn to crime to support your habit.

Bloody Red

In September1975 he was arrested in Biloxi with James Diggles for burglary, pled guilty and convicted. The judge sentenced him to 2 years in prison. In the mid to late 1970's, imprisonment in Mississippi meant being shipped to the famed prison farm at Parchman.

In prisons and jails, nearly everyone has a nickname. Colorful names flourish in jails and prisons and are part of jail culture. They are bestowed based upon appearance, personality, backgrounds or prior criminal activity.

So "Bloody Red" was not as ominous on the inside as it sounds to those on the outside. It was normal or typical for a confined person to have a nickname, which reflected terror or violence. Indeed, that was part of the reasoning – if you have a bad ass nickname, that may be enough to get respect or keep people away from you. Indeed, it's all about respect!

Nicknames in the area partly were created or adopted because neighborhoods often created the reputation to which you were entitled. Being a resident of the tough Desire projects had given him a tough status, whether he was or not.

Hyperbole also followed Clayton like a blanket. Because he had been in and out of jail and imprisoned before, the stories of what had happened were repeated. The joke in the family was often about his criminal exploits, normally property crimes. While real, the facts or circumstances of the crimes were distilled and expanded like old fish stories.

There was the escapade with a savings and loan institution, which he allegedly broke into in Milwaukee, Wisconsin. When the silent alarm tripped, and he was aware that police were emerging into the area, he allegedly hid in a large garbage can and pulled the top shut, ala the cartoon character "Top Cat." As police searched the area outside of the garbage it became evident to them, for some reason, that he was inside and serious, but also amused, they banged their billy-clubs on the sides and tops and demanded "Come on out buddy". He was arrested, pled guilty, and sentenced to 2 years imprisonment in a Wisconsin state prison.

Similarly, the circumstances surrounding his arrest in Biloxi for burglary, which led to his imprisonment, was also exaggerated. The way the story goes, he had allegedly broken into the Williams' Clothing store on Howard street in the city. Again, a silent alarm tripped, alerting police that the store was being burglarized. When he recognized that police were closing in on the store, he dressed in some of the clothes from the store and posed as a mannequin. Like the "Top Cat" character, he was quickly arrested and charged with burglary.

His nickname should have been "Top Cat," rather than "Bloody Red" or "Bubba". And, he had more than his share of silent alarming.

Life on the Farm

Clayton was sent off to the renowned Parchman prison in 1975, located in the northern part of the state. Along with Angola prison in Louisiana, Parchman was the largest prison, by acreage, in the country. It was a small city in itself (about 28 square miles) containing more than twenty buildings. As men were delivered to the prison farm, they were issued classic white cotton, black-striped prison wear, similar to that which Martin Lawrence and Eddie Murphy wore in the movie *Life*.

Parchman was constructed in 1904 in Sunflower County, along the Mississippi Delta. It was infested with mosquitos during the summer and rodents during the winter. It was without air conditioning (just fans), although temperatures in the summer reached into the 90's. And it was still beset with violence and

Bloody Red

corruption. And nearly half of the inmates had substance abuse problems.

It was the largest prison in the poorest state in the country. That in itself tells one something about how it was operated and administered. More telling, it reflected all of the vestiges of slavery in Mississippi. It had some of the features of a plantation, with mules, gardens and massive cotton fields. Indeed, it was not far different from what the fields resembled during slavery. It was also adorned with gun towers and blood hounds, to search for and capture escapees, and three cemeteries for the many inmates who expired on the premises.

There, the faces were often solemn, barren of expression or burdened with a scowl of anger. Some described the conditions as close to death or slavery, or both. It boasted a population of a majority of black inmates.

It was ending its trusty system which had existed for decades. Under this system, violent inmates were used to guard or harass other prisoners, as the leading supreme court decision described the trusty system which was used to operate the prison.

Shortly before Bloody arrived on the premises at Parchman, federal trial and appellate courts had found the prison existed in essentially an unconstitutional setting. Nearly every essential operation was significantly deficient.

In *Gates v. Collier*, 501 F.2d 1291 (5th Cir. 1974), the court found that the state had violated the Eighth Amendment prohibition against cruel and unusual punishment in its utilization of corporal punishment, flagrant inmate abuse, and utilization of the trusty system.

With respect to corporal punishment, the court found that the state was "*handcuffing inmates to the fence and to cells for long periods*

Bloody Red

of time, ... and forcing inmates to stand, sit or lie on crates, stumps, or otherwise maintain awkward positions for prolonged periods."

Overall, it found the prison's general conditions were sub-human.

With respect to the trusty system, it declared:

Armed trusties guarded each of the prison camps, oversaw inmates while working in the fields, and on occasions were left in sole charge of the fields. Penitentiary records indicated that some of the armed trusties had been convicted of violent crimes, and, that of the armed trusties serving as of April 1, 1971, thirty-five percent had not been psychologically tested, forty percent of those tested were found to be retarded, and seventy-one percent of those tested were found to have personality disorders. There was no formal program for training trusties.

Trusties were instructed to maintain discipline by shooting at inmates who got out of gun line; in many cases trusties had received little training in the handling of firearms. In addition to abusing their authority and engaging in loan sharking, extortion and other illegal conduct, the trusties shot, maimed or otherwise physically maltreated scores of inmates subject to their control. .... The record revealed at least eighty-five instances where inmates had physically assaulted other inmates; twenty-seven of these assaults involved armed attacks in which an inmate was either stabbed, cut or shot.... There were assaults, fights, gambling and drugs.[137]

But Bloody was hardly soulless or sullen, and survived Parchman!

In 1981, he pled guilty to another burglary and again sent off to prison. But due to overcrowding in the prisons, fortunately at the time, corrections authorities shipped him out to the Biloxi Harrison County jail, to serve his sentence and transition back into society.

He would serve his time there and then be released.

Bloody Red

He could receive visitors (some of his closest relatives were within walking distance) and he began making plans for his release. He had a fantasy about what his prison after-life would be, when he would no longer exist as a number in the system. In his conversations with his mother, he had been talking about the future and becoming closer to God. He knew, however, that mere prayers were not going to cure his drug problems. Thus, there was a glint of hope for Bloody.

Signage leading to Parchman Prison, courtesy Friends of Justice

The Biloxi jail where he was shipped was a one-story-brick and concrete building, situated on Delauney and McElroy streets, which had been built in the mid 1960's, as a police station and courthouse for the city. However, in 1975, the city sold the premises to the county and it was converted into a jail for additional county jail space. As part of the contract, the City agreed to pay the County $3 per day to house and feed its prisoners.

The jail was one of two operated by the county, with the main jail in Gulfport, eight miles away. Moreover, in the late 70's voters in the city had twice rejected proposals to raise taxes to build a new jail.

Ironically, even in its condition, it was considered one of the better jails in the state.

Bloody Red

More critically, overall jails and prison conditions in Mississippi had been the subject of a federal lawsuit brought by private lawyers for the prisoners beginning in 1971, challenging their inhumane conditions. The Department of Justice had joined in the lawsuit on behalf of the prisoners, but later switched positions after a Mississippi Congressman wrote a letter arguing against federal inspections of the county jails. Biloxi's jail was among those which were subject to inspections under the parameters of the lawsuit.

The jail on Delauney was two streets over and a few blocks down from Reynoir, near where Clayton grew up. Indeed, it was less than ½ mile away. Clayton's grandparents had also lived on Delauney Street, decades before the fire.

The jail was co-ed, with more than 20 of the inmates being female. Many of inmates at the jail, such as Clayton, were state prisoners who were housed there because of overcrowding in state facilities or awaiting transfer to a state facility (corrections authorities initially reported that 22 of the inmate victims were state prisoners). Consequently, some were serious felony offenders. Others were being held on misdemeanor charges and could be expected to be released in the following days. For instance, one of them had been recently arrested for stealing a small amount of beer.

The jail was designed to hold 102 inmates, and there were 20 cells in the jail. In addition, safety deficiencies had been noted at the jail and as noted above, it was the subject of an investigation by the United States Department of Justice for civil rights violations, including jail conditions. In fact, the department had sent a letter to the county merely three months before the murders, wherein it referenced that one of the issues it would be reviewing was "serious fire hazards".

Mislaid in the furor and excitement regarding the fire deaths was an underlying political debacle within the Department of Justice.

Bloody Red

The department had filed a motion to inspect the jail as part of the *Gates* case, because state prisoners were housed there. They received push back from Mississippi Representative Trent Lott and withdrew the motion before the court. When the Section Chief in the Civil Rights Division first requested that the department investigate the jail, months before the fire, the Assistant Attorney General for the Civil Rights Division had replied that the "federal government had no authority to act as a roving commission."[138]

The lawyers were finally allowed in for a tour about three weeks before the fire and noted fire hazards, among other deficiencies. When they returned after the fire, they got to see the charred outlines of where dead jail prisoners had lain. It was clear that "[t]he Biloxi jail was severely overcrowded, it lacked a fire evacuation plan, and it was in flagrant violation of fire safety codes."[139] It was too late then – politics had overcome reason! Even some of the department's previous lawyers were highly critical of what had occurred, or more appropriately had not occurred.

Moreover, jails were supposed to be even safer than prisons because most of those confined are not yet convicted, enjoying greater constitutional rights to contact with family and legal counsel. They were to be accorded all of the rights which were not inconsistent with the need to assure their appearance in court.

One of the critical aspects of its conditions was that although the jail had jailers on duty at night, emergency lighting, and a fire alarm system, it did not have water sprinklers or fire safety devices to open all of the doors. Additionally, each of the cells had manual locks. Although there were two sets of keys, one set was at the guard desk and the other set was locked in a cabinet in an administrative office at the jail.

Fiery Incident

It was near midnight when Biloxi police received a call of a

Bloody Red

disturbance at Amelia's Lounge, near the beach, on Sunday, November 7, 1982. Named after the female aviator, Amelia Earhart, it was the hotspot for late-nighters in the city. In attendance would be soldiers from neighboring Keesler Air Force base, exotic dancers, and stragglers from other bars. It had mirrored dance floors and non-stop disco music.

Robert Eugene Pates, 31, a drifter from Granite City, Illinois was among those at the bar. A former high school wrestler and football player, and all of 240 pounds, he was well known to police since he had been arrested on Saturday, the day before, and brought to jail but was released. He was now drunk and at Amelia's again raising havoc, less than 6 hours after his release from jail.

Side of the jail – courtesy NEFPA

He had a broken leg because he had recently been struck by a car while in Florida. Another family informed the media that Pates had visited with them for several weeks in Mobile, Alabama prior to him traveling to Biloxi. They attempted unsuccessfully to have Pates obtain mental help but he refused. He had said he would report to a mental health clinic in Alabama, but instead got on a bus to Biloxi a few days before his appointment. He had been in and out of mental health facilities in several states.

Bloody Red

When police arrived at the lounge, they believed they had no choice but to arrest him again. He was incoherent and acting irrational. As a Chancery Clerk later commented, he was a big man and out of control. As a consequence, they charged him with public drunkenness and then petitioned for a "lunacy" determination.

"We decided to arrest him rather than let him get hurt or hurt somebody," arresting officer Bill Reynolds said later. One officer in his police report, related that he talked with Pates for about 45 minutes and could not understand what he wanted. The police also contacted his mother in Granite City and his brother, a police officer in Illinois, who claimed that he had mental problems and could become very violent. In addition, they informed police that he had escaped from mental facilities more than 20 times.

Another relative of Pates' said that he had been taken to a mental health facility in Illinois, a week before his arrest in Biloxi, but the facility placed him in a taxi and suggested that he leave town.

Jailers signed commitment papers for a commitment proceeding for Pates, and Chancery Clerk Nicky Creel, after seeing the 240-pound Pates act violently, banging and kicking the cell walls, determined that the drifter should be held in jail rather than the hospital. "That man weighs 240 pounds and had a history of violence," Creel said. "I'd hate to think of what might happen if he got loose in that hospital." [140]

The thinking by law enforcement was that it was necessary to arrest him for his own protection, as well as to protect others. He would be behind bars and both he and the public would be safe.

The police van pulled up to the bay of the jail and escorted the unruly Pates inside. Jailers stripped him down to his underwear and placed him in a padded cell in the north tier of the jail. He was alone in the cell, which was intended as a protective unit, and for inmates with mental health issues or concerns regarding suicide.

Bloody Red

The door to his cell was a heavy framed steel door, with outlets or openings for viewing and passage of food. The door and walls were padded, with concrete floors and ceilings.

Locked up alone in the padded cell, early Sunday, he refused to be released. His conversation then, officers said, was still bizarre, and impossible to understand. Authorities decided to hold him for a mental examination.

According to the commitment papers, his family had revealed to police that Pates had been confined to mental institutions regularly for the previous 10 years. He was scheduled for a hearing before the judge on Monday morning.

While in the jail on Sunday, he caused disruptions and havoc with the other inmates. He was spitting at people hanging in the hall as well as those across the hall. As a result, at about 1:15 a.m. on Monday, one of the jailers closed and locked him behind the heavy steel door of his cell. He had not been in the cell long that night when the fire broke out in his cell, about 1:25 a.m., triggering the jail's fire alarm system.

The other inmates at the jail were asleep when the fire started. There were three jailers on duty and 94 jail inmates, 7 of whom were trusties, all of whom were unlocked in their separate trusty cell. They were alerted when the fire alarm went off, and Pates began yelling "fire in the hole"!

The padding in Pates' cell was afire, but he had covered himself with his mattress. The enflamed padding contained plastic polyurethane a deadly substance, which, when set afire or burned, releases toxic smoke and gases. The county had purchased the padding on an emergency basis after some had complained about the lack of padding in cells at the jail holding mentally ill inmates.

As described later by Investigator James R. Bell: "The jail officer

Bloody Red

took the set of keys and entered the confinement area of the jail. He was followed by a second male jail officer and a jail trusty. As he approached the padded cell, he smelled a light odor of smoke in the corridor, but saw no visible smoke. He placed the key in the cell's lock and unlocked the door. The jail officer reported that when he pulled the door open approximately two inches, an "explosion" blew the door open, knocking him down the corridor. A "large ball of fire" rolled out of the cell, and the corridor instantly began to fill with thick black smoke."[141]

Tom Miller, the jailer who had opened Pates' door, was one of the three jailers on duty that night and had run to the cell to see what was transpiring. But when he and the other jailer opened the door slightly, and were literally blown off their feet, the keys remained in Pates' door cell lock. The explosion resulted from what is termed a "flash over" – when a slow burning fire is energized by a fresh insurgence of oxygen, and literally explodes.

Miller was overcome by the choking smoke and fumes and passed out. His valiant efforts landed him in a local hospital in critical condition. Upon seeing the fire and thick smoke, the third jail officer, who was approaching the door to the units rushed back to the guard desk, which was about 12 feet away, and pushed a panic key on the phone to connect with the Sheriff's Department Communications Center, and yelled "Fire in the jail, "send the fire department!"

The smoke from the burning polyurethane padding spread rapidly through the ventilation system and the hallways into much of the rest of the jail. The flames from the fire did not last long, but it was not easy to extinguish at first. Nevertheless, the smoke trenchantly marched into each cell unit, leading to utter chaos.

The jailers and one of the trusties obtained fire extinguishers, which were at the jail, and sought to extinguish the fire. But the smoke was too tough and menacing and they could not get to the key ring. "Repeated efforts to retrieve the key ring were unsuccessful because the cell door was engulfed by the fire coming from the cell."[142] Inhalation of the black smoke eventually temporarily incapacitated the three of them.

It spread rapidly with thick black, oily smoke consuming the jail, rendering it difficult to see or move about and trapping the inmates in their cells. Smoke wedged its way into the entire jail, making it virtually impossible to escape. They were in a fire trap!

Fire personnel arrived less than 5 minutes after the alarm, at about 1:34 a.m., and were able to put out the blaze in about 5 minutes. But they were stifled by the smoke and the inability to unlock the cells because the keys were nowhere to be found. Rescuers with air tanks and face masks had arrived and crawled on their hands and knees searching for the jailer and keys.

With the jailers and one trusty incapacitated, another trusty bravely "donned a fire department self-contained breathing apparatus (SCBA) and entered the building with fire fighters."[143] After obtaining the keys from the door, they unlocked cell doors in the north cell block. But that trusty's air supply was depleted and he too became incapacitated.

Then, one of the jail officers on the outside took the ring of keys and without any breathing apparatus re-entered the jail, but he too was quickly knocked unconscious. Fire fighters entered the building and rescued him, retrieving the key ring.

Next, the jail warden attempted to enter the administrative area in order to obtain the second set of keys, but the heavy smoke prevented him from doing so. He then called for a tow truck which could use be used to pull out bars and windows. The tow truck appeared instantly. It would use its hydraulic winch to break the

Bloody Red

lock on the jail's entrance and the adjacent bullpen, freeing the remaining inmates.

Initial attempts with the tow truck were unsuccessful until the warden had the tow truck move to the other side of the building where he entered and opened the unlocked interior exit door located at the west end of the corridor, in front of Bullpens 3 and 4. He then attached the cable to the doors to the bullpen cells, which the tow truck pulled open. Prisoners were alive in this bullpen area but they still needed to open Bullpens 1 and 2. Those doors were more difficult to open, even though policemen worked at it with a crowbar and fire axe. When they were opened it was too late; most of the men inside had passed (10 of the 30 deceased). See Exhibit 2.

The breathable air in the jail had worn thin and desperation turned to exasperation. The inmates were quickly overcome by smoke from the smoldering polyurethane padding.

Asked to describe the smoke and aftereffects, Police Officer LeBlanc describes that as the soot from the smoke settled on the walls, it was oily and difficult to wipe away. Given that the jail did not have windows which could open, the smoke appeared to linger in the building for an extraordinary period of time.

One surviving trustee recalled that the smoke burned your throat and the only way to avoid the feeling was to hold your breath.

Pates was one of the first inmates rescued, with minor injuries. He had covered himself with a mattress, then when the door exploded open, hobbled quickly past Jimmy Ellis, one of the 3 jailers. From his cell, he went into a laundry room and covered his face with a wet mop. He was dragged to the outside, coughing and spewing but was still cursing and acting out. He was hollering and screaming. He had fire burns to his back, which were later deemed not serious, but he was alive.

Still, even while under guard outside the jail, with his left lower leg in a cast, he limped around, being obstinate, cursing and uncontrollable, as responders prepared to transport him to the hospital. He did not stop acting up, until one policeman told him to "shut up."

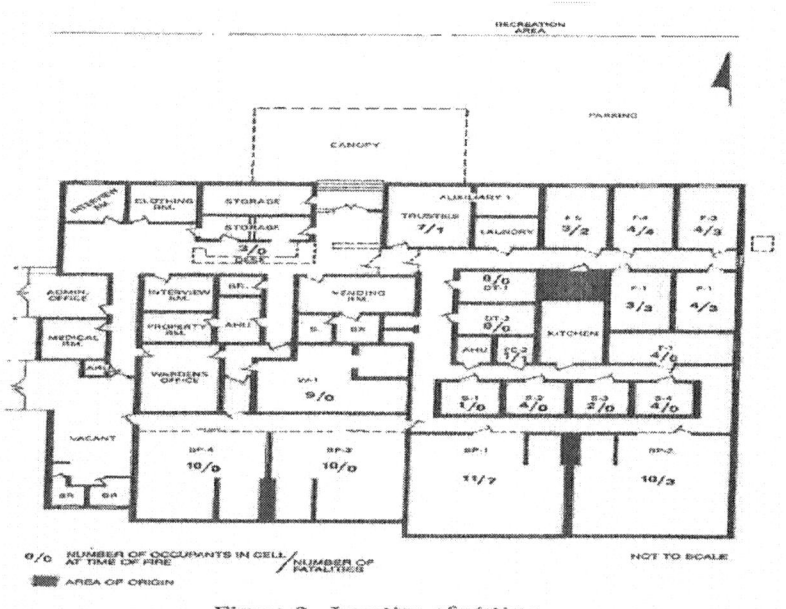

Figure 2. Location of victims.

Exhibit 2- Schematic of cells and location of victims-courtesy of Fire Journal

As mentioned, the flames themselves did not last long. Inmates died from inhaling the thick black smoke from the cell's padding. Once the smoke engulfed the building, the options available to stop it were extremely limited. That left the only practical option as getting all of the inmates from the jail as quickly as possible, even risking that some might attempt to escape. None did even attempt such.

Some prisoners, put rags beneath their cell doors in a desperate

Bloody Red

attempt to save themselves. Others raced to lavatories for wet towels or got in the showers and turned on the water.

Paramedics treated the injured briefly at the scene and then took them to the hospital. Firefighters, policemen and inmates rushed in and out of the jail bringing out prisoners alive and dead. The injureds' breathing was strained and labored and they were in obvious need of prompt medical care. They were transported to three area hospitals. It is estimated that approximately one hour had passed before all of the inmates were removed from the locked cells.

NEFPA photos of fire

Photo 3. View looking east toward Padded Cell-1 on right. Intense heat and flames from the cell vented into adjoining corridor. NFPA

Figure 2. Location of victims

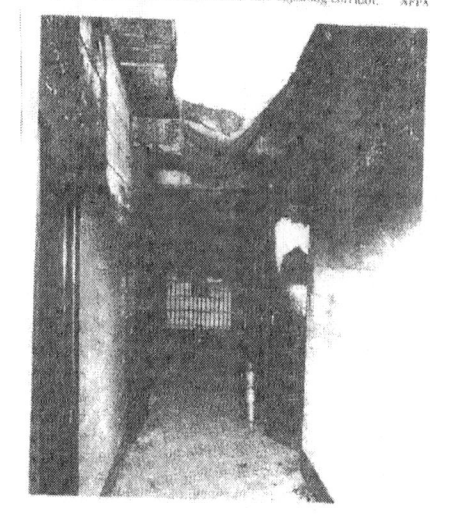

Photos taken showed many of the survivors on the outside of the jail laying prone, hooked to oxygen tanks, with paramedics and emergency personnel attending them. First responders also lined the dead bodies on the grassy area outside of the jail and covered them with sheets. They all had died - essentially because they couldn't breathe, leading to cardiac arrest. The bodies were encrusted with soot but identifiable. Many had the classic manifestations of carbon monoxide (CO) or cyanide (CN) poisoning - cherry red cheeks.

Clayton Is Among the Dead

Clayton was one of the more well-liked inmates in the jail. He was in cell F3, along with 17year-old David Thomas Gray and 27-year-old James K. Franklin, whose brother (Tommy) was also locked in the jail, but around the corner in one of the bullpens. Similar to Clayton, James had served in the military, with the U.S. Navy. There was another unidentified inmate in their cell, who miraculously survived. Their cell was situated on the northeast corner of the jail, katty-corner from Pates' cell, about 12 feet away.

Clayton was among those killed. Those in his section of the jail appear to have died early during the incident. See Exhibit 2. His burglary codefendant, James Diggles, also confined at the jail, was also killed. So were both of the Franklin brothers. The two female inmates, whose cell was about 4 ½ feet from Pates', and who had allegedly (but later contradicted) given the cigarette to Pates, were also dead. Tragically, there were 24 other persons who were killed. There were 28 males and 2 females who were victims.

Those inmates who were closest to the fire suffered the greatest number of casualties. See Exhibit 2. Only 3 of the 18 inmates in Section F, on the northeast side of the jail, survived.

According to authorities, the dead included two murderers, two rapists, three kidnappers, three armed robbers, three forgers and 10 burglars. Several of the deceased were military veterans.

The bodies of the victims were loaded onto trucks and then flown to the state Medical University in Jackson for autopsies. Autopsies confirmed that the cause of death was a combination of carbon monoxide (CO) and cyanide (CN) poisoning by smoke inhalation for all of the deaths. Medical examiners found soot and particulate in the victims' airways, including their mouths, singed facial and nasal hairs, as well as swelling and inflammation in the airways.

Authorities initially didn't know how Pates started the fire. They reasonably assumed that he used a cigarette. The polyurethane padding in the cell "was supposed to be fireproof," according to Chief Deputy Sheriff Craig Monroe. He says it charred like a burnt marshmallow.[144]

Jail policy allowed for an inmate to smoke in the padded cell, but only if a jailer observed the inmate smoking and put the cigarette out.

Exhibit 3- Bodies lying outside the jail – credit Fire Journal & Pat Sullivan

At the outset, authorities were hesitant to conclude what had occurred for several obvious reasons: they were unsure, concerned with indicting their own actions or lack thereof, and it would have been premature. They noted, nonetheless, that there were issues about whether the mattresses were flame retardant. Likewise, with respect to a cigarette which they found in a corner of Pates' cell, they declined to link it to the fire at that time.

"We understand the inmate may have first ignited the mattress on his bed and this spread to the padding," coroner Ed Little said. "The flames were limited to one cell but the ventilation system quickly carried the smoke to the rest of the building", he added.[145]

Many of the victims' relatives gathered in front of the jail before dawn, in distress, some crying and shaking their heads in apparent disbelief. 'How did this happen?' one woman asked softly, her question directed to no one in particular.[146] Mildred Showers cried out hysterically, that her 19-year old daughter was being held on a misdemeanor, and had to "die for nothing." Others contacted a local television station, inquiring whether their relatives were among the deceased, or about their medical condition.

Among the dead were those awaiting trial, convicted and sentenced, or awaiting sentencing. There was a 17-year old who had been sentenced to 3 years for burglary and grand larceny, just 2 months before the fire; a 34-year-old who was sentenced in September to 5 years for carrying a concealed weapon; and a 52-year-old from Texas who was sentenced to 1-year for forgery.

In its wake, the killings and fire caused extensive human and property damage. There was significant smoke and water damage, on the interior. Black soot covered inside walls of the jail and there was an inch of water on the floor. The outside of the building, however, bore little evidence of the devastation inside other than some broken windows. Mattresses and clothes lying on the ground were blackened.

The human toll physically and emotionally was monumental. In addition to the dead, 61 were injured, with 45 of the surviving prisoners hospitalized, and 12 were in critical condition, some with permanent brain damage. Sixteen of the first responders also required hospitalization.

And the families of the victims had a lifelong era of grief ahead of them. The deaths were followed by stoic obituaries, with some of the inmates being residents of neighboring states Alabama and Louisiana and others as far away as Indiana.

It was also gut-wrenching for some of the responders, since they had never encountered a fire or crime scene with so many victims.

The Killing Fumes

Clayton, more than likely, died a horrible and painful death. Depending on the density and heat of the smoke, it may have taken 2 to 10 minutes for him to lose consciousness or die.

Fire burns oxygen, removing the breathable air in a confined space, so as a fire continues to burn, more oxygen gets removed from the room.

That all of the victims in Biloxi died as a result of smoke inhalation was not surprising. This is because smoke inhalation is the number one cause of death for victims related to indoor fires. It is estimated that 50–80% of fire deaths are the result of smoke inhalation, including burns to the respiratory system.

Smoke inhalation occurs when you breathe in the products of combustion during a fire. The hot smoke injures or kills by a combination of thermal damage, poisoning and pulmonary irritation and swelling, caused by carbon monoxide, cyanide and other combustion products. The most common gas, carbon monoxide, can be deadly, even in small quantities, as it replaces oxygen in the bloodstream.

Smoke is a mixture of heated particles and gases. It is impossible to predict the exact composition of smoke produced by a fire. The products being burned, the temperature of the fire, and the amount of oxygen available to the fire all make a difference in the type of smoke produced. Depending upon the materials which burn, the smoke normally triggers deaths from acute exposure to CO or CN, or a combination of both.

In CO cases, smoke then places carbon monoxide into the lungs, which prohibits oxygen entering the body and carbon dioxide getting released from the body. Persons who die from CO typically lose consciousness or pass out before dying and even if they survive, may suffer brain damage. Research has established that 15 minutes of straight smoke (0% oxygen) would kill a person, and 5-10 minutes would cause permanent brain damage in humans.

CO disrupts the normal lining of the respiratory tract. This disruption can potentially cause swelling, airway collapse, and respiratory distress. Heat from the fire is also a respiratory hazard, as superheated gases burn the respiratory tract. When the air is hot enough, one breath can kill.

However, in a house or building fire the smoke is more toxic due to the gases released from other burning objects, such as furniture and plastics. Once a human starts to inhale the smoke, they simply do not get enough oxygen to survive.

On the other hand, CN is one of the most rapidly acting poisons. As Dr. Marc Bayer relates: "People who inhale significant concentrations of cyanide gas "are dead within minutes . . . basically, the person internally suffocates."[147] It is so potent that it is one of the substances used as part of legal injections in death penalty executions.

Acute cyanide poisoning causes the failure of a person's cells, eventually leading to death. Sufferers will first feel nausea, which is then often followed by confusion, loss of co-ordination, rapid deep breathing and gasping, further leading to muscle spasms and loss of consciousness.

"Oxygen deprivation causes potentially painful muscle contractions, convulsions and abnormal heart rhythms, all of which may develop before the cessation of breathing and death."[148] Death is often the result of cardiac arrest.

And this is what happened to the Biloxi victims.

Determined to know how and why these people died, Delahousey sought scientific and medical answers. Finding it odd that most of the victims were not cyanotic (blueness of the skin due to lack of oxygen) - instead their skin was cherry red - he suspected cyanide poisoning. "A good friend of mine was Chief Medical Officer at Keesler AFB Emergency Room. He is board certified in emergency medicine. We took some of the patients to Keesler AFB emergency room. They had better medical laboratory capability than the civilian hospital ERs and he quickly ran blood cyanide levels on the patients and they were all elevated. Our investigation led to the conclusion that when you burn the type of Styrofoam found in the padded cell, one of the by-products is lethal hydrogen cyanide gas."

Dr. Barbara Levin, who examined some of the materials from the fire, also concluded that it produced as much hydrogen cyanide as it produced CO, and hydrogen cyanide is washed out by water.[149] This explains why some inmates survived, as they doused themselves with water.

Eyewitness Accounts

There were numerous eyewitnesses to the fire and rescue efforts. They provided chilling glimpses into the horrors and devastation, but also the hearts and compassion of those who were part of the rescue effort, including inmates.

Policeman Dan Russell was one of the officers who had arrested Pates and also among the jail rescuers. With respect to the arrest at Amelia's, he said: "We thought we ought to pick him up for his

Bloody Red

own protection," Russell said. "I wish now we hadn't."[150]

The media also interviewed several of the inmates who were rescued. Charlie Acevedo, one of the trusties at the jail, who was interviewed while hospitalized for smoke inhalation, said, there was "a chemical in the smoke. You could smell it when you breathed it in, and it would just about knock you out."[151] "The ones that stayed alive got wet towels and wrapped them around their face of got in a shower and put wet blankets over them," Acevedo said.

"The ones that didn't, died."

Acevedo related that the two women inmates, whom he sought to help first, were screaming but then immediately quieted by the exterminating smoke. Those women were, undoubtedly, Joan Johnson and Bobbie Showers.

Biloxi Patrolman Walter "Tiny" Chatagnier, described a similar setting, saying: "I remember running through that jail and slipping around in the dark," Chatagnier said, adding that he had yelled at prisoners to "wet a rag in the commode and lie down and breathe through it. Some of them did it, and they lived. Others didn't, and we brought them out dead. "I remember it," Chatagnier said.[152]

The first Biloxi firefighter to enter the jail, Rocky Smith, said he felt helpless. "I tried my best to help them," said Smith, who went from cell to cell opening each door so crews could bring out prisoners. "It wasn't enough. It was like I couldn't move fast enough. "You couldn't even see a foot in front of you," Smith said. "I was trying to unlock a (cell) door, when this white face just appeared in front of me. This man was begging me to save him. He said, 'Let me out. Please, let me out' Then it just disappeared."[153]

One of the most compelling and graphic accounts was provided by Brian Gillespie, a jail trusty, an inmate who was not locked-in

Bloody Red

because of his trusty status. There was panic and hopelessness. He "remembers frantic hands reaching though cell bars." "I remember those hands. Those screams, 'Help me, help me,' " Gillespie said. "God, it was terrible." Gillespie said that, as a trusty, he was not locked in a cell. "I was luckier than most of them," he said. "I could get out." Gillespie, who was hospitalized for smoke inhalation, said he and another inmate ran outside and started breaking windows with bricks. "We were trying to let some of the smoke out," he said. "I remember we called out names. I remember not getting any answers."[154]

Another trusty, Leon Ratcliff, recalled that he was in his bed on the other side of the hall from Pates when he heard a lot of commotion, and then a "boom". He ran across the hall, with one of the jailers, and helped remove some of the screaming inmates from their cells.

"When we first got there, the inmates were hollering out for help, but there was nothing we could do until we found the keys," said fire-fighter Danny Boudreaux. "By the time we got to all the cells and got them unlocked, most everybody was unconscious," Boudreaux said. "Some were curled up in the corner of the cells. Others had tried to get under beds. They were lying all over the place."[155]

According to Officer LeBlanc, "the smoke was like 3 feet off the ground, and very black." Others relate how some inmates called on God to help them.

"All we could do was feel our way, feel under the bunks or wherever people were huddled. "Some of them were trying to block the cells with rags to keep the smoke out before we got there, said Deputy Fire Chief Bruce Marie."[156] "We were locating bodies by feel," he said.

"We looked in beds and we looked in corners." ... Some of the victims were in respiratory arrest, but their hearts were still

Bloody Red

beating," paramedic Steve Delahousey recalled. 'We tried aggressively to resuscitate them."

According to one firefighter, "There were a lot of people out on the ground. The medical people were putting IVs (intravenous injections) in their arms and giving them oxygen and determining which people were salvageable and which were not." [157]

LeBlanc described the inmates as worried and frightened but collegial, as they helped in the rescue effort, pulling other injured or dead inmates out of the building. "These guys may be hardened criminals, but at a time like this they really showed themselves to be good people," he had replied to the media.[158]

The jail emerged as a crime scene. It was simply deadly and ghastly. Relatives gathered outside the jail, holding their breaths. Some held their heads in tier hands, sobbing uncontrollably. Others relate that they were so stressed by not knowing what had happened and who had survived that they could not breathe.

The chorus of concerned citizens was made up of varied family members of the victims, but one stood out: Laura Pyles. She attended the various court proceedings, and was agitated and vocal, stoking the consciousness of the protesters regarding the injustice of her brother and others being killed.

Trial

Police shipped Pates immediately to Parchman, but shortly thereafter he was transferred to the mental ward of a hospital. When questioned by police initially he said that a female inmate, who was locked up in a cell across from him, had handed him a lighted cigarette and he had fell asleep while smoking. He then was awakened by the fire and toxic fumes. Thus, he denied intentionally setting the jail afire.

The Harrison County prosecutor initially charged him with 27 counts of murder, which was amended to 29 counts later, after 2 additional inmates died. Law enforcement initially refused to answer whether Pates' story would change their prosecution decision.

Prior to trial, sympathy for him in the Biloxi community seemed to be in short supply. Prosecutors initially claimed Pates, a drifter, set the fire to get attention or escape. They believed that he started the fire by inserting a lighted cigarette through a funnel made of playing cards and blew on the cigarette to generate enough heat within the card funnel to ignite the polyurethane foam on the walls and mattress.

To several people, Pates' actions were hardly surprising. Even his relatives did not deny that he was capable of violence and acting out in an extreme manner. They had seen it before on many occasions.

One of his high school classmates, and then a local judge in Pates' hometown, said that Pates had appeared before him on several occasions, before the incident, and commented: "He was a time bomb waiting to go off." He would often go to bars, get drunk, and start fights. He had once slammed a steel door in a jailer's face at the jail in Carbondale, Illinois.[159]

Biloxi authorities discovered that he has been in mental hospitals in at least three states. One of his attorneys provided a glimpse of his defense prior to trial. He alleged that one of his client's friends had revealed how he had been with Pates, in Florida in October when Pates had left a cigarette burning in a Florida hotel room. This occurred even though Pates was on his medication.

The first step in the criminal process was an arraignment to determine how Mr. Pates would plea to the charges. Sheriff's deputies rolled him into the Harrison County courthouse courtroom in a wheel-chair. His head was hung low, he was unshaven, and

Bloody Red

bearded. Wearing an orange jump suit, he had been driven to court in a police van from Gulfport Memorial Hospital where he has been held in a psychiatric ward since the fire.

What would normally have been a serene quiet scene in a courthouse was transformed into an electrical commotion. Appearing nervous, and handcuffed to the wheelchair, he was whisked into the Harrison County Courthouse past nearly a dozen shouting people, relatives of inmates killed or injured in the jail fire, who surrounded the police van. There was tight security at the courthouse and all those entering the court were searched. There were no compassionate faces among the crowd. The dozen or so angry spectators were packed with emotions and seeking justice.

"You killed my brother," Laura Pyles of Biloxi shouted as Pates headed for the courthouse door. She had to be restrained by another spectator. Ms. Pyles' brother, Michael Pyles, died in the early Monday fire. "You are going to die", one of the survivors yelled to Pates. Laura also commented to the media: "They didn't deserve it. Can you imagine them kids standing at those bars, choking on the smoke that killed them? It's horrible," she said.[160]

There were several threshold issues for the judge to resolve: (a) who would represent Pates and (b) was he mentally competent to stand trial.

Once inside the courtroom, Judge Daniel Guice told him that his arraignment would have to be delayed because no Biloxi attorneys had come forward to represent him. Pates then agreed to let two attorneys from Gulfport defend him. Because they were not present, no plea was entered at the hearing.

Judge Guice appointed Jim Rose and Earl Stegall, to represent Pates after the defendant said he has been drawing Social Security disability benefits and had no money to hire a lawyer. The judge ordered him held without bond.

Bloody Red

Pates mother also came to his defense. She claimed that he had been a student at Southern Illinois University and was mentally ill, resulting from the use of LSD on a single occasion, 10 years prior to his arrest in Biloxi.

She was concerned that her son could be "railroaded into the gas chamber to cover up negligence by local jail officials." She told the media that she had warned police and jail officials that Pates was mentally ill and could be dangerous when locked up.

Mrs. Pates said in a telephone call she had warned a deputy from Harrison County about her son's mental illness and his long record of arrests and commitments for mental disorders. The deputy had called to inform her of Pates' arrest Sunday for public drunkenness. She said another son, also had warned deputies in Harrison County of Pates' problems and potential for violence.

Pates was the second oldest of 9 children. She averred that sometimes he did not take his medicine - lithium.

Her criticism was not limited to his mental condition. Pates' mother criticized jail officials for placing Pates in a padded cell and then failing to prevent him from getting the matches or cigarettes that started the fire. "It's negligence on their part," she said. "They should not have put him in that cell where there could be problems."

Pates' arraignment did not occur until June of the following year, when the charges were amended to 29 murders. His arraignment was delayed so that Pates could undergo a battery of psychiatric tests to determine his mental competency to stand trial. When it did happen, his arraignment lasted more than half an hour as the judge asked him his plea with respect to each murder. For each, he asserted "not guilty".

After another examination and hearing, the judge also determined that Pates was competent. Thus, the criminal trial was scheduled to go forward. Before it began, however, defense counsel filed a motion for contempt against the district attorney, contending that he had prejudicially released to the public a psychiatric report concerning Pates.

Another of defense counsel's first actions was filing a motion with the court for a change of venue, where the trial would be held. They alleged that Pates could not receive a fair trial in Biloxi and it would be impossible to get an impartial jury because of the number of victims from the city, anger by survivors, and the pervasive pretrial publicity. The judge granted the motion and changed the location of the trial to Gulfport, and trial was scheduled before Judge James Thomas.

The trial, which lasted 5 days, began Tuesday, October 26, 1983, about a year after the fire. After selection, the jury was sequestered and remained in a local hotel during the trial. Among those following the trial was Mildred Spicer, whose 24-year old son Freddie was killed, Armand Broussard, whose brother was killed, and Laura Pyles', whose brother Michael was among the dead.

Although Pates did not raise insanity as a defense, his lawyers argued during opening statements that he did not have enough sense to know that his actions were imminently dangerous. His lawyers alleged that he was a manic depressive who was not taking his medication; thus, he could not control his actions. Prosecutors countered that these arguments were mere "smoke screens". District Attorney Albert Necaise laid out to the jury that he would show that Pates set the fire to get out of jail. The applicable law, he asserted, was whether the defendant knew the difference between right and wrong, and a psychiatrist had already reported that he knew such differences. Heavily sedated, Pates sat quietly through the opening statements, testimony and closing arguments during the trial.

Bloody Red

The core of the trial concerned the issues of intent and Pates' mental condition at the time of the incident. The prosecution presented evidence from the jailers, as well as the Fire Marshal and others, to establish that Pates set the fire intentionally. The start of the fire, only minutes after an angry Pates was forced into his cell, was circumstantial evidence of further motive on his part.

To establish intent, prosecutors opened the trial with statements which Pates had made to a policeman and hospital assistant and the observations of the government psychiatrist. The police officer testified that 2 days prior to the fire, when he arrested Pates, the defendant told him, "fire will strike, the devil is coming" and [the police officer] "was going to burn in hell". While he was hospitalized after the fire, a hospital transport worker testified that Pates threatened him, if the worker did not give him a cigarette. "He said if I didn't give him any cigarettes he'd burn down …. The hospital, just like he had done the … jail", the worker claimed.

The Deputy Fire Marshal testified that he found about 6 inches of materials in a pile in Pates' cell. Among the pile was socks, chicken bones, paper towels and a paper cup. He opined that the origins of the fire were in the materials.

One of the jailers testified that he had searched Pates before he was placed in the cell and did not find either playingcards or matches.

The State psychiatrist testified that Pates was sane, but a manic depressive. Rather, he was manipulative, asserted the psychiatrist. However, the psychiatrist's notes did contain notes, stating Pates was "nuts" and "mentally unstable".

Prosecutors also presented testimony from two forensic experts, who testified that a cigarette did not start the fire as Pates contended. One opined that Pates set the fire by using a match, but Judge Thomas disallowed that testimony, because a match had not been found among the cell's charred debris.

Bloody Red

The prosecution also presented testimony from an FBI lab expert who testified that material found in the fire debris matched the material from the cast on Pates' leg. This testimony was offered in support of the prosecution theory that Pates set the fire as part of an escape attempt.

Later, Douglas Fielder, a trusty in the jail at the time of the fire, testified that jailer Tom Miller asked another trusty for a cigarette, about an hour before the fire, to give to Pates. As part of the prosecution testimony, however, Miller had denied that he gave Pates a cigarette.

There was certainly conflicting testimony about where he got the cigarettes. Eventually, it came out during testimony that one of the things which Pates was so argumentative about was wanting cigarettes. Some trusties and inmates acknowledged giving him cigarettes. The two jailers whom he identified as providing him a cigarette denied doing so.

Pates testified in his own defense. On the stand for nearly 2 hours, he said he carelessly flicked a menthol cigarette to the corner of his cell. According to him, because the cigarette "didn't taste right", it was of no use to him and he flicked it away. He further testified that one of the jailers had provided him the cigarette which caused the fire.

On cross-examination, the prosecutor sought to establish the incredulity of Pates' testimony:

Prosecutor: "Why didn't you just put it [the cigarette] out on the concrete floor?"

Pates: "I believe if I thought if I just flipped it, it would go out and I'd smoke the rest in the morning."

Prosecutor:" Didn't you do it because you wanted to get out of your cell?"

Bloody Red

Pates: "No, sir".

Pates further admitted that he had some playing cards in his cell, which had been given to him by a trusty, which may have caught afire.

The defense also presented a psychiatrist, who had examined Pates, who testified that the defendant was a manic-depressive person and needed medication. He explained, similar to the government's expert, that Pates threats were "manipulative", simply as a way to get cigarettes. But, the psychiatrist explained, his actions were neither evil nor intentional.

Indeed, in their closing argument Pates' lawyers not only sought to eradicate intentionality on his part but place the blame for the fire on the government. They argued that the padding in Pates' cell had been improperly installed and what a few of the victims' family members had contended - Pates was a scapegoat for the actions or lack thereof of the government. In essence, the government were the real murderers!

After deliberating about four hours, a jury acquitted Pates of all charges, after his attorneys had argued that the fire started because he flipped a cigarette into a corner of his cell and fell asleep. In essence, although he may have been careless, they asserted, it did not constitute the type of intentional conduct which would render his actions criminal.

Part of the difficulty with this defense was that Pates' brother, a police officer, had told authorities that his brother did not smoke. "He doesn't even smoke. How the hell did a guy in a padded cell get matches?" he said. "He was probably trying to attract a little attention to himself."[161] Moreover, Pates had used various means to escape form confinement before, so it was believed by prosecutors that this was but another attempt or deadly ruse by Pates to escape.

Bloody Red

The prosecution, however, suffered from the lack of eyewitnesses to Pates' actions. There were no cameras in that section of the jail and possible witnesses in neighboring cells were dead or could not see into the cell enclosed by a solid steel door. In addition, the prosecutor would possibly have been required to rely upon the testimony of inmates, whom he was also prosecuting for other crimes.

Moreover, the State's evidence or theory was arguably unclear. Was the fire started by a cigarette which was already lighted by Pates or someone else, or by a match which Pates used to ignite debris in his cell?

Pates acknowledged that as the jury deliberated, he was nervous about the potential outcome. Hearing the jury verdict, Pates was ecstatic, turned to his family members attending the trial and proclaimed loudly, "I'm going home." His mother also proclaimed she was thrilled by the verdict. Pates said he wanted to return to college.

After his acquittal, Pates returned to Illinois, and never returned to college. Instead, he was arrested several times in that state and others, before he passed away in 2014, at the age of 63.

Most of the victims' survivors did not accept the jury verdict acquitting Pates. For many, their hearts lurched at the announcement of the verdict, as though it were a nightmare. There were no happy stories or easy answers and many wondered openly about how the city and county could allow this to happen to human beings – caged animals were better treated.

Some, therefore, believed that the government was as responsible for their deaths, if not more so. If Pates did not murder their loved ones, the government did by failing to maintain a jail which would adequately protect them from such a tragedy. The questions would never go away, or doubts were raised, about the actions which the city had taken upon arresting Pates and its alleged negligence and recklessness in the lack of an adequate fire safety system at the jail.

Aftermath

Although Pates' acquittal left the survivors with very little justice to chase in the criminal justice system, there were other remedies and issues which were important to the families and the corrections community. The survivors wanted to make sure that Pates' actions, trial and media coverage, did not overshadow the lives of the victims and those who were seriously affected.

First, it was critical that those persons who risked their lives should be recognized. And certainly, there were heroes. In fact, maybe the most compelling story through this monumental crisis was how all those associated with the jail - jailers, inmates, firefighters and policemen – bonded together to save lives. It gave credence to what social scientist had explored for decades – that in times of crisis and acute stress (such as war and natural disasters), rather than causing conflict and lack of trust, people often bind together, continuing our collective survival.

For example, several of the injured jailers, and first responders fought through the dense smoke to drag inmates or others assisting from the building. Some went into the building even though they were not equipped with breathing devices. Similarly, one of the trusties had lost his life assisting when he could easily have sat on the sidelines. The warden had reentered the building several times, without breathing equipment, seeking to rescue the inmates.

Steve Delahousey, who has continued to work in EMS and serves as the National Federal Liaison Officer for American Medical Response, confirms the story of heroism and unity. "When I arrived the inmates and other first responders were all having difficulty breathing. Biloxi Police Chief Bob Payne (I think we was the chief), kept running back into the building, trying to rescue people, until he too became overcome with the toxic smoke. I tried several times to hold him back and administer oxygen to him, but he kept slipping away and going back into the building. When we finally convinced him to go to the hospital, I recall placing him in one of my ambulances along with a jail inmate. One of the police officers on the scene questioned the logic of placing a law enforcement official in the same ambulance with an inmate. My response was "they are all patients to me". Mr. Payne had "no objection."

Police Officer Chatagnier was also one of those recognized. He earned the Police Department's Metal of Valor for his efforts to save inmates at the jail. In addition, he was hospitalized for four days recovering from smoke inhalation. Similarly, Miller was hospitalized with smoke inhalation after seeking to unlock the cells manually, in the face of the fire and smoke. Officer Leblanc was also hospitalized for smoke inhalation.

Coroner Little also praised the efforts of firemen and law enforcement: "The death toll might have been higher except for the 'quick reaction' of the firemen and law enforcement agencies," he said. He claimed he didn't know of anything that could have been done to save the lives of the dead. "It was one of those stupid things that happen".[162]

In addition, the fire led to several reforms at the jail and at other facilities throughout the country. It was the catalyst for soul searching in the corrections community and beyond, including hearings by Congress on fire safety in commercial buildings.

More poignantly, the fire accelerated changes in Harrison County. Afterwards, the Sheriff's Department installed an automatic fire system in the jail that could open cell doors automatically in the event of a fire.

Guilt and innocence of the dead and injured inmates were no longer the primary concerns of many in the community, including the governor. For instance, one of the inmates had just landed in jail that day for theft of a radio and another had been there for two days, charged with a misdemeanor, while her family sought to raise bail to get her released.

Governor Winter pushed for prison reform. And a federal judge ordered that the state conduct inspections of all of the correctional facilities, as well as ease overcrowding.

As a threshold thought, Bob Farmer, former chief deputy for the Maury County jail, had commented, in retrospect, after the Tennessee fire: "I've had time to think about this. If we'd have electric doors, if we'd have a button to push I would have pushed that button and let them all run. We could catch them later, rather than lose a life."[163]

Finally, within a month, families filed civil damage lawsuits, against the county, State, and local governments, totaling more than $200 million. Initially, the governmental bodies disclaimed responsibility, asserted various defenses regarding others being responsible. As if reflexively, the defendants began to blame one another with, e.g., the county contending it was the state's responsibility to inspect the jails and even arguing that some survivors were not entitled to damages because their loved ones were in incarcerated and thus could not show them much love and affection. Eventually the defendants settled the claims.

Settlement was their only feasible option: it was clear, as the Department of Justice had observed, that the jail was overcrowded and riddled with fire code violations; the prior fires in other states had provided clear markers for what could happen if the code violations and lack of an evacuation plan was not remedied; and the manufacturers of the polyurethane padding had abundant notice of the toxic fumes which could develop from a fire. All of this was compounded by placing a disruptive arrestee in a cell essentially

Bloody Red

with a toxic cocktail of matches and materials, which he utilized to destroy the lives of nearly 30 men and women.

Nevertheless, that was not the only profound thing to occur as a result of the incident. Several investigations also emerged from the killings - one by the state fire marshal, another by the County Board of Supervisors, and a third by the district attorney.

Analysis following the fire revealed that the polyurethane met all government flammability standards, but would burn under certain circumstances. The Biloxi jail had many safety features, including night jailers, a fire alarm system, an emergency lighting system, and a working smoke detection system. However, its design created one dead-end corridor where smoke backed up. Two other corridors were not visible from the jailers' desk. The temporary loss of one set of keys made the manual locking system hazardous. Other hazards were overcrowding and, perhaps, lax enforcement of the rules. In addition, the plans for dealing with large numbers of injured prisoners were inadequate, and security was initially lax at the local hospitals.[164]

The Justice Department, which had received complaints about conditions at the jail at Biloxi and began its investigation several months before tragedy struck, now accelerated its review. In February 1984, a department official testified before the Committee on the Judiciary of the U.S. House of Representatives, and provided the following striking revelation of the department's communications with county officials prior to the fire: *We actually were investigating the Biloxi jail prior to the tragic fire that occurred there and had, indeed, advised the jail authorities prior to that fire that we thought they ought to remove the mattresses and padding that were in the jail because if a fire took place, it could be disastrous for the prisoners. Tragically, a fire did break out and some prisoners were killed.*[165]

319

Bloody Red

One of the critical reports regarding the fire was authored by James R. Bell, who had investigated many of the mass fires in the country during that period.[166] In his final report, he did not absolve the state of responsibility with respect to their actions or lack thereof preceding the fire, writing:

The following major factors contributed to the fatalities and injuries in this fire:

- *Lack of detection and extinguishment of the fire in its incipient stage before it became life-threatening.*
- *Once ignited, the synthetic foam-plastic cell padding material created an intense fire characterized by a rapid rate of burning, high heat release, and a large amount of dense smoke.*
- *Lack of smoke barriers and compartmentation allowed unrestricted spread of smoke throughout the jail.*
- *Inability of jail officers to rapidly release the inmates in all cells in the confinement area, using the key system.*[167]

The Biloxi jail fire was the third deadliest jail or prison fire in history.[168] The deadliest fire in U.S. history had occurred at the Ohio state prison in 1930 in Columbus, when 322 inmates died from smoke inhalation, where jailers refused to unlock their cells.[169] Closer in time, in 1975, 11 inmates died in a Sanford Florida jail, and five years later 10 inmates died in a jail fire in South Carolina.

Corrections officials had previously become aware of the potential danger of jail fires like the one in Biloxi and some had taken steps to avert it, by, for instance, prohibiting mattresses that are not fire retardant. And there had been many articles, trainings and conferences emphasizing fire safety.[170] Indeed, prior to the fire, Harrison County had already started some modifications to the building and its policies, but had not completed its actions.

Bloody Red

Five months earlier, an eerily similar incident had happened in New Jersey:

Perhaps the most painful memory is from April 15, 1982. Early that morning, in the darkness, there was a lighting of matches (an item that was apparently admissible and readily available). A small fire broke out in Cell 8-7 on the eighth floor; attempts to extinguish it were made inside the 20-by-20-foot dormitory cell by seven prisoners. But the flames spread. Security guards on duty attempted to open the cell but were overcome by intense heat and severe smoke. Keys could not be readily located to set the prisoners free, wasting valuable time and causing confusion among arriving firefighters.[171]

The story line was all too familiar. Another strangely similar incident had occurred at Maury County jail in Tennessee in June 1977, five years before the Biloxi jail fire. Then, a 16-year-old had killed 42 persons when he started a blaze in his padded cell. All of the persons there died as a result of the smoke from the burning polyurethane padding in the padded cell. There, both inmates and visitors were killed because the fire occurred during a visitation period; thus, some of the victims were there temporarily as visitors to the one-storied jail.

At Maury, the first indication of the fire came when the teenager in the padded cell yelled, "I'm on fire!". As officers opened the door to the padded cell, flames and heavy black smoke erupted and engulfed the area quickly. Similar to Biloxi, the jailers' keys were lost when in the mass confusion the deputies collided with fleeing visitors and keys were lost to the cellblock and the locked visiting section. It took about 12 minutes for the keys to be found and about an hour before a bulldozer arrived.

The similarities to what occurred in Biloxi were striking. Both jails were made of fire-resistant concrete and cinder block with few

Bloody Red

combustible building materials. For both, there were no sprinkler systems, only fire extinguishers to fight a fire, if one started. More critically, the padding in the padded cells was flammable.

The assailant in Tennessee was described as a "misfit" with mental problems, similar to Robert Pates. Initially, the teenager admitted that he set the fire deliberately. He suffered some burns as a result of the fire. His lawyers later asserted, however, that his actions were not intentional. He eventually pleaded guilty to 42 counts of manslaughter and served 18 months in prison.

Combined Grief and Anger

In the weeks that followed the Biloxi fire, the victims' survivors had competing feelings of grief and anger. Most had probably never heard of the Maury County jail incident, which was similar to the Biloxi killings, or the Oakley prison fire from decades earlier. Instead, they sifted through all of the scenarios wherein their loved one was about to be released or, for some, would only be in for a mere night or two.

On the date of the arraignment, as noted above, family members began to arrive early, in a confrontational and aggressive mood. The survivors were angry because it was like an unfair fight – their loved ones had no way of escaping the fire, in light of the iron bars which were in place to keep them locked in. If it had been so easy to get out some probably would have escaped before the fire. Moreover, Pates had never shown any remorse or concern for their loved ones, whether his actions were intentional or reckless. Instead, he yelled, cursed and stomped around.

The day of judgment finally came – and went - when the jury acquitted Pates. It was a head-scratcher like no other in life. In the end, they believed Pates did not suffer any consequences for his actions. Practically, he could not be sued civilly because he simply had no assets or funds.

There were significant lessons learned and the Biloxi incident has been cited in many scientific, medical and corrections journals, as exemplary of a factual portrayal from which policies and customs may be developed. Thereafter, part of the modified fire safety plans for jails and prisons emphasized the need for saws for steel or concrete, or even a cutting torch and tow trucks. Additionally, the trainings emphasized that staff should become familiar with the many different security devices and systems used in the facility for which they are responsible in protecting persons.

Clayton's death, as well as that of the other inmates', were in many ways unconscionable emotionally. They were trapped! And they were dead within minutes, which probably felt much longer to them. Many probably sensed that they would not survive, after they screamed out for help, since responders were present, but could not help them under the circumstances. But it was also a horrifying and cruel death, physically.

Another author, describing fire deaths in similar circumstances, captures what was likely the horrifying death scenario which Clayton and the other inmates faced:

Prior to death those in the galley would have endured a rising level of fear, bursts of panic that overwhelms the body and mind, as well as a flicker of hope. Others on the brink of death in sudden disasters have testified to the crushing sense of unfairness, disappointment almost, that this is it. The inhalation of smoke would have brought a choking, a burning sensation in the lungs, the build-up of sooty deposits in the nose and throat, but each poisoned breath increased the level of carbon monoxide in the bloodstream which brought about confusion, bewilderment and ultimately unconsciousness.[172]

The Austin family took Clayton's death hard. For his family, the intensity of their pain was triggered by the pain which he endured before succumbing to the smoke, the senselessness of his death, and that he was scheduled to be released to the "free world" in a matter of months. How could this have happened, they thought.

Although living apart at the time and with some financial distress, Clayton's partner, Theola, and their kids' lives took a free fall. They moved from one place to another and suffered great financial strain. Clayton's mother, had waited with great anticipation for his release. She had spent many hours on her knees, in prayer. He had said to her that his mind was not shackled and he had been editing his life. But, suddenly, Bloody was gone. The heaviness of the occasion weighed on her for many years.

Not only Clayton's family – but all victims' families were affected tragically. The families of the 29 other victims also took the deaths of their loved ones hard. Overall, the killings left undetectable psychological wounds for the injured survivors, the families of the dead men and women, as well as the rescuers. The grieving also affected their health. Afterwards, many injured inmates, survivors and family members passed away prematurely. Laura Pyles, for example, who protested valiantly for justice on behalf of her brother, Michael, died upon reaching her early forties.

There were too many unanswered questions and lingering pain for them simply to "get over it", and that is not an appropriate response anyways. They cried out for answers about how this could have happened. There was sadness throughout the community and it had a public face – the one-story, charred, jail house. The psychology of collective sentiments and communal grief was most evident at the court proceedings, however, where they cried and protested together.

Only two months later, 16 of the surviving women jail inmates from Biloxi were subject to another fire, while housed at the women's side in Parchman. But they survived again, with one inmate having been hospitalized in both incidents. This was eerily similar since one of the guards there shouted that he could not find the keys to unlock the cell doors and corrections officials believed it was the result of arson, and thus an intentional attempt to kill.

Several of the surviving inmates and rescuers reported that they still had bad dreams about that horrible early morning, even many years later, reliving the screams of the deceased as they begged for help. Some family members recall reliving the tragedy even years later, claiming to smell smoke and seeing them die.

Addressing this issue, Delahousey says that he continues to think about the Biloxi fire. For years afterwards, he often spoke about the incident with his father, who was a police officer on the scene. Even though he became the county coroner in 1984, investigated thousands of deaths, and disasters throughout the country, the fire at the jail, about a mile from his home, stands out. "This was the first time I'd seen 27 dead bodies from a single event, so it was etched into my memory."

The catastrophe demonstrated, however, the positive side of humankind. If only for the hour while the incident transpired, people's actions transcended all of the other things which may have divided them before the fire - race, class, poverty, status, etc. On that early morning, they acted in concert to save the lives of their fellow human beings, with inmates and trusties working with jailers and first responders. As the adage goes, the worst of times often brings out the best in people.

Nevertheless, despite the victims being jail inmates, and some having been convicted of felonies, it still represented the taking of the lives of innocent people, whom neither a court nor jury had decided they deserved the death penalty! Thus, the lives of the inmates and their jailers and rescuers became intertwined for life - and it still haunts the survivors.

Bloody Red

The lives of the victims' families were splattered. Similarly, and symbolically, scattered throughout the debris in the aftermath of the fire were chess and checkers sets, inmate clothing, and novels and bibles. Tellingly, one inmate had written Psalm 23 of the Bible on one notebook page in his cell, which was still visible and protected from the flames:

The Lord is my shepherd, I lack nothing.
He makes me lie down in green pastures,
He leads me beside quiet waters,
he refreshes my soul.
He guides me along the right paths
for his name's sake.
Even though I walk
through the darkest valley,

I will fear no evil, for you are with me;
your rod and your staff,
they comfort me.

That said, and engraved in the minds of the survivors, it is noted that more than thirty-five years have passed since the Biloxi fire. Clayton's sister, Eudith, offers this closing perspective: *It has been about thirty-five years since my brother was killed. Although what happened seems like a fairy tale or television program, it was real and lasting. While the pain, anger and frustration have subsided, I still am reminded of the tragic incident from time-to-time. The horror of such a death can not be understated nor understood. What is most troublesome is that there was no resultant justice applied to either the killer or the officials. And there is no time limit on injustice and the pain which it causes. It will always stick out as an ugly scar on the state and city. Luv u Bubba!*

CHAPTER 8
GENERAL EULOGY AND HONOR

Pain and Grief

A much less obscure issue, aside from its obvious sensationalism, is the psychological effects of murder. Survivors often articulate or act out their grief and pain. It has been shown that the process of grieving changes as it changes survivors.[173]

Nearly anything can trigger the memory of the murder and the resulting pain. Survivors relate how even the ringing of the phone at wee hours causes flashbacks. Birthdays, holidays, and other deaths can cause a rush of emotion. A media piece concerning murder can similarly cause an emotional setback.

In part, we often live with illusions of immortality or that it simply will not happen unexpectedly to us or the ones we love so dearly. We feel this way despite the fact that, for some, their friends had been slain, shot or suffered permanent injuries before they were themselves killed. Or they were involved in high risk lifestyles or in a drug culture. But for many they were going about life as most of us do - normally.

It presents one of life's challenges for which you cannot prepare. For the survivors and loved ones, nothing in life prepared them for this. There are no classes or seminars which could ever mimic the raw feelings from such an untimely, unforeseen tragedy. This even applies to families who suffer multiple homicide victims over time.

Like the recent television commercial regarding if we knew we were going to suffer a heart attack that day we would have taken the appropriate medication, hardly any victim woke up believing they would be murdered. As one mother put it, related to her

Eulogy

personal tragedy related to her son, Armstrong: "If I had known that morning when I talked to my son it was going to be for the last time, I would've taken him and held him in my arms and kept him with me all day," Armstrong's mother, Doris Hayes, told the court before turning her attention to Adams [the murderer].[174]

It is an irrevocable act, so no matter how sorry the killer professes, it may not help. It is not like a marriage where someone cheats, or an accident where a leg is broken and "sorry" or an apology or monetary damages helps the healing process.

There is almost always collateral damage associated with murder - a shrapnel effect. Long range, the murders may affect existing as well as future attachments and relationships for survivors.

Murder results in a convulsion of stressors. With the ultimate violation of mankind, comes grief like no other. It encompasses not only dealing with your own feelings but dealing with the feelings and reactions of others, whether they are family, friends or strangers. A common assumption, often erroneous, is that their deaths were the result of being involved in some illegal activity.

Less obvious to many are the long-range effects of the killings on survivors, i.e., life beyond the burial of the victims. Just as you cannot begin a story in the middle you also can not end it in the middle (the death of the victims). Funerals are not the end of the story.

This intrusion into survivors' lives is unwelcome, serious and immediate. They often ask themselves, "Now what do I do with the rest of my life?"

How do You Get Past What You May Never Get Over?

One mother, surviving the murder of her son in the Washington D.C. area, says she struggles with and lives by the credo of "how to get past what she will never get over". Mental health

Eulogy

professionals have advised her that realistically it will take a lifetime for her to cope with her son's murder. She attempts to cope with her grief by helping others who have suffered similar tragedies.

Mental health and support groups identify certain stages of grief. It means coping or struggling with a stream of competing concerns: anger, guilt, addressing holidays and anniversaries and birthdays, and the criminal justice and judicial systems. It is a shock to everything normal about life. However, behavioral scientists, criminologists and various professionals have not been able to provide a complete answer to the question of "why"; thus, there is no holy grail upon which law enforcement or behavioral professionals can rely in either predicting who will commit homicides.

Like what occurs with other less serious, stressful circumstances, the mind becomes singularly focused, not allowing the grieving person to cope with any other life functions. That grief can turn into anger or depression.

The range of emotions spans from guilt to anger. For some survivors, the anger never goes away. There is guilt from not shielding or protecting loved ones, to not being able to move on with their lives. Just as their loved ones were removed, they became invisible. They felt betrayed by those whom they thought cared and would be there in support for them, but were not.

Centuries ago, in many cultures it was customary for a victim's family to avenge his murder or retaliate against the killer. Even now, for some, retaliation is expected because of "rules of the game", cultural norms, or lack of confidence in the judicial system. Survivors are often left waiting for justice. In contrast to physical and emotional pain, there is often gross frustration with the criminal justice system.

Eulogy

Often the emotional pain is replaced by the hunger for justice. Many are still wondering when justice will come. There is not a long road to justice for some survivors – instead, the road has been washed out. For them, more than 20 years have transpired without even a telephone call or further inquiry from police or prosecutors.

Many never attend a trial because the murderer was never arrested; but that does not mean authorities do not know the identity of the killer. Then for some, their loved one's case became a cold case and justice never comes because a perpetrator was never identified or prosecuted. Even for others, where there was a prosecution, justice did not end with the trial, since there was an acquittal or, in their view, an unjust sentence.

A flurry of questions often invades their brain. They ask: Does this mean that my brother, sister or cousin was not important enough to warrant a more informed and detailed investigation? Did my brother's or father's investigation end on the night of his murder or the following week?

The portrait is that of a long, tortured grief. For some it is hard to break through the silence. Some have even suggested that they live under the philosophy that death stalks life, and it is not unusual.

A mother never stops being a mother even in death – her grief simply lasts a lifetime. There is no way to measure the hurt and despair for the families of victims or even that of those convicted.

Some only can trust their spirituality – God is their refuge. They then answer the questions of "why", solely on a spiritual basis. The sermon notebook is consulted to soothe the pain of family, friends and loved ones. For others, their faith is not deep enough to get them through grief.

As noted above, murders have communal effects on some neighborhoods more than others. According to some theorists,

Eulogy

these neighborhoods also appear to cope with murders by relying more heavily on friends and family and spiritual connections than on formal or government support networks.

It is a bit sterile to believe that people fall solely or merely into one personality category. The intersection of bad guy and good guy is difficult for many to understand, but it exists as a survival mechanism for many. As a result, some of those in urban environments (urban survivalists) tend to characterize the issue of good and bad quite differently.

The Children

Most problematic is a killing's affect upon the victim's surviving children. Murder almost always leaves young children in its wake. Many leave behind young children who only have a photograph as a "daddy". And children appear to suffer the effects in a different, more perplexing, manner than adults and sometimes are referred to as forgotten grievers.

Profound emotional reactions may occur in children. These reactions include anxiety attacks, chronic fatigue, depression and thoughts of suicide. An obsession with the deceased is also a common reaction to death.

Because we live through our children – it also murders our dreams – because it is instinctual to want to protect kids. Murder permeates everything, from school to putting children to bed at night.

Even when one of their family is not victimized, children have been seriously impacted. They are often at the scenes as police investigate, remove the body, and remember the reactions of the victim's family and friends at the scene.

According to a recent report concerning the effect of the exposure of violence on children in New Orleans, the researchers found that violence can: (a) cause premature cellular aging through the shortening and fraying of the tips at the end of chromosomes (relying upon the American Association of Pediatrics) which can cause heart disease, diabetes and mental illness; and (b) impair the immune system, which can cause permanent damage to their ability to fight off diseases (relying upon the American Psychology Association).[175]

And how do you respond to the victim's kids when they ask where is daddy or what happened to my daddy? These are horrifying questions without simple answers.

The Cleveland Clinic has published a resource which identifies some of the common fears and questions which children raise, after a family member was murdered, e.g.:

- What happened?
- Was it my fault?
- Did I do something bad?
- Am I going to die?
- Will others I love die?
- Who will take care of me?
- What does dead mean?
- Where do people go when they die?
- Where is heaven?
- Don't people get cold, hungry, or scared underground?
- Why would God take him/her away?
- When is (deceased's name) coming back?[176]

Symbiotic Connection between Grief and Health

For some survivors, the grief is too much and they die much sooner than they would have otherwise. The saying by many survivors has become common - "when he killed my son, he killed me too." This is beyond a mere aphorism.

The nexus between human emotional and physical states is

Eulogy

indisputable. Thus, the connection between the psychological and the physical is exposed. As a result, survivors often suffer physical symptoms such as sleep disturbance, intestinal upsets, and fatigue. They express, "I am weary". Their preexisting conditions may worsen or new conditions develop for which they were not previously disposed.

Generally, research has found that grief increases the grievant's susceptibility to disease, aggravates physical pain, raises blood pressure, and increases the risk of a stroke or heart attack, particularly within the first few months of loss.

The medical and mental health communities have drawn distinctions between "normal" and "complicated" (traumatic) grief. Those suffering traumatic stress have poorer mental and physical health. Unfortunately, those who had the greatest levels of grief were less likely to seek medical help.[177]

More critically, research has shown that survivors of homicide victims have a higher risk factor for illness and dying early.[178] The emotional stressors can weaken the heart and body. It can lead to what is classically referred to as a "broken heart." Medically, it is real and termed broken heart syndrome. This syndrome is often misdiagnosed as a heart attack because the symptoms and test results are similar. The difference is that in contrast to a heart attack, the patient's heart arteries are not blocked.

In broken heart syndrome, a part of your heart temporarily enlarges and does not pump well, while the rest of your heart functions normally or with even more forceful contractions. Researchers are just starting to learn the causes, and how to diagnose and treat it.

When family members of murder victims die, it may not be attributed to the killing, although it is linked medically. Correspondingly, because family members often die as a result of

Eulogy

the stress and grief, it breeds survivors of survivors, because those family and friends who die then leave an additional set of survivors.

The Financial Side

Aside from the devastating loss of human life, there is also a significant financial side to coping with the loss of a loved one or being a victim of a nonfatal shooting. The financial byproduct is usually unknown to the public and hardly discussed.

There have been various studies and reports which have sought to gauge or estimate the costs of murder, and more particularly gun violence. One often cited study concluded that every murder costs society $10-12 million. A more recent study by Iowa State University Sociology Professor Matt DeLisi concluded that each murder costs society about $17.25 million per offense.[179] Even these studies do not account for the long-range costs to survivors. Aside from the loss of human lives, the economic cost for victims, and concomitantly their families, is staggering. The costs associated with gun violence alone is estimated to be $228 billion annually.[180] The cost to survivors or co-victims is often difficult, if not impossible, to track or account for. Undoubtedly, the expenses related solely to the survivors are overwhelming.

Although the government bears the expense of most homicide victims, because they were uninsured, some are left to be paid by the survivors, usually tens of thousands of dollars. Less recognized or publicized are the costs associated with mental health and counseling for the survivors. For instance, in its series concerning the costs of gun violence, *Mother Jones* describes the plight of one survivor whose 18-year-old son was murdered.

The mother revealed: *The few hours when Terrell clung to life in the hospital cost about $10,000, which was mostly covered by the family's health insurance. Later, Bosley spent thousands of dollars out of pocket on therapy and antidepressants for herself and*

Eulogy

another family member, who was hospitalized at one point for depression. Bosley also lost several thousand dollars in earnings during a six-month leave of absence from her operations job at a bank. ... She twice attempted suicide. "I could be okay one hour, then the next minute I could look at something and be broken down," she says. She regained some balance, but when she returned to her job, her coworkers' chatter about their kids, and her memories of Terrell visiting her at work, were too much to bear. She took a job at another bank.[181]

The cost to the family: $23,500.

Consequences for Perpetrators

On the left-hand side of the equation, perpetrators have also left devastating consequences for their families. Since they have precipitated the violence and caused the grief and pain, the consequences of their actions cannot be viewed equally to that of the victims' survivors. Nonetheless, it still amounts to further communal suffering, pain and societal issues.

Although perpetrators have acted based upon their own rules and peculiar notions of truth or justice, or even mental incompetency, it hurts those who love or are close to them.

Many of the killers come from broken families, some suffer from mental health or psychological infirmities, yet others emerge from stable, well-functioning families. Nevertheless, their families often have to absorb the shock, guilt and embarrassment of their actions. They act without consideration of the harm to their parents or siblings and the stigma and isolation which their acts may cause for their loved ones.

For some, even though they may know and lived with a different side of the killer's personality, it is difficult to reconcile those personality traits with taking the life of another human being. In some instances, killing another human being constitutes a badge of

Eulogy

honor or respect. Even then, there are family members who are seriously scarred or subject to retaliation. And there are usually no assistance or social programs designed to address their psychological problems.

As I have sometimes commented to youth about the consequences of violence or murder, along these lines: "Do you want to send your mama to prison, because that's what your crime does? She is the one who often cannot sleep, wondering whether you are okay in prison, or are going to be victimized in retaliation. She is the one most often riding the blue (or whatever color) prison bus to visit you, oftentimes your only visitor? From your "boys" perspective, you are "hood dead" and out of mind. She has to sacrifice her meager funds to finance your prison "account". Did you even imagine, just a little, the tremendous pain which would fall on her with you being in prison? She is the one, in some instances left attempting to apologize to the victim's family or shunning neighbors who look at her disapprovingly. Well, when you killed that other person, and indirectly their family, you also shortened or took your mother's life!"

In the event that the victim was a child, or killed by a serial killer or mass murderer, the perpetrator's family may be ridiculed, shunned or rejected, or lose their job. For instance, the mother of Lee Malvo, who was convicted of killing 10 persons and responsible for possibly 17 other murders, contends she was ostracized and fired from her job as a result of his actions. Even more problematic are instances where victims' families or fellow gang members have retaliated by murdering the killer's mother.

The lesson or reasoning continues: "What about the impact of imprisonment on your children? Was the disrespect someone exhibited towards you enough to trade that for a lifetime of disrespect by others in prison. Who's going to protect or guide your children while you do all of that time? Why should they be punished for your selfish actions? You are also putting your son or daughter at a huge disadvantage economically, because children who have parents in jail are more likely to be impoverished and have to turn to crimes themselves. By the time you get out, if you get out, will their lives be ruined?

Even if only limited to their children, the effects are distressing. The research shows, among other things, that children of imprisoned inmates, have issues related to progress in schools, problems with attachment and separation to loved ones, and diminished cognitive abilities.[182] It operates primarily through antisocial adjustment and behavioral problems in children, rather than cognitive abilities.[183]

Recovery

Killings shatter families and communities. Each death claims or enraptures other people along the way. There is an entire industry behind every death, including those deaths which are the result of murder. There are a blizzard of people surrounding murders, including government and private services, as well as entrepreneurs. There are the homicide detectives, and clean-up crews, doctors and nurses, and morgue personnel and funeral directors, and florists, and ministers, and burial site administrators, and balloon and teddy bear manufacturers, and now RIP T-shirts, life-size cut outs, and poster producers and video technicians.

In fact, there are some whose job is to work with death every day, such as personnel for the various medical examiner offices and funeral directors. How does it affect them and how can they do it with the required level of sensitivity?

Sheila Garner, writer and minister, opines that homicide survivors' grief is similar to others, but they tend to gain a close relationship with God, which helps them recover sooner.

Eulogy

Although there have been numerous local initiatives regarding reducing murders, the FBI or federal government has not set forth initiatives on a national level. The reasoning for lack of a national plan is that it is reasoned that murder is a local phenomenon with unique characteristics and factors in each locale. The federal government has funded research at the local level to address those concerns but, as noted below, the funding has been insufficient.

On a national level, the CDC has declared murders from gunshots a national public health crisis, elevating the discussion beyond criminal justice observers and experts. Prosecutors' offices and state legislators have also embraced the establishment of grief and victims' assistance units. These units usually have victim coordinators and provide booklets to survivors regarding how to place their loved ones' deaths in perspective and where to obtain assistance.

For instance, the United States Attorney's Office for the District of Columbia, publishes a handbook for survivors of homicide victims. One page from the booklet reads as follows:

The death of a loved one is deeply painful. Grief is a common experience. People experience grief when they leave familiar places, when they divorce, when someone they love dies. But grief for families of murder victims is different. It is more intense, it lasts longer, and is more complicated. [184]

There also has been a dramatic and significant shift recently in how the media reports about murders and their expanding effects in many locales. The media in cities such as New Orleans, Chicago, Los Angeles and Wilmington, Delaware, have started to better profile homicide and humanize victims and the impact of their deaths on survivors; all being cities with histories of the traumatizing effects of gun violence on their populace.

Eulogy

For some sensational murders, the media attention has been both helpful and hurtful. This is one factor which distinguishes murders from other deaths; what would normally be a private matter becomes public, along with the loss of privacy. In commenting on the police shootings of Alton Sterling and Philando Castile, Michael Brown's mother commented:

Death isn't pretty for anyone, but what these families now face is the horror of seeing their loved one die over and over, in public, in such a violent way. They face the helplessness of having strangers judge their loved one not on who he was or what he meant to his family but on a few seconds of video. Mr. Sterling died in a very lonely way, surrounded by his killers. Can you imagine a lonelier death? Mr. Castile died with his girlfriend and her young daughter watching as he was gunned down.[185]

Aside from the government programs and more sensitized media attention, citizens, particularly mothers, have turned pain and grief into purpose. They have used the tragedies to help others deal with murder and violence. One example is the mother in the San Francisco area who embraced such role after emerging from years of depression caused by the murders of her 22-year-old twin sons in 2000. She created the nonprofit, 1,000 Mothers to Prevent Violence, serving as a counselor, pastor, diplomat and advocate. Another father in Los Angeles used his son's murder as a catalyst for him to broker a peace treaty between rival gangs.

Similarly, in Charlotte, North Carolina, mothers created Mothers of Murdered Offspring to support families through the cycle of grief and devastation that murder causes, and created support programs and activities that focus on the prevention of violence.

Others work on gun violence prevention, such as Philadelphia-based, Mothers in Charge or Moms Demand Action.[186] Often bringing together women from different backgrounds, it provides

Eulogy

grief support, public education, and on the other side, working with anger management in schools and with prisoners. Even those who have sought to be peace interventionists, however, have sacrificed their lives and become victims of gun violence, such as a former gang member who had tried to bring rival gangs together.[187]

These efforts are consistent with research and studies which show that homicide survivors often "seek to benefit others or give significance to the survivor's life."[188]

Murder Wall, Saint Anna's Episcopal Church, New Orleans

Then there are even a few unusually courageous or uncanny stories of parents forgiving their sons' murderers, and openly forming a relationship with them.

And there are the many commemorative digital murder walls or crosses, such as those at churches such as St. Sabina's in Chicago, Highland Baptist Church in Louisville, and St. Anna's Episcopal church in New Orleans, and at municipal parks, such as those in Houston, Texas, and Orlando, Florida. They reflect the communities' cognitive lens and conscience.

Eulogy

Forgiveness

Some survivors have privately forgiven the killers, believing that they must do so based upon religious tenets or moral reasons. Others have perceived forgiveness as driven by a survival instinct rather than compassion, because it is the first step to moving forward with their lives.

Some families have gone beyond private forgiveness and responded with amazing redemption publicly, forgiving the murderers or those charged with the murder. One of the more notable instances of forgiveness involved some of the relatives of the victims who were killed inside the historic Emanuel African Methodist Episcopal Church in Charleston, S.C. At the killer's bond hearing, they did not speak in anger. Instead, they offered him forgiveness and said to him and the court that they were praying for his soul, even as they described the pain of their losses. Again, at his sentencing, prior to him being sentenced to death, and speaking to him directly, they offered forgiveness.

For instance, the response of the family of Tyson Gay, world class and Olympic sprinter, to the murder of his 15-year old daughter, who was killed as an innocent bystander in Lexington, Kentucky, was similarly noteworthy. The family released a statement which proclaimed, "The family appreciates the outpouring of support during the loss of our beautiful Trinity. She will be truly missed by all. She touched so many people on so many different levels. We ask for your continued prayers and privacy during this difficult time."

The family added that, "We are a family that believes in love and forgiveness. We are also asking for prayers for the 3 men accused and their families during what is also a difficult time for them."

Another noteworthy stroke of forgiveness was offered by the mother of Cherica Adams, a pregnant mother who was murdered

Eulogy

by NFL player Rae Carruth. As a result of the murder, Cherica's and Rae's son was born prematurely and with cerebral palsy. Saundra Adams says she has forgiven Carruth for selfish reasons, so that she can love her grandson unconditionally. She also intends to bring her grandson to the prison on the day of Carruth's release, so that Carruth can see his son and the fine young man he has grown to be.

In a recent murder which was aired live on Facebook by the killer, who chose his victim randomly in Cleveland, the victim's family, amazingly and quickly, responded with an olive branch of forgiveness. One of the victim's daughters (Tonya Godwin-Baines), speaking for the family, said: "Each one of us forgives the killer, the murderer," …"We want to wrap our arms around him."

One of the more memorable instances of hate and forgiveness came from Martin Luther King's father, in commenting on the murders of both his son and his wife and that he did not hate either murderer. "Nothing a man does takes him lower than when he allows himself to hate someone".[189]

One of the surviving mothers, relates how her spirit of forgiveness, was constructed, brick by brick, so to speak. When she went to her minister for assistance after her son was murdered, he reminded her of forgiveness and how the perpetrator's family did not have a voice. Then she attended a rally for survivors of homicide victims, where one victim's mother discussed how she sought out the killer's mother in order to comfort her, because she knew that she was likewise in pain.

Even more amazing or odd instances, are stories of mothers who not only have forgiven their sons murderers but actually become parts of their lives. The story of Mary Johnson and Oshea Israel is one such story. Israel killed Johnson's 20-year-old son when he was 16 years old. While in prison, she visited him and forgave him.

Eulogy

They made peace. When he was released from prison, she assisted him in getting an apartment - next door to where she lived.

Moreover, murderers who have asked for pardon or forgiveness report feeling relieved or unburdened by their request and training on repentance. In a *New York Times Magazine* story about national reconciliation in Rwanda between victims and survivors of genocide, amazingly the formalized reconciliation process by a non-profit organization met with amazing success, wherein if forgiveness was granted both parties agreed to be photographed together and many went forward to establish relationships. The statement of one of the perpetrators exemplified the thought process of some of those who wreaked havoc on their fellow countrymen: **Ndahimana**: *"The day I thought of asking pardon, I felt unburdened and relieved. I had lost my humanity because of the crime I committed, but now I am like any human being."*[190]

Shaka Senghor, convicted of murder and having served 19 years in a Michigan prison, adds to the level of forgiveness he believes appropriate. He had this to say about forgiveness:

People had told me about the power of forgiveness, but it had taken me until now to understand that forgiveness wasn't only about letting other people off the hook. It was about me. I had to free myself from the anger, fear and hurt of my past. I had to forgive the people I hated. Most important I had to forgive myself.

In a letter to the victim (although deceased), he wrote: *saying I am sorry for robbing you and your family of your life seems too small of a gesture. .... I know that saying I'm sorry can never restore your life. But I believe in the power of atonement, and I have taken responsibility for my actions by dedicating my life and talents to making amends for the pain I have brought into this world.*[191]

In their last statements, condemned prisoners usually express love to their families and those who have represented or assisted them.

Eulogy

Some are contrite, others still defiant, and others are philosophical. Then there are those who refuse to make any last statements or more simply express having found God in their lives. Some however, address the families of victims and express sorrow or ask for forgiveness. Below, is an example:

To the victims, I'm very sorry for everything that happened. I am not the malicious person that you think I am. I was real stupid back then. I made a great many mistakes. What happened was wrong. I was a kid in a grown man's world. I messed up, and I can't take it back. I wasn't old enough to understand. Please don't carry around that hurt in your heart. You have got to find a way to get rid of the hate. Trust me, killing me is not going to give you closure. I hope you find closure. Don't let that hate eat you up, find a way to get past it.

.... To the victims again, I hate the way all of this happened to ya'll. I don't think any good will come of this. I am going to see ya'll again. I love ya'll, be strong for me. Keep your heads up. ... Warden, go ahead. I am sorry for the victim's family. Murder isn't right, killing of any kind isn't right. Got to find another way.

Beunka Adams – Texas inmate, Last Statement on day of execution, April 26, 2012

On the other hand, forgiveness is against the natural instincts of man and not wanting, or having the capacity, to forgive does not mean a survivor is a bad person. It may simply mean it is not healing for them at that time or they feel they can only do it if they are not pressured by others to forgive. Forgiveness, they reason, may be more important to the person applying the pressure than the survivor who is victimized.

Others believe spiritually that they do not have the power to forgive, because only the victim can do such. And since the victim was killed, it renders murder unforgivable. Under some religious

Eulogy

tenets, the consequences are more dire: the family of the victim may: pardon the killer; request monetary compensation; or take the life of the perpetrator.

Additionally, some survivors believe they are not in a position to forgive because the truth of what happened is elusive, or that forgiving is a betrayal of full justice on behalf of their loved one.

What to Say and Not Say

A difficulty most of us share is how to respond to a survivor or what to say. One survivor offers some of her thoughts:

For those who don't know what to say...
PLEASE, don't ask me if I'm over it yet.
I'll never be over it.
PLEASE, don't tell me they're in a better place.
They aren't here with me now....
PLEASE, don't tell me you know how I feel,
Unless you have lost a loved one this way.[192]

Seeking to have the rest of the public understand her feelings concerning the loss of a child, one mother eloquently shares the following: *There is no "moving on," or "getting over it." There is no bow, no fix, no solution to my heartache. There is no end to the ways I will grieve and for how long I will grieve. There is no glue for my broken heart, no exilir for my pain, no going back in time. For as long as I breathe, I will grieve and ache and love my son with all my heart and soul. There will never come a time where I won't think about who my son would be, what he would look like, and how he would be woven perfectly into the tapestry of my family. I wish people could understand that grief lasts forever because love lasts forever; that the loss of a child is not one finite event, it is a continuous loss that unfolds minute by minute over the course of a lifetime.*[193]

Or the sentiments may not be as polished, but just as impactful, as

Eulogy

the views of one mother in Chicago who lost her son to gunfire:

Theres no words that can or will ever shine lite on thiz senseless situation. Thers a part of me that has been taken, n it will never and cannot be replaced! I cant even explain how much my son, meant to me, to us, to people, to individuals, to family, and to friends, he wasnt just no ordinary young man, he was like my, and our sunshine to a dying flower, he made me bloom on my worse days when no one else could. The pain I have had since the call on Feb 25, 2011, at round 2p.m., will "stain my heart for life" I work in the medical field so I just knew that I could make it there to save him and everything would be ok, but no, I arrived to a dark tunnel.

T. Collins.[194]

ENDNOTES

Introduction

[1] Connolly, J., & Gordon, R., *Co-victims of homicide: A Systemic Review of the Literature*, Trauma, Violence and Abuse, 2015 Vol 164(4), 494-505, http://citeseerx.ist.psu.edu/viewdoc/download?doi=10.1.1.957.5718&rep=rep1&type=pdf.

[2] See, Samuels, A., *Weeping for Her Sons, from Africa to the streets of Boston, Cape Verdean Mother tries to stop a wave of violence*, Ebony, (Feb 10, 2008) 123, Vol 63 No. 4 (also discusses how one mother in Boston area has lost 2 sons and three nephews to murder).

[3] Vega, C., *Richmond family grieves for 4 dead sons*, August 18, 2009 ABC7News, file:///Richmond%20 family%20grieves%20for%20four%20dead%20sons%20_%20abc7news.com.htm.; Reckdahl, C., *Gun violence claims all four sons in one New Orleans family*, NOLA.com, (February 3, 2012), http://www.nola.com/crime /index.ssf/ 2012 /02/gun_violence_claims_all_four_s.html; Lucie, C., WSB-TV Atlanta, *Mother pleads for end to violence after losing 3 sons*(Aug 20, 2012), http://www.wsbtv.com/news/local/mother-pleads-end-violence-after-losing-3-sons/242921807; Corley, C., NPR, *Gun Violence Robs Chicago Mother of 4th Child* (Feb. 5, 2013), http://www.npr.org/2013/02/05/171130943/gun-violence-robs-chicago-mother-of-remaining-child.

[4] Hertz, D. *The Debate Over Crime Rates is Ignoring the Metric That Matters Most: 'Murder Inequality,* The Trace, 'https://www.thetrace.org/2016/07/crime-rates-american-cities-murder-inequality/ (July 25, 2016).

[5] Dukmasova, M., *A Young Chicago Woman Has Lost 23 Loved Ones to Gun Violence. She Wants You to See Their Faces,* The Trace (March 28, 2016), UPDhttps://www.thetrace.org/2016/03/chicago-woman-loses-23-loved-ones-gun-violence/.

[6] See Webster, R. & Bullington, J., *The 28*, NOLA.com (June 14, 2018) https://projects.nola.com/the-children-of-central-city/the-28/#incart_big-photo.

[7] McLaughlin, E., *New Orleans violence 'beyond the pale of reason and sanity',* CNN (April 18, 2016) http://www.cnn.com/2016/04/18/us/new-orleans-will-smith-causes-of-violence/.

[8] Ivers, D., *In Newark schools, coping with violence a tragic matter of routine,*http://www.nj.com/essex/index.ssf/2014/11/in_newark_schools_coping_with_violence_a_tragic_matter_of_routine.html NJ.com (Nov. 20, 2014).

Endnotes

[9] Lazara, G., *Las Vegas man knew many of the Orlando shooting victims* (Jun 13, 2016) 13 ABC Action News, http://www.ktnv.com/news/las-vegas-man-knew-many-of-the-orlando-shooting-victims.

[10] Not only do certain communities suffer greater numbers of murder, but also far fewer clearances than the remainder of the country. In a detailed investigative report, the Washington Post analyzed more than 50,000 homicides nationally from 50 of the nation's largest cities, and identified the places in dozens of American cities "where murder is common but arrests are rare." Referring to these areas as "pockets of impunity", it found that there were areas with virtually no arrests, let alone convictions. In these areas, the arrests rates were made less than 33 percent of the time. Identifying further disparity, it noted: "An arrest was made in 63 percent of the killings of white victims, compared with 48 percent of killings of Latino victims and 46 percent of the killings of black victims. Almost all of the low-arrest zones are home primarily to low-income black residents." Lowery, W, Kelly,K, Mellnik, T., Rich, S., *Where Killings Go Unsolved*, The Washington Post (D.C., June 10, 2018): A.1.

[11] See, Daniels, A.K., *"City's Violence can take hidden toll*, Baltimore Sun (Dec. 14, 2014) at 21; https://www.aaas.org /sites/ default/files/BaltSun%20 Collateral%20Damage%20series% 20(2)% 20(1).pdf; C. Shawn McGuffey, & Tanya L. Sharpe, Ph.D., *Racial Appraisal: an integrated Cultural and Structural Response to African American Experiences with Violent Trauma*, Journal of Sociology and Social Work, December 2015, Vol. 3, No. 2, pp. 55-61; http://jsswnet.com/journals/jsswOne.

[12] See, Myers, J., *Notes on the Murder of Thirty of My Neighbors - 00.03 (Part Four);* The Atlantic Monthly *(*March 2000*); Volume 285, No. 3;* page 72-86 *(*discussing murders occurring in neighborhood near Capitol Hill).

[13] This narrative discusses the lives of 7 victims and a sequel will discuss other victims.

[14] http://www.murderdata.org/p/blog-page.html.

[15] One study estimated that between 2006 and 2014, there were more than 700,000 emergency room visits for firearm-related injuries, with about 8 percent dying during their visit. See, Gani, F., Sakran, J.V. & Canner, J.K., *Emergency Department Visits for Firearm-Related Injuries in The United States, 2006–14,* Health Affairs (Oct. 2017).

[16] CDC, *Nonfatal Injury Reports, 2001-2014,* https:// webappa.cdc. gov/ sasweb/ncipc/nfirates2001.html.

[17] Redelings, M, Lieb L, & Sorvillo F, *Years off your life? The effects of homicide on life expectancy by neighborhood and race/ethnicity in Los Angeles county,* J Urban Health. 2010 Jul;87(4):670-6.

[18] For instance, in Miami-Dade County for the period 2004-2007, 76% of the Black, Non-Hispanic homicide victims were within the 18-24-year-old age category. See, Velis, E., *Victim's profile analysis reveals homicide affinity*

Endnotes

for minorities and the youth, J. Injury & Violence Res.2(2), 67-74, 71 (Jun., 2010).

[19] As Borck puts it, when it comes to the deceased: "We are their last physicians." https://www.theguardian.com/lifeandstyle/2016/aug/31/new-york-city-deaths-chief-medical-examiner-job.

[20] *Carruth v. State*, 165 So.3d 627, 635 (Ala. Cr. App. 2014).

[21] Mattiuzzi, P., http://www.everydaypsychology.com/2008/07/, why-do-people-kill-typology-of-violent.html#. V7cu1 TVWOA8.

[22] See, e.g., December 11, 2014 *Bowman guilty of 1st-degree murder in wine steward's slaying*, Posted by Sara Jean Green, http://blogs.seattletimes.com/today/2014/12/bowman-guilty-of-1st-degree-murder-in-wine-stewards-slaying/; Conley. A., *Omaha man was killed execution-style as target practice, police officer testifies,* Omaha World-Herald (Mar 2, 2017), http://www.omaha.com/news/crime/omaha-man-was-killed-execution-style-police-officer-testifies/article _8289e574-fe9e-11e6-834b-eb410d598b06.html.

[23] See, e.g., United States v. Romeo Blackman (Goonie Boss gang), for, among other things, 10 murders in 3 years (federal indictment for racketeering, Oct. 2018).

[24] UPI, *He Regretted his Life*, St. Petersburg Times, (Nov. 5, 1975) at 2.

Chapter 1

[25] For a discussion of sundown towns, see Loewen, J., *Sundown Towns, A Hidden dimension of Segregation in America* (New Press 2005).

[26] See, http://www.michaelcorcoran.net/archives/1688.

[27] Armstrong, J.B., *Mary Turner and the Memory of Lynching* (UGA Press 2011), at 273.

[28] Byrd's murder eventually led to Congress passing anti-hate legislation, which was signed into law by President Obama in 2009.

[29] Lyman, R., *Man Guilty of Murder in Texas Dragging Death*, NY Times (Feb.4, 1999).

[30] See, *Young v. Pierce*, 628 F.Supp. 1037 (E.D. Tex. 1985).

[31] *Young v. Pierce*, 822 F.2d 1368, 1373 (5th Cir.1987).

[32] *Fair Housing Issues, Hearings Before the Subcommittee on Civil and Constitutional Rights*, 103rd Congress, 2d Session, (Sept. 28, 1994), at 404.

[33] *HUD & Ross Dennis v. Edith Marie Johnson*, HUDALJ-06-93-1262-8 (Jul.26, 1994).

[34] NY Times, *Weary of the Hostility, a City's Blacks Will Go* (Aug. 29, 1993).

[35] Pressley, S.A., *A New Residence and a Tragedy*, Wash. Post (Sept. 3, 1993).

[36] See, *Who Is Responsible?* The Galveston Daily News, (Sept. 5, 1993) at

Endnotes

p.6 (Vidor's mayor crying about Bomber's murder, saying it was not possible to control individuals' mouths).

[37] *Hale v. Texas Knights of the Ku Klux Klan*, No. 93-074143 (261st Dist. Ct., Travis County, Tex., Feb. 3, 1994).

[38] *State of Texas v. Knights of Ku Klux Klan*, No. 94-40425 (5th Cir., July 25, 1995).

[39] Brewer & Shockley, *Klan Rally Attracts Few Supporters, Hecklers*, The Beaumont Enterprise, February 21, 1993 at 1B, col. 1.

[40] See *Young v. Cisneros*, Civ. Action No. P–80–8–CA, Final Judgment and Decree, (E.D.Tex. March 30, 1995).

[41] Langford, T., *Black Mother of 5 Finds Home--and a Hug: Texas: So far, five minority families have moved into previously all-white housing complex. Officials are holding units open for 10 more.* LA Times, (Feb. 20, 1994).

[42] *Ex Parte Lowe*, 887 S.W.2d 1 (1994). In another ironic twist, one of the organizations which filed an amicus brief on the Klan's behalf - the Thomas Jefferson Center for the Protection of Free Expression - is considered a liberal organization, yet committed to the protecting the First Amendment. See, Amicus Brief, before the Supreme Court of Texas (No. D4506).

[43] See, AP, *Black Families Ready to Pack Up and Leave 1 Year After Moving in Desert News.com,* (Jan. 12, 1995).

[44] See Boudin, K., *Maull Murder Trial Begins, Olean Times Herald,* (Jan. 14, 2016).

Chapter 2

[45] During the period 1993-1997, the CDC found that 50% of non-fatal gunshots victims received wounds to the extremities (feet, legs, arms, hands), and 25% received wounds to their trunk, with the remainder to the head or neck. Strom, K., Zawitz, M., *Firearm Injury and Death from Crime, 1993-1997,* BJS (Oct. 2000), NCJ 182993.

[46] HUD reported that in 1998, there were 44 gun-related murders in New Orleans' public housing projects; which were more than Chicago, Las Angeles and Houston. See HUD, *In the Crossfire, The Impact of Gun Violence on Public Housing Communities,* (2000) at 16.

[47] At [Charity], gunshot victims took up one-third of the orthopedic beds and consumed 20 percent to 30 percent of hospital resources. Because 51 percent of gunshot victims were uninsured, the hospital had to eat $6 million in costs in 1994. See, Jackson, D., *Taxpayers paying for Gunplay*, Kansas City Star (Aug. 9, 1999) at B5.

[48] Ecker, R. et.al, *Gunshot Wound head trauma,* (update May 2015) http://www.aans.org/Patient%20Information/Conditions%20and%20Treatments/Gunshot%20Wound%20Head%20Trauma.aspx; see also, Murphy, P.,

Endnotes

et al., *Shootings: What EMS Providers Need to Know* (April, 2010), http://www.emsworld.com/article/10319706/gunshot-wounds.

[49] See, Anderson, E., *The Code of the Streets*, The Atlantic, (May 1994); http://www.theatlantic.com/magazine/archive/1994/05/the-code-of-the-streets/306601/.

[50] See, La. State Museum, *Small Shoes, Giant Steps*, La. Cultural Vistas, Vol.21, Issue 3, (Fall 2010).

[51] A 1997 Department of Justice study of 8 cities, including New Orleans, which examined the correlation between the number of murders and clearance rates found a negative relation between the two factors. In concluding such, it found: "In New Orleans, interviewees reported that the typical serious violent offender did not believe that he was likely to be arrested for any one violent act, and that over the last decade arrest for a violent offense was perceived as increasingly less likely. Interviewees felt that lack of police manpower and equipment contributed to that perception." Lattimore, *Homicide in Eight U.S. Cities: Trends, Context, and Policy Implications,* USDOJ NIJ, NCJ 167262 (Dec. 1997).

[52] Zawitz, M. & Strom, K., *Firearm Injury and Death from Crime*, 1993-97 (Oct. 2000), NCJ 182993, Bureau of Justice Statistics, at 3.

[53] See, https://www.ronbrown.org/class/2014/herbert-spurlock-iii.

[54] See, e.g., Harrison, A., *Grisly coincidence or written in the stars? One zodiac sign is attached to more serial killers than any other,* The Mirror (May 15, 2018).

[55] See, e.g. http://www.annperrynumerologist.com/.

[56] See, McLellan, E., *The Power of Numbers or Name Vibration*, (Oakland, Cal. 1925).

[57] All charges were dropped against Ashton's killer about 6 months later and he was released from jail. However, within about 6 months after his release he was arrested again and charged with a similar shooting. Coincidentally, the latest incident occurred in the *1100* block of a street in Austin, which was north of East *11th* Street.

[58] The three sisters have also lost several cousins to murder - Brock, Jason, and Jimmie "Slick" – the latter whose killing is discussed in another chapter.

Chapter 3

[59] Creighton University, Archive of Prayer Requests 2010, http://onlineministries.creighton.edu/CollaborativeMinistry/Prayer-Requests/prayer-archive-10.html.

[60] Perez, K., *Questions remain after body found*, The Daily Nonpareil (Oct. 25, 2010),http://www.nonpareilonline.com/archive/questions-remain-after-body-found/article_4b152f74-b4d5-5c9f-a6c7-ac6bc88de8f6.html.

Endnotes

[61] McIntyre, J., *Body Found is That of Missing Woman,* Wowt news (Oct. 24, 2010), http://www.wowt.com/home/headlines/Body_Discovered_At_40th_And_Ames_105606053.html.
[62] See OPD Annual Report, http://police.cityofomaha.org/images/Annual Reports/2010AnnualReportFinal.pdf.
[63] Moorman, L., Baker, J., & Mastre, B., *Murder Details Revealed in court* (Dec. 30, 2010), http://www.wowt.com/home/headlines/Police_Arrest_Two_For_October_Murder_112596159.html.
[64] *Man Talks About Killing of Omaha Businesswoman,* KETV NewsWatch 7 (Oct. 17, 2011), http://www.dipyoutube.com/watch?v =eZ41sMlmWGw.
[65] Cooper, T., *Life sentence in slaying of landlord,* Omaha.com (Nov. 14, 2012).
[66] Nowatzke, J., *Creighton Professor Laid to Rest,* http://fox42kptm.com/archive/famil (Nov. 8, 2010).
[67] Project Jason, *College Moves forward following Professor's Murder* (Oct. 25, 2010), https://projectjason.org/forums/topic/2407-found-deceased-karen-jenkins-ne-10172010/.
[68] Kulper, J., *Friends to honor woman's memory* (Nov. 1, 2010), http://www.nonpareilonline.com/archive/friends-to-honor-woman-s-memory/ article_39d1aa9 -57d7-5592-92bc-9bee4838bb8a.html.
[69] Jenkins, Karen, "How African American women handle conflict in the workplace: An assessment of the impact of race, gender and class" (1997). Student Work. 1131. http://digitalcommons.unomaha.edu/ studentwork/1131.
[70] Cooper, Nov. 14.

Chapter 4

[71] See Benson, S., Brannen, D.E., & Valentine, R.,*"Sharecropping and Tenant Farming." UXL Encyclopedia of U.S. History.* Vol. 7. Detroit: UXL, 2009. 1400-1401. *U.S. History in Context.* Web. (Sept. 2016); http://libraries.state.ma.us/login?gwurl. http://ic.galegroup.com/ic/uhic/
[72] Courtesy of the Southern Tenant Farmers' Union Records #3472, Southern Historical Collection, Wilson Library, University of North Carolina at Chapel Hill.
[73] Id.
[74] See, See, DeJong, G., *With the Aid of God and the F.S.A.": The Louisiana Farmers' Union and the African American Freedom Struggle in the New Deal Era,* Journal of Social History, Vol. 34, No. 1 (Autumn, 2000), pp. 105-139.
[75] See, PBS, http://www.pbs.org/tpt/slavery-by-another-name/themes/sharecropping/.

Endnotes

[76] See, *Good Record for Pointe Coupee's FSA Farmers,* Pointe Coupee Banner, (Jan. 20, 1938), 1, 4.

[77] See DeJong, G., *A Different Day, African American Struggles for Justice in Rural Louisiana, 1900-1970* (Univ. North Carolina Press, 2003).

[78] See, DeJong, G., *With the Aid of God and the F.S.A.*

[79] Federal Bureau of Investigation, FBI Files, *Louisiana Farmers Union* (Farmer's Educational and Cooperative Union of America, Louisiana Division) Sept. 27, 1941, File 100-45768, La. Farmers Union.

[80] In the early 40's, sharecroppers often earned less than 75 cents a day. The regulations provided for men to be paid $1.20 per day and women to be paid $1.00. De Jong, G., *African American Struggles.*

[81] See Taylor, O.C.W., *The Crescent City Pictorial, Dedicated to the progress of the Colored Citizens of New Orleans*, (1925).

[82] Eig, J., *A Project Named Desire*, Time Picayune (June 19, 1989) at A-6.

[83] Office of Policy and Planning, *Desire Area Neighborhood Profile*, (New Orleans, 1978) 3.01-3-07.

[84] See, *Wards of New Orleans.* Bureau of Governmental Research (New Orleans, La.) (1961).

[85] See, http://newbirthno.wixsite.com/newbirthno/aboutus.

[86] See discussion about what it became years later, Beaulieu, L., *Life is Crime, Poverty, Fear, For Housing Project Dwellers,* Times Picayune, Jan. 7, 1980. According to the NOPD for 1979, "Based on reported index offenses, zone 5Q, which contains the 5000-unit Desire Housing project, is one of the most violent areas in the city. In 1979, it ranked first among police zones in the number of reported rapes (18) and aggravated assaults (228) and ranked third in the number of murders (8). Also, zone 5Q ranked second in the number of burglaries (398) in 1979 among all police zones".

[87] Eig, J., *"Desire Pays Price for Shortcuts,"* Times Picayune, (June 19, 1989).

[88] Bragg, R., *New Orleans's Hopes Rise as Crime Rate Decreases*, NY Times, (December 25, 1995), http://www.nytimes.com/1995/12/25/us/ new-orleans-s-hopes-rise-as-crime-rate-decreases.html.

[89] See, Conway, J., *117 Homicides in Orleans Parish already this Year*, Times Picayune, (Nov. 3, 1966) at 30.

[90] Stabbings were more prevalent in some cities. For instance, in New York City knives held the lead over handguns until 1969. In 1959, there were three times as many murders by knife than gun in New York. See, Greenberg, J., *All About Crime*, New York Magazine (Sept. 3, 1990) at 27.

[91] Rousseau, J., *3 are Knifed to Death within one Hour, Slashed to Death on Way Home from Church,* Louisiana Weekly (May 21, 1966).

[92] https://www.aft.org/resolution/nathaniel-h-lacour.

[93] See, Ward, S., *Arthur Hunter Jr.: From cop to judge to fighting recidivism,* ABA Journal (Sept. 10, 2015), http://www.abajournal.com/legalrebels/

Endnotes

article/Arthur_l_hunter_from_cop_to_judge_to_fighting_recidivism.

Chapter 5

[94] To protect the privacy of the family, pseudonyms have been used for the victim and survivors.
[95] *Murder conviction for Delco mom in child death*, Action News, (Dec. 12, 2016) http://6abc.com/news/murder-conviction-for-delco-mom-in-child-death/1652402/.
[96] Russo, M., *UPDATE: details of Dell Rapids child death* KSYTV, (Dec. 8, 2016), http://kwsn.com/news/articles/2016/dec/08/update-details-of-dell-rapids-child-death/.
[97] Ovalle, D., *North Miami-Dade father beat his fussy baby daughter to death, police say* Miami Herald, (March 30, 2016), http://www.miamiherald.com/news/local/crime/article68969347.html.
[98] http://www.oddee.com/item_98679.aspx.
[99] Dostis, M., *Chicago teen hid pregnancy from family and threw newborn out window minutes after giving birth: police* NY Daily News (Nov.16, 2015), http://www.nydailynews.com/news/crime/chicago-teen-hid-regnancy-threw-newborn-window-article-1.2437016.
[100] Burgess, Z., *Unthinkable Crime in Detroit*, Mich. Chronicle, (4/16/2015), https://michronicleonline.com/2015/04/16/unthinkable-crime-in-detroit/.
[101] See, e.g., Plunkett, J., *Resuscitation injuries complicating the interpretation of premortem trauma and natural disease in children*, J Forensic Sci. 2006 Jan;51(1):127-30. (Minor soft tissues injuries are common in both adults and children who have had cardiopulmonary resuscitation (CPR). Potentially life-threatening injuries are rare…it may be difficult if not impossible to distinguish resuscitation injuries from pre-existing accidental or inflicted trauma).
[102] Dept. of Health and Human Services, Centers for Disease Control and Prevention, National Center for Health Statistics, http://www.cdc.gov/nchs/data/nvsr/nvsr 50/nvsr50_15.pdf Table 35, National Vital Statistics Report, Vol. 50, No. 15, (September 16, 2002).
[103] Id., Table 9.
[104] Child Trends Data Base, *Infant Homicide, Indicators of Child and Youth Well Being,* (Feb. 2015), https://www.childtrends.org/wp-content/uploads/2015/02/72_Infant_Homicide.pdf.
[105] Id., Table 10.
[106] Murray, I., *Juvenile Murders: Guns Least of It,* CS Monitor, (March 27, 2000), https://www.csmonitor.com/2000/0327/p9s1.html.
[107] Overpeck D., at the National Institute of Child Health and Human Development; Kunz J, Bahr S., *A profile of purental homicide against*

Endnotes

children. J Fam Violence 1996; 11:347-362; Scholer SJ, Hickson GB, Mitchel EF Jr, & Ray WA., *Persistently increased injury mortality rates in high-risk young children.* Arch Pediatric Adolesc Med. 1997; 151:1216-1219; Ortega, H.W., Vander Velden, H., Kreykes, N.S., & Reid, S., *Childhood Death Attributable to Trauma: Is There a Difference Between Accidental and Abusive Fatal Injuries?* The Journal of Emergency Medicine 45, (2013) at 332-337; Fajardo GC, & Hanzlick, RL, *A 10-year epidemiologic review of homicide cases in children younger than 5 years in Fulton County, GA*: 1996-2005. PMID: Am J Forensic Med Pathol. 2010 Dec;31(4):355-8.

[108] Maryland Vital Statistics, Dept. of Health and Mental Hygiene, Vital Statistics Administration, Annual Report 2000, http://dhmh.maryland.gov/vsa/Documents/00 annual.pdf.

[109] http://healthybabiesbaltimore.com/uploads/file/pdfs/ 2013_07_29 FIMR%20 Annual%20Report%20FY%202013.pdf.

[110] Cooper A. & Smith, E., BJS, *Homicide Trends in the US*, 1980-2008, https:// www.bjs. gov/content/pub/pdf/ htus8008.pdf (Nov., 2011).

[111] Child Welfare Information Gateway. (2016). *Child abuse and neglect fatalities 2014: Statistics and interventions.* Washington, DC: U.S. Department of Health and Human Services. https://www.childwelfare.gov/pubPDFs/fatality.pdf.

[112] Starling, S.P., et al., *Abusive Head Trauma: The Relationship of Perpetrators to Their Victim*, 95 Pediatrics 259, 260 (1995). See also, Sorenson, S.B., et al., 1 J. Aggression, Maltreatment & Trauma 189, 193 (1997) (study found that offenders in homicides of children under four years old from 1980 through 1989 were family members in 77% of cases, nonfamily members known to the victim in 7% of cases, and strangers in 2.5% of cases).

[113] See Brewster A.L., et al., *Victim, Perpetrator Family, and Incident Characteristics of 32 Infant Maltreatment Deaths in the United States Air Force*, 22 Child Abuse & Neglect 91, 100 (1998) (58% of perpetrators who killed an infant 12 months old or younger reported an infant's crying as preceding the abusive episode).

[114] Friedman, S., Cavney, J., & Resnick. P., *Child Murder by Parents and Evolutionary Psychology,* Psychiatric Clinics of North America 35, 781-795 (2012); Friedman, S, Cavney, J., & Resnick, P., *Mothers Who Kill: Evolutionary* C.K., Lathrop, S.L. (2010) *Child Abuse-Related Homicides in New Mexico: A 6-year Underpinnings and Infanticide Law. Behavioral Sciences & the Law* 30:10.1002/bsl. v30.5, 585-597 (2012); Fajardo, G.C., & Hanzlick, R. *10-Year*; Lee, *Retrospective Review. Journal of Forensic Sciences* 55:10.1111 /jfo.2009.55.issue-1, 100-103.

Endnotes

[115] See e.g., West, S.G., *An Overview of Filicide*, Psychiatry (Edgmont), (Feb. 2007) 4(2): 48–57.

[116] See also, Romero, M., *Fatal child abuse cases highlight risks when the boyfriend moves in* Desert News (May 16, 2015) http://www.deseretnews.com/article/865628841;http://baltimorecitypolicedept.org/citypolice/baltimore-police-districts/northwest-district.html.

[117] Barnes, J., "*The Boyfriend Problem,*" Weekly Standard, (December 14, 1998); Overpeck, M., et al. "*Risk Factors for Infant Homicide in the United States,*" New England Journal of Medicine, October 22, 1998; Richards, C.E., *The Loss of Innocents: Child Killers and Their Victims*. Wilmington, DE: Scholarly Resources, 2000.

[118] Stiffman MN, Schnitzler PG, Adam P, Kruse RL, & Weighman BG, *Household composition and risk of fatal child Maltreatment*, Pediatrics. 109(4):615-21 (April 2002).

[119] Bou-Saada, K., Hunter, WM, Catellier, DJ, & Kotch JB, *Are father Surrogates a risk factor for child Maltreatment?* Child Maltreat. 2001 Nov;6(4):281-9.

[120] More recently, a man in Baltimore was charged with killing his girlfriend's baby less than 5 years after pleading guilty to abusing his own son, which led to the son's death. See, Lambert, J., *Man charged with killing his girlfriend's baby also did time for death of his own son*, Fox45 News (July 24, 2018), http://foxbaltimore.com/news/local/francois-browne-charged-for-the-murder-of-an-18-month-old-baby.

[121] Pediatrics 2005;116: e687–e693; www.pediatrics.org/cgi/doi/ 10.1542/peds. 2005-0296.

[122] Schnitzer, P. & Ewigman B., *Child Deaths Resulting From Inflicted Injuries: Household Risk Factors and Perpetrator Characteristics*, Pediatrics. (2005 Nov); 116(5).

[123] Holler, J., *Child Homicide/Death Investigations*, http://www.Marylandchildrens alliance.org/wp-tcontent/uploads/2014/08/2016-Child-Homicide-Death-Investigations- DAY_HOLLER.pdf (undated); Diebold, K. Chapter 7, *Sudden, Unexplained Infant Death Investigation* https://www.cdc.gov/sids/pdf/guide manual/chapter7_tag508.pdf CDC, (undated).

[124] Li, Ling, Fowler, D., Liu, L., Ripple, G., Mary, Lambros, Z. & E Smialek, J. *Investigation of sudden infant deaths in the State of Maryland (1990-2000)*, Forensic Science International. 148(2-3):85-92 (April 2005). In a retrospective study of Office of Chief Medical Examiner (OCME) cases between 1990 and 2000, the researchers found that there were 1,619 infant fatalities, of which 802 infant deaths were determined to be SIDS, (50%), 523 deaths (31.8%) were due to natural diseases, 128 (7.9%) were accidents, and 74 (4.6%) were homicides. For 92 infants (5.7%), the manner of death

Endnotes

could not be determined after a thorough scene investigation, review of history and a complete postmortem examination. Of the 74 homicide victims, 53 (70%) involved infants less than 6 months of age.

[125] See generally, Hanzlik, R., Clark, S., & Jentzen, J., *Infant Death Investigation: Guidelines for the Scene Investigator* Department of Health and Human Services, Maternal and Infant Health Branch Division of Reproductive Health Centers for Disease Control and Prevention, (Atlanta, Ga.), https://www.cdc.gov/ sids/pdf/508suidiguidelinessingles_tag508.pdf (Jan. 2007); see also, American Academy of Pediatrics, Division of State Government Affairs, *Child Death Investigation Act: Model Bill*. (Elk Grove Village, IL): American Academy of Pediatrics 99.

[126] Walsh, B., *Investigating Child Fatalities, Portable Guides to Investigating Child Abuse*, Office of Justice Programs, Partnerships for Safer Communities, www.ojp.usdoj.gov Office of Juvenile Justice and Delinquency Prevention (Aug. 2005), www.ojp.usdoj.gov/ojjdp; https://www.ncjrs.gov/pdffiles1/ ojjdp/209764.pdf.

[127] American Academy of Pediatrics, *Distinguishing Sudden Infant Death Syndrome from Child Abuse Fatalities,* Pediatrics, Vol 107, No.2 (Feb. 2001)http://pediatrics.aappublications.org/content/pediatrics/107/2/437.full.

[128] Overpeck, M., Brenner, R., Trumble, A., Trifiletti, L., & Berendes, H., *Risk Factors for Infant Homicide in the United States,* N Engl J Med 1998; 339:1211-1216 (Oct. 22, 1998) http://pediatrics.aappublications.org/ content/pediatrics/107/2/437.full.pdf; American Academy of Pediatrics Committee on Child Abuse and Neglect Distinguishing Sudden Infant Death Syndrome from Child Abuse Fatalities, Pediatrics 2001 107; 437.

[129] One of the groups dedicated to helping survivors (Compassionate Friends) describes the difficulty of the most basic of tasks following the death of a child: "One major decision which all seem to struggle with when their child was young or not married is what to do with their belongings whether it be toys, clothing, furniture, car, or any other possessions. Some feel they are pressured to quickly remove these items from the home. For some, their child's possessions may cause too much pain and are stored or given away soon after the death. Many parents, however, have reported that seeing the child's belongings helped them face the reality of their loss and helped them grieve. Sometime later, some of these items became important memories of their child to hold onto." https://www.compassionatefriends.org/wp-content/uploads/2018/10/ compassionate-grief.pdf.

[130] Sharkey, P., The *Acute Effect of Local Homicides on Children's Cognitive Performance*, Proc Natl Acad Sci U S A. (Jun 29, 2010); 107(26).

Chapter 6

[131] See Times Picayune, April 9, 1976 at 8. Ironically and mystically, forty

Endnotes

years later, in 2016, with an age differential similar to that between Aaron and Arnold (about 10-11 months apart), another man in the city was charged with killing his brother – Aaron Jackson.

[132] See, Kennedy, A, "The History of Public Education in New Orleans Still Matters" (2016). *History Faculty Publications.* Paper 5. ("In 1938, Louisiana's State Superintendent of Education, T. H. Harris, ... admitted there was 'no serious intention in most of the parishes to provide school facilities for Negro children,' and there was no 'serious concern' about the matter." p.16). http://scholarworks.uno.edu/hist_facpubs/5.

[133] Gebo, E., *A Contextual Exploration of Siblicide*, Violence and Victims, Vol. 17, No.2 (April 2002).

[134] http://www.wisegeek.com/what-is-fratricide.htm

[135] See, Fulton, V., *How to Handle Siblings After the Death of Your Parents*, (Jun 25, 2015), Livestrong.com, http://www.livestrong.com/ article/80290-handle- siblings-after-death-parents/.

Chapter 7

[136] Surprisingly, it was not the largest number of prisoners to die in a prison fire in the state. In 1913, 35 inmates had burned to death at the Oakley Convict farm, near Jackson. The difference was that the fire was considered as resulting from an accident, while Biloxi was considered as a murder.

[137] *Gates v. Collier*, 501 F.2d 1291, 1307-1310 (5th Cir. 1974).

[138] Testimony of Robert Plotkin, *Civil Rights of Institutionalized Persons Act Hearings*, Committee on the Judiciary, House of Representatives, (Dec. 7, 1983 and Feb.8, 1984) at 16.

[139] Id at 16.

[140] Grove, R., *Night of fire haunts prisoners and police*, November 16, 1987, Clarion-Ledger from Jackson, Mississippi, Page 11.

[141] Bell, J., *Twenty-Nine Die in Biloxi, Mississippi jail fire / James R.*, November 8, 1982, Fire Journal Vol. 77 (6) (November 1983), 44-49. Many of the facts concerning the fire and rescue efforts set forth herein were culled from Mr. Bell's report, with confirmation of much of the depictions from other sources.

[142] Bell at 48.

[143] Bell at 48.

[144] *Keys lost to Cells in Jail Blaze*, Asbury Park Press, Asbury Park, New Jersey (Nov. 9, 1982), p.2.

[145] McCormack, D., *Ex-mental patient charged in fatal fire*, The Courier-Journal, Louisville, Kentucky (Nov. 9, 1982), p.2.

[146] *27 Inmates Die in Jail Fire at Biloxi, Miss.*, The Republic from Columbus, Indiana (Nov. 8, 1982), p. 1.

Endnotes

[147] Steinbrook, R., *Cyanide Gas Kills by Blocking Body's Ability to Use Oxygen,* LATimes, (April 11, 1992).
[148] Ibid.
[149] Levin, Paboo, Gurman, Harris & Braun, *Toxicological Interactions Between Carbon Monoxide and Carbon Dioxide,* Toxicology 1987; 47: 135–164 at 318, Proceedings of The Sixteenth Conference of Toxicology October 28-30, 1986 Dept. of the Navy Medical Research Institute (Dec 1987).
[150] www.gendisasters.com/mississippi/4104/biloxi%2C-ms-prison-fire-kills-27- inmates%2C-nov-1982; Beitler, S., *Mississippi Jail Fire Kills 27 Inmates, 61 People Injured.*; The Index-Journal from Greenwood, South Carolina, (Nov. 9, 1982), p 3.
[151] Beitler, *General Disasters.*
[152] Grove, ibid.
[153] Grove, ibid.
[154] Grove, ibid.
[155] Williams, F., *Similar fire Doubtful in Lee Jail, Officials say,* News-Press, Fort Myers, Florida (Nov. 9, 1982), p.6.
[156] Muller, L., *Fire Kills 27 in Mississippi Prison,* Iowa City Press-Citizen (Nov. 8, 1982) p.1.
[157] *27 Inmates Die in Jail Fire at Biloxi, Miss.*
[158] *Keys Lost to Cells in Jail Blaze,* p.2.
[159] UPI News Track, *Pates: 'A time bomb waiting to go off'; What he's done doesn't surprise me',* Newswire (Nov. 9, 1982).
[160] UPI, www.upi.com/Archives/1982/11/10/A-former-mental-patient-rolled-into-the-courtroom-in/9325405752400/ (reviewed 9/22/2017).
[161] *Violent Inmate Sets Fire, Kills 27,* The Indianapolis Star (Nov. 9, 1982) p. 5.
[162] *Biloxi Jail Fire Kills 27 Inmates,* Logansport-Pharos Tribune, (Nov. 8, 1982) p.1.
[163] Coggins, A., *Tennessee Tragedies: Natural, Technological, and Societal Disasters in the Volunteer State,* (Univ. Tenn. Press 2012), at 113.
[164] Levinson, MR, NCJ 086689, *In Biloxi, a Ten-Minute Fire Kills 29,* Corrections Magazine, Vol. 9 Issue:1 (Feb. 1983) pp:10-15.
[165] See, Hearings before the Subcommittee on Courts, Civil Liberties and the Administration of Justice, 98th Congress, (Dec. 7, 1983 & Feb, 8, 1984), at 126.
[166] Bell, J., *Twenty-Nine Die in Biloxi.*
[167] Bell at 55.
[168] Historically, a former Biloxi jail had been set ablaze by an inmate in March 1875, about midnight, as he set the fire as part of an escape attempt. He died from smoke inhalation.
[169] As one newspaper reported: "Frantic men suffocated like vermin behind

Endnotes

their steel bars". See *Report on the Ohio State Penitentiary Fire*, Ohio Inspection Bureau (1930), https://www.nfpa.org/-/media/Files/News-and-Research/Resources/Fire-Investigations/ohio_state_penitentiary.ashx?la=en

[170] See, e.g., Schafer, N.E., 1982: *Fire Safety in Jails - Planning for Emergencies.* 46 (3) Federal Probation 41-45 (Sep. 1982); NCJ #85712.

[171] Gomez, J., www.nj.com/jerseyjournal150/2017/04/horrific_jail_fire_in_jersey_city_claimed_7_lives.html (May 2, 2017).

[172] McGinty, S., *Fire in the Night, The Piper Alpha Disaster*, (PanMcMillan Press, 2010), at 57.

Chapter 8

[173] http://www.nmha.org/conditions/coping-loss-bereavement-and-grief.

[174] Johnson, A., *Defiant Triple Killer Sentenced to Death*, LATimes (July 31, 2003).

[175] See Webster, R.& Bullington, J., *Science of Trauma*, NOLA.com (June 13, 2018) https://projects.nola.com/the-children-of-central-city/science-of-trauma/.

[176] *Common Fears & Questions of Grieving Children* https://my.clevelandclinic.org/ccf/media/Files/bereavement/understanding-death-grief-mourning-resources-manual.pdf?la=en.

[177] See, *Report on Bereavement and Grief Research,* Center for the Advancement of Health (Nov. 2003) at 36-40.

[178] Harper, M., O'Connor, R.C. & O'Carroll, R., *Factors associated with grief and depression following the loss of a child: A multivariate analysis*, Psychology, Health & Medicine, (2013). One study which examined mortality data after 20-years found that bereaved parents lived shorter lives than non-bereaved parents, even after controlling for age and gender. The longitudinal analysis showed that parental bereavement was a significant predictor of mortality at 20-year follow-up. Cohen-Mansfield, J., Shmotkin, D., Malkinson, R., Bartur, L, & Hazan, H., *Parental bereavement increases mortality in older persons.* Psychological Trauma: Theory, Research, Practice, and Policy, Vol 5(1), Jan 2013, 84-92.

[179] *ISU team calculates societal costs of five major crimes; finds murder at $17.25 million,* Posted Sep 27, 2010, https://www.news.iastate.edu/news/2010/sep/costofcrime.

[180] *The True Cost of Gun Violence in America*, Mother Jones, http://www.Motherjones.com/politics/2015/04/true-cost-of-gun-violence-in-america/2/. It should be noted that the estimates related to the cost of gun violence varies wildly, with some estimates much lower.

[181] Follman, M., Lurie, J., & Lee, J., *What does Gun Violence Really Cost?*

Endnotes

The Survivors, Mother Jones, (May/June 2015), http://www.motherjones.com/ politics/2015/04/survivors-of-gun-violence.

[182] Parke, R.D., & Alison Clarke-Irvine, K., *From Prison to Home: The Effect of Incarceration and Reentry on Children, Families, and Communities, Effects of Parental Incarceration on Young Children*, (December 2001), https://aspe.hhs.gov/basic-report/effects-parental-incarceration-young-children.

[183] Travis, J., & Western, B., eds., *The Growth of incarceration in the United States, exploring Causes and Consequences*, Committee on Law and Justice, Division of Behavioral and Social Sciences and Education. National Research Council of the National Academies (National Research Council 2014).

[184] https://www.justice.gov/sites/default/files/usao-dc/legacy/2013/08/07/coping_after_homicide.pdf.

[185] McSpadden, L., *Michael Brown's Mom on Alton Sterling and Philando Castile* NY Times (July 8, 2016), https://www.nytimes.com/2016/07/08/opinion/michael-browns-mom-on-alton-sterling-and-philando-castile.html?_r=0.

[186] Vaisvilas, F., *Gun victim's mother speaks out against gun violence at Kelly*, Chicago Tribune, (Mar 16, 2016), http://www.chicagotribune.com./suburbs/daily-southtown/news/ct-sta-cleo-pendleton2-st-0320-0160319 -story.html; Ivers, D., *Newark mother who lost 3 sons to gun violence: 'Stop killing my kids'* (Jan.1, 2016); http://www.nj.com/essex/index.ssf/2016/01/newark_mother who_lost_3_sons to_gun_violence_stop.html; see also, Vives, R., *An answer to deadly question of gang violence; 'Where you from?' Woman campaigns for peace, inspired by last words grandson heard*, Los Angeles Times; Los Angeles, Calif. [Los Angeles, Calif]10 Jan 2019: B.1 (grandmother starts billboard campaign after grandson and his father killed within 3-month period).

[187] See, Chang, C., *Three suspects arrested in killing of gang intervention worker celebrated as a peacemaker*, Los Angeles Times (Online), Los Angeles: Tribune Interactive, LLC. Aug 15, 2018.

[188] Armour, M., *Meaning making in the aftermath of homicide*, Death Studies 27(6):519-40 (Aug. 2003) at 534.

[189] Farris, C., *Through It All* (Atria Books, 2009), at 198.

[190] Hugo, P., & Dominus, S., *Portraits of Reconciliation*, New York Times Magazine, (April 6, 2014), https://www.nytimes.com/interactive/2014/04/06/magazine/06-pieter-hugo-rwanda-portraits.html?_r=0.

[191] Senghor, S., *Writing My Wrongs Life, Death, and Redemption in an American Prison*, Random House (2016), at 3.

[192] From a poem by Rita Moran, appearing in Compassionate Friends, Ft. Lauderdale Newsletter; http://www.svlp.org/support/whatnottosay.html.

Endnotes

[193] Miller, A., *7 Things I've Learned Since the Loss of My Child* (Oct. 31, 2015) https://abedformyheart.com/7-things-since-loss-of-child/.
[194] http://www.illinoisvictims.org/index.php/resources/il-victim-groups-and-organizations/moms/.

Back cover by Raenell Pollard